Decolonial Futures

Postcolonial and Decolonial Studies in Religion and Theology

Series Editor: Sheryl Kujawa-Holbrook, Claremont School of Theology

Series Editorial Board
Jon Berquist, Stephen Burns, Cláudio Carvalhaes, Jennifer Te Paa Daniel, Lynne St. Clair Darden, Christine J. Hong, Wonhee Anne Joh, HyeRan Kim-Cragg, Boyung Lee, Aprilfaye Tayag Manalang, Loida Yvette Martell, Stephanie Y. Mitchem, Jea Sophia Oh, Nicolas Esteban Panotto, Jeremy Punt, Patrick Reyes, Joerg Rieger, Fernando Segovia, Melinda McGarrah Sharp, Kay Higuera Smith, Jonathan Y. Tan, Mona West, and Amos Yong.

This series responds to the growing interest in postcolonial studies and re-examines the hegemonic, European-dominated religious systems of the old and new empires. It critically addresses the colonial biases of religions, the academy, and local faith communities, in an effort to make these institutions more polyvocal, receptive, and empowering to global cultures and epistemologies. The series will engage with a variety of hybrid, overlapping, and intersecting definitions of postcolonialism—as a critical discursive practice, as a political and ideological stance concerned with exposing patterns of dominance and hegemony, and as contexts shaped by ongoing colonization and decolonization. Books in the series will also explore the relationship between postcolonial values and religious practice, and the transformation of religious symbols and institutions in postcolonial contexts beyond the academy. The series aims to make high-quality and original research available to the scholarly community. The series welcomes monographs and edited volumes which forge new directions in contextual research across disciplines and explore key contemporary issues. Established scholars as well as new authors will be considered for publication, including scholars "on the margins" whose voices are underrepresented in the academy and in religious discourse. Authors working in subdisciplines of religious studies and/or theology are encouraged to submit proposals.

Titles in the Series
Colonialism and the Bible: Contemporary Reflections from the Global South, edited by Tat-siong Benny Liew and Fernando F. Segovia.
Ecologies of Participation: Agents, Shamans, Mystics, and Diviners, by Zayin Cabot.
Feminist Praxis Against U.S. Militarism, edited by Nami Kim and Wonhee Anne Joh
Postcolonial Preaching: Creating a Ripple Effect, by HyeRan Kim-Cragg
Decolonial Futures: Intercultural and Interreligious Intelligence for Theological Education, by Christine Hong

Decolonial Futures

Intercultural and Interreligious Intelligence for Theological Education

Christine J. Hong
Foreword by Marcia Y. Riggs

LEXINGTON BOOKS
Lanham • Boulder • New York • London

Published by Lexington Books
An imprint of The Rowman & Littlefield Publishing Group, Inc.
4501 Forbes Boulevard, Suite 200, Lanham, Maryland 20706
www.rowman.com

6 Tinworth Street, London SE11 5AL, United Kingdom

Copyright © 2021 by The Rowman & Littlefield Publishing Group, Inc.

All rights reserved. No part of this book may be reproduced in any form or by any electronic or mechanical means, including information storage and retrieval systems, without written permission from the publisher, except by a reviewer who may quote passages in a review.

British Library Cataloguing in Publication Information Available

Library of Congress Cataloging-in-Publication Data

Names: Hong, Christine J, author.
Title: Decolonial futures : intercultural and interreligious intelligence for theological education / Christine J. Hong ; foreword by Marica Y. Riggs.
Description: Lanham, Maryland : Lexington Books, [2021] | Series: Postcolonial and decolonial studies in religion and theology | Includes bibliographical references and index.
Identifiers: LCCN 2020051036 (print) | LCCN 2020051037 (ebook) | ISBN 9781498579360 (cloth) | ISBN 9781498579384 (pbk) ISBN 9781498579377 (epub)
Subjects: LCSH: Theology—Study and teaching. | Decolonization. | Religion—Study and teaching.
Classification: LCC BV4020 .H57 2021 (print) | LCC BV4020 (ebook) | DDC 230.071—dc23
LC record available at https://lccn.loc.gov/2020051036
LC ebook record available at https://lccn.loc.gov/2020051037

For my grandfather Yoon Jong Sung who transitioned in his 100th year while I wrote this book. Grandpa, 할아버지, your faith, hope, and love live on through Tae-Sup and Tae-Jin. May we honor your legacy.

Contents

Foreword by Marcia Y. Riggs	ix
Preface	xiii
Acknowledgments	xv
Introduction: Decolonial Futuring in Theological Education	1
PART I: DECONSTRUCTION	**13**
1 Undoing Competency	15
2 Unbinding Liberation	39
3 Upsetting the White, Christian, Patriarchy	61
4 Uncivilizing Teaching and Learning	79
PART II: RECONSTRUCTION	**97**
5 Reclaiming Epistemologies	99
6 Retelling Histories as Story and Story Formation	111
7 Reframing Religious and Cultural Borderlands	129
8 Restoring Genealogies of the Intangible	145
Conclusion: Begin Again	169

Notes	173
Bibliography	191
Index	197
About the Author	209

Foreword

Teaching with Intercultural and Interreligious Intelligence

I was introduced to the content of this book during a Dean's Lunch at Columbia Seminary where Dr. Hong and I are on the faculty. As is the custom, she had shared a couple of chapters from the working manuscript prior to the lunch so that we could prepare to engage in a dialogue with her. Just those two chapters made me want to read more. Dr. Hong's narrative-analytical writing style opens up difficult concepts from decolonial studies and educational theory as she uses personal and communal experiences to illuminate further these concepts.

As an ethicist I was particularly drawn into the book's argument that begins thus:

"Theological education and its teaching institutions are going through a crisis of conscience" (my emphasis). With that opening assertion, Dr. Hong pushes us to enlarge our conversation about how to "save" theological education institutions *from what we might do* (i.e., address declining enrollments or query about whether or how theological education can be effectively (authentically) rendered digitally) *to who we are*. To speak of "a crisis of conscience" is to make ethical inquiry a crucible for our conversations about theological education. From my perspective, the ethical inquiry in this book widens the focus from what's gone or going wrong in theological education to *who we are as moral agents responsible for transforming our teaching institutions*. This book makes a strong case regarding the necessity of intercultural and interreligious intelligence as central to our moral agency as educators.

Part one of the book is entitled Deconstruction. Deconstructing how we define competency is critical in the ethical quest to mend the crisis of conscience in theological education. Dr. Hong exposes how competency is tied to assimilation to "white and Christian norms." This means that instead of asserting competency as mastery of the western educational and

Christian canon, she proposes that educators must develop intercultural and interreligious intelligence. Whereas the concept of intelligence as mastery has been weaponized against minoritized persons and groups of color, Dr. Hong defines intercultural and interreligious intelligence as an "embodied posture," "a specific posture and expectation towards listening and understanding across difference." Most of us have embraced Gardner's multiple intelligences. Dr. Hong explicates the next important implications of multiple intelligences. She engages Gardner's multiple intelligences in this way: "The value in interreligious and intercultural intelligence is its potential for integrating known forms of multiple intelligences to expand cultural and religious awareness towards more inclusive expressions and understandings."

In sum, Dr. Hong invites us to live for an anticolonialist revolution in theological education; in her words:

"Anti-colonialism as a daily practice begets intercultural and interreligious intelligence as a posture for teaching and learning. The concept of mastery and its sidekick competency are illusory for the posture of intercultural and interreligious intelligence. Intelligence framed as posture does not seek mastery over knowledge to wield it against others but aims to be open to it. It seeks accountability to how different peoples, cultures, and homelands understand what intelligence looks, sounds, feels, and tastes like."

The character of the theological educator who participates in this revolution is grounded in "humble modesty." This virtue affirms the inextricable relationship between our character, our commitments, and our actions. Indeed, humble modesty is both a theological virtue and social ethical value. Theologically, we are reminded that theological educators are humans who have an inspired vocation, and we educators can oppress or liberate those whom we teach, thus the need for humble modesty. Likewise, we must affirm that what we do has social ethical consequences for the world in which we live. With humble modesty, we never forget that we will see some of those consequences, for good or evil, but many of the consequences will come to fruition in the future. If humble modesty is a central virtue for theological educators, then, hopefully, there will be a future of human and planetary flourishing for which we planted seeds in the present.

Overall, part one of the book is deconstruction at its best. Her criticism and analysis are hard-hitting in ways that break through our urge to oversimplify complex issues while inviting us to understand these issues for the sake of a future in which we will all flourish. Dr. Hong exposes historical harms of education that are embedded in white and Christian supremacy by showing us both why we should and how we can free ourselves from captivity to such.

Part two of the book is entitled Reconstruction. There are four Rs of reconstruction: (1) reclaiming, (2) retelling, (3) reframing, and (4) restoring. We must reclaim and reintegrate the creativity of Indigenous knowledges; Dr. Hong explicates this point with the theological constructs of *woori* from her Korean background. Retelling histories is about the importance of stories for persons and communities of diaspora, exile, and displacement. These stories inculcate resistance so that "both teachers and learners of one another's stories might be utterly transformed and convicted to break coloniality in every corner of our lives." Reframing is about classrooms reframed by the "religious and cultural borderlands" of minoritized people and communities into spaces of learning that honor "transpiritualities" and "hybridity." Restoring communal genealogies of learning and knowing stresses the need "to validate or verify the existence of alternate genealogies of epistemologies, stories, and fluidities, against the dominant culture." The four Rs of reconstruction provide the needed scaffold for teaching and learning in the twenty-first century.

In the conclusion, Dr. Hong issues a call to commitment and action; she says:

"I invite you to make a commitment to the decolonial futuring of theological education through tangible anti-colonial work. Your commitment, *our* commitment, is a beginning. The decolonial futuring of theological education is an embodied dream. It is not a figment of our imaginations but the very real commitment to the daily pursuit and practice of liberation unbound." Thus, the book ends with an ethical call to action. Again, we are called to be intentional moral agents who break the bonds of oppressive education in order to construct education that liberates. Our constructive moral agency requires mutuality and solidarity for which this book is the road map. In Hong's eloquent words: "We story ourselves into one another's lives as a way to tell truths about ourselves and our communities of accountability, the loving work of resistance to a coloniality that seeks to overcome, erase, and diminish personhood and peoplehood."

This book is compelling because Dr. Hong is doing what Patricia Hill Collins calls "intellectual activism," that is, she has "placed the power of [her] ideas in the service of social justice." Dr. Hong theorizes and educates us. In this book, she is the theological educator that she calls us to become. As I write this Foreword, the COVID-19 pandemic has challenged us to find ways to flourish amid uncertainty, pain, suffering, and death. If you want insight about how to engender hope that can get you through this time and prepare you for tomorrow, you should read this book.

Near the conclusion of the Dean's Lunch to which I referred at the beginning of this Foreword, a white male colleague asked: "Who's the audience for this book?" The audience is everyone who is willing to sing with Sweet Honey in the Rock, an acapella African American women's group, "We who believe in freedom cannot rest until it comes."

Marcia Y. Riggs, PhD
J. Erskine Love Professor of Christian Ethics
Columbia Theological Seminary
Decatur, GA

Preface
We will Teach

I love spoken word poetry. Over the years, I've learned poetry is an epistemology of relationships: to self, community, the world, and the Divine. Poetry can cut us to the bone and pierce our hearts better than most scholarly texts. This book engages the ideas and truths of poets alongside the work of academics. When I wrote this book, the world burned and it does still. It's been burning since long before my time. Watching the smoke, I felt a deep urgency to get every thought and emotion down on paper. Sometimes, the words I wanted to say and the grief and sorrow I felt seemed to consume me. Poetry and teaching helped me survive.

One of the poems which helped me get through the hardest days was *Oral Traditions*, written and performed by celebrated Samoan and Korean-Hawaiian spoken word artists, William Nu'utupu Giles and Travis T. When they perform this piece the air feels thick. With each word, they harness incredible emotion to describe the destructive histories of colonization on island people. With each punctuated syllable and movement of their hands they celebrate the power of their ancestors who survived and thrived in the face of attempted genocide. In tandem, they shout, "I will teach a hundred years of colonizers that a language is the most dangerous weapon you can give a bloodline of storytellers, culture keepers, with responsibilities to speak no matter their split tongue."[1] I am moved to tears every time I hear these words. I hear pride, anger, struggle, yearning, passion, joy, and purpose. I witness the roar of their ancestors rising in a mighty multitude behind them. I feel the rhythm of their exhortation in my gut and heart.

This single line of poetry is how I understand my work and imagine the work of theological educators who are religiously and racially minoritized. Giles and T. speak into the lives of those of us who struggle against white and Christian supremacy in theological education. Their words speak to all of us who live under the white gaze and live through the constant attempt to domesticate and civilize our names, languages, stories, voices, and bodies. Giles and T. invite us to turn the education weaponized against us into tools to multiply our truths through teaching. They remind us to teach the stories of our people in full color, to honor the ancestors and elders who pushed and willed us through the doors of the academy even as institutions tried to shut us out. This book is for the teacher-poets who are embracing the chaos of uncivilized spaces, who are proclaiming their truths against all odds and shaping the decolonial futures of theological education as the world burns. I celebrate you.

We will teach, though you refuse to see us
We will teach and *make* you hear us
We will teach and you will know us
   by our mother-tongue names
We will teach though we are weary
We will teach though we are angry
We will teach the discipline of hope
We will teach love with sharp edges
We will teach the dream of a different world
   and usher in its arrival
We will teach freedom coming
We will teach because we are here
Now.

Acknowledgments

Every book is a communal effort. Educators weave together a tapestry of wisdom from ancestors, guides, elders, mentors, friends, and family. Their wisdom sustains us and reminds us of our rootedness and belonging. None of us have ideas borne in a vacuum. Our best ideas are seeded in us by our communities: the words, songs, dreams, visions, and hopes of our people. We nourish the seeds and they grow to become our collective longing for a better world. I could not have written a book about decolonial futures without the many seeds of wisdom and support from my villages.

From the village of scholars and colleagues, I would like to thank series editor Sheryl Kujawa-Holbrook for her encouragement throughout my scholarly life. Sheryl, you are an incredible pedagogue, and I've learned so much by simply by watching you teach. I want to thank my co-teacher of some eight years, Najeeba Syeed, who invited me to stand beside her and teach fearlessly and compassionately. You believed I had something to say and helped me become a better educator year to year. A warm thank you to my editor Michael Gibson, who helped bring this book forth in the middle of a pandemic.

Thank you to the Louisville Institute and the Forum for Theological Exploration for inviting me to mentor doctoral students of color. It was at LI and FTE I discerned I wanted to write a book for new teachers. Thank you, Edwin Aponte, Don Richter, Ralph Basui Watkins, Carmen Nanko-Fernández, Jean-Pierre Ruiz, Patrick Reyes, and Elsie Barnhart for your collegiality and friendship. Deepest thanks the Wabash Center for Teaching and Learning in Theology and Religion. I have the sincerest appreciation for Lynne Westfield's and Paul Myhre's phenomenal leadership. Their work of bringing together communities of scholars to dig deeper into innovative teaching continually feeds my spirit.

I could not have written this book without faculty colleagues at Columbia Theological Seminary. In particular, Mindy McGarrah Sharp who partners with me daily in teaching and life. You are a wise friend and scholar. Thank you to Marcia Y. Riggs and Kathy Dawson. You are two educators I look up to in all things regarding integrity and excellent pedagogy. To the Practical Theology Area women at CTS, I am grateful for your friendship. Thank you, Lisa Weaver, Rebecca Spurrier, Anna Carter Florence, and Sue Kim Park for the prayers and hard conversations. I also want to thank three students who assisted in the research for this book: Garam Han, Dana Kim, and Hannah Sucharitha Injamuri.

I also could not have come this far without the support of the women of PANAAWTM. Their scholarship and friendship have impacted me in immeasurable ways. They ground me in my Asian and Asian American community and accountabilities. In particular, a deep 90 degree bow to Kwok Pui Lan, Haruko Nawata Ward, Grace Kao, Boyung Lee, Helen Jin Kim, Wonhee Anne Joh, Su Yon Pak, and Mai-Anh Le Tran. You shifted worlds within me.

From the village of friends and family, I want to thank Laura Mariko Cheifetz and Jessica Vazquez Torres. I could not have written this book without the friendship of these two brilliant humans. Keep truth-telling. You are two of the best teachers I know. Neighbors, forever! I want to thank my childhood friends and sisters, Carol Shin Park and Joyce Pak Lee. I love you both. You remind me to be my best self and I'm so glad we can raise our kids together across the miles.

Finally, I want to thank my family. Thank you to my *Umma,* Yoon Kyung Hee. You helped us raise Tae-Jin for her first two years so I could steal away to write. I don't have the words to express how grateful I am for the gift of your presence in our home and my life. You were my first teacher. You taught me about embodied love. Thank you, Halmi. Thank you to my *Appa,* Hong Sung Chi, for cheering me on across the distance, checking in on me, and believing in me. Thank you to my brother, Andrew, who somehow always makes it into my writing. Remember when I used to read you comics before bedtime? You were my first student! A deep well of love and gratitude for my partner Roger and his steadfast care and support in all things. Thank you especially for being parent number one when I am hunkered in the writing cave. Finally, thank you to my two wild and beautiful babies, Tae-Sup and Tae-Jin. *Umma* loves you. *Umma* will help build a better world for you.

Introduction

Decolonial Futuring in Theological Education

WE HAVEN'T ARRIVED, YET

Theological Education and Decolonial Futures

Theological education is experiencing a crisis of conscience. Despite vocal and public commitments to justice and liberation, institutions of theological education are still ultimately colonial and Christian enterprises. Many were built on the lifeblood of enslaved African people and on stolen Indigenous land. Outside of historically Black institutions, institutions of theological education in North America were established for white Christians alone. Some theological schools claim mission statements that center justice and liberation, but without contenting with their histories of entangled oppressions. Some schools remain staunchly reluctant to face their complicities and crimes. There exists an internal paradox at the heart of institutions of theological education and those of us who teach therein. Institutions of theological education have expertly dominated, stolen from and erased entire peoples. Rinse, and repeat. Can such institutions thrive and flourish in the face of such deep contradictions?

On the one hand, theological education hopes to change the world for the better, and on the other hand, it has difficulty holding a mirror up to its white supremacist, settler-colonial, and Christian hegemonic histories and practices. Theological institutions might say they want to become decolonial and turn away from colonial histories and practices but this would require them to carefully come to terms with the questions, "What is our complicity in empire? How are we perpetuating the conditions of coloniality today?" "What are we willing to give up or return to communities from which we have stolen?" When we examine the answers and realize our institutions have reaped the benefits of multitudes of oppressions, including settler-colonial histories, we might come to understand, as educators Eve Tuck and K. Wayne Yang suggest, there is not a path to complete decoloniality other than through indigeneity and reparations, the return to an Indigenous way of life and the return of stolen land.[1] That is just the start. There is more owed to Black, Indigenous, Latinx, Asian, Queer, and religiously minoritized people, than theological education could or would ever repay. Decolonization must be one of theological education's goals, but we are not there yet. We are yet unwilling.

As much as we teach postcolonial theory, we are not quite postcolonial. Our institutions still thrive on coloniality. The colonial enterprise is still with us and in us. It is not yet behind us. What are those of us committed to freedom and justice in theological education to do? What does pedagogy look like when it embraces justice in a movement toward decolonial dreams within unjust systems and structures? When confronted with our present colonial reality, could we commit ourselves as teachers toward strategic anticoloniality through the constant work of liberation from supremacist and settler-colonial entanglements? Could we oppose coloniality at large in our institutions by working to dismantle the reality and threat of violence as we create and reconstruct what gives life? Could educators do this by finding ways in our teaching and learning to see and hear the most minoritized among us? Can we imagine for a moment, the impact of teaching and learning that honors intercultural and interreligious differences as a commitment to collective anti-supremacist work?

In my life and education, I am aware of the power of both white and Christian supremacy in theological education. As a woman of color, I am an intruder in a space not meant for me. Not as I am. As a member of academic guilds and a teacher in theological schools, I know the feel, sound, smell, and taste of institutional white supremacy and Christian hegemony. I have rarely been part of theological educational spaces where the knowledge of my "unbelonging" does not surround me like an inescapable vapor. I learned and am learning about myself as a scholar and as a person through what institutions and people tell me I am not. As I came through different stages of theological education, I was like many others, defined through the lens of white normativity. As a non-Black and non-Indigenous woman of color, I am also familiar with the powerful lure and lie of white adjacency, white junior partner-ism,[2] and settler-colonialism. As Frank B. Wilderson III teaches me, by being a non-Black person, I am both a target of white supremacy and also the agent and beneficiary of anti-Blackness.[3] I know what it's like to discover religious bias, racial bias, and patriarchy imbedded under my skin through a lifetime of internalizing whiteness and the white framework of Christianity as normative. I have a responsibility to both undo and remake the ways in which I have been formed and conditioned by white supremacy, Christian hegemony, and their entangled saccharine poison.

Life in theological education has been a series of undoings and remakings. The experience of undoing reminds me of a scene in one of C. S. Lewis' Chronicles of Narnia books, *The Silver Chair*. A boy named Eustace becomes a dragon as a punishment for his selfish choices. Through a series of selfless acts, Eustace learns the error of his ways. He desires to shed his dragon skin but un-dragon-ing is not easy. Aslan, the lion, Lewis' metaphor for the Christian G-d, uses his claws to rip dragon scales from Eustace's flesh until he once again becomes a boy.[4] This scene is in my mind's eye as I imagine the decolonial dream for theological education. Undoing the violence of coloniality is not an easy nor instantaneous task. Un-dragon-ing is painful, but it is a communal effort to undo the colonial enterprise, scale by scale.

To press for movement toward decolonial and anticolonial teaching and learning in theological education, is to first acknowledge the crime of violence worked by white supremacy and Christian supremacy in theological education and on the lives of teachers and students as a colonial project. The premise of this book acknowledges that most institutions of North American theological education are still predominantly white and Christian. Institutions of theological education are mainly Christian institutions founded on Christian principles and theologies that have historically othered nonwhite and non-Christian people and their communities. This book acknowledges these very same historically white and Christian identifying institutions are growing and learning to serve a more interreligious, transnational, and racially diverse body of students. However, institutions of theological education have not left colonial Christian, and racist histories and events behind. They cannot hope to contribute to a new and just future without understanding the impact of those histories. In student bodies and on faculties of theological institutions, are people who have lived and experienced the atrocities of white supremacy and Christian hegemony.

This book is for theological educators who recognize that we are in the throes of a return to neocolonial white and Christian supremacist ideology in North America, and who are fighting back tooth and nail starting in their practices of teaching and in their institutions. Therefore, this book undertakes the reframing of theological education through anticolonial commitments in teaching and learning, toward a decolonial futuring. There is nothing systems and structures of oppression and violence hate more than minoritized people refusing to remain minor, and who are possessed with joy. A decolonial futuring is built on the grasping of joy in the face of our shared understanding that white and Christian supremacy are everywhere and tenacious as hell. White supremacy and Christian hegemonic structures and systems are at the core of how we experience teaching and learning. They exist as frameworks in everyday biases, degree program curricula, syllabi, the production of knowledge, assessment, grading, and in our relationships with students and colleagues. To take on intercultural and interreligious intelligence as a posture and a goal in theological education is to face head-on the damage white supremacy and Christian supremacy have inflicted on our lives. The pursuit of anticolonial commitments and decolonial futuring in teaching and learning and the frameworks of intercultural and interreligious intelligence, are concrete and subversive acts of love. The love of and for a theological education that is not soft but has edges. A love built on accountability pushing institutions of theological education into the future and at the very least, to the brink of transformation.[5]

NAVIGATING WHITE AND CHRISTIAN SUPREMACY CULTURES

For minoritized people, white supremacy and white Christian supremacy are realities we negotiate every time we teach. The first time I entered the classroom as a professor, I almost hyperventilated. I want to believe my face portrayed calm, but my heart was racing and I could feel the blood pounding in my temples. My hands and voice shook. I had trouble taking up space and could feel myself physically shrinking, crossing my arms over my chest, holding myself with the fear and defensiveness rooted in vulnerability and insecurity. As I strode to the front of the room, eighty pairs of eyes at my back, I viscerally felt the dynamics of power and privilege set into motion. Students began assessment. I was a problem. Race, ethnicity, gender, and age, combined with the fact that the Christian professor was decidedly *not* a white male, were part of the equation.

Black, Indigenous, and other people of color, particularly women of color, are presumed incompetent regardless of expertise. They enter classrooms with the odds stacked against them.[6] Knowing this, I felt an urgency to quickly establish my place as an expert. How else would students know I was in charge? Imposter syndrome was and still is very real. I had to flex my knowledge, vocabulary, and assert myself, while at the same time garnering the best possible evaluations for my teaching. The feeling of urgency around quickly proving my expertise carried significant weight. At that moment, my students and I, both alike and differently, were caught up in a cycle of western, whitewashed patterns of theological education. My embodiment instantaneously disrupted student's expectations of what learning should look and feel like. Meanwhile, my struggle to take up space by mimicking my white and male counterparts triggered my discomfort and fear of failure. Presumed incompetence doesn't mean students are apathetic to educators of color, it means we elicit extreme responses from both our colleagues and our students to our bodies, words, and teaching. Grace Chang, in the anthology *Presumed Incompetent*, talks about the way her students respond to and evaluate her courses in women of color studies. One student shared, "you either love her, or you hate her." Another student wrote that Chang made "the white community feel unsafe and uncomfortable."[7] Black, Indigenous, and other people of color, in particular, religiously minoritized BIPOC, challenge spaces of teaching and learning, evoking strong reactions from white students and white-serving institutions.

I remember a particular student interaction where I experienced first-hand the harsh reality of the negative response of white students to my embodiment as a teacher. After teaching a session on Christian histories and theologies in light of religious pluralism, a white man raised his hand in response to my comment on Karl Rahner's anonymous Christianity. In frustration, he mimicked my voice and repeated something I had said. His intentional caricature of my voice sounded like a little girl whining to an adult. After this odd and inappropriate exchange, I approached the student after class. He stated, "I'm not used to unqualified professors teaching Christian history and theology." His comment knocked the wind out of me. Only later did I realize the part of me he deemed unqualified was my race, gender, and perceived age. How often had this student and others like him been exposed to scholars of color who taught core subjects in theological education, rather than the carefully curated and domesticated areas of expertise in "cultural and ethnic" fields? I imagine if I had not been a Christian, the backlash would have been more severe. Never mind the fact that white and Christian academics have taught the histories of nonwhite and non-Christian peoples for centuries. This classroom interaction reminded me of what a senior Asian scholar once told me when I inquired about what I should expect in academe. She advised me saying, "They'll expect you to teach Buddhism and Asian histories, even if they aren't your subjects of expertise. Even if you know nothing about them."

Understanding this extraneous expectation for scholars and students of color is similar to the DuBois-ian double consciousness, the awareness of oneself through two distinct lenses and embodied realities. W.E.B. DuBois describes double consciousness in the lives of Black and African diasporic peoples as the ever-present discord of two competing understandings of self as "a peculiar sensation, this double-consciousness, this sense of always looking at one's self through the eyes of others, of measuring one's soul by the tape of a world that looks on in amused contempt and pity."[8] An additional way double consciousness presents itself is as code-switching, the necessity for Black, Indigenous, and other people of color to move between the expectations of the dominant white and Christian culture of theological education and that of their own communities of cultural and religious accountability. Though institutions might prop up code-switching as a valuable skill and a form of cultural savvy, it bears the question, why should *only* minoritized people have to cultivate this ability? In theological education, there is the added layer of theologizing and spiritualizing the struggle of racially and religiously minoritized scholars who live in multiple and competing worlds at once. This theologizing and glorifying the struggle of double-consciousness and code-switching as a commodifiable soft skill is systemic oppression working to justify the way minoritized scholars must operate within white supremacist and white Christian supremacist systems of theological education.

What theological education needs is not more minoritized scholars who can code-switch, but new frameworks of theological education altogether. How we teach and learn are constructs of a specific type of western educational system that came to different places and people via the vehicle of coercion and colonial oppressions. The three Ms of colonization, mission, mercantilism, and militarism[9] brought with it systems of education invented to obscure and erase the epistemologies of Indigenous communities and peoples. The three Ms of colonization established methods and realities of dominance and subjugation that began with the destruction of people and continues today through the internalization of settler-colonial and white supremacist ways of looking at oneself, others, and the world. Ways of knowing that edify and honor minoritized communities are systematically wiped out by western forms and systems of academe. We base scholarship and efficacy in the classroom on how well scholars can emulate and reify the very oppressive constructs of education that stifle their innate and vibrant understandings of self, community, and the world.

THE DREAM

Let us dream together. What if teachers and learners alike could walk into classrooms without bias? Both bias attributed to us and bias attributed to others? What if our classrooms were wall-less, creatively chaotic, and disruptive to oppressive educational frameworks as a method of normative education? What if education itself was not about coming to understand how much we know, but coming to terms with how much we must undo and how much we will never grasp or understand? Is it possible to move toward the coformation of educational models, especially in contexts rich with intercultural and interreligious differences? What might this require? What might we have to give up? What might we have to take on? Learn and unlearn?

This book on teaching and learning is guided by the questions, "What makes education intercultural and interreligious?" "How might we rethink and redesign spaces of learning as hospitable to cultural and religious differences and dismantle the coloniality of theological education?" "How might we subvert traditionally colonial spaces to model the engaged intercultural and interreligious world we seek?" This book aims to help theological educators deconstruct and reconstruct teaching and learning by centering interreligious and intercultural intelligence through the voices, experiences, and narratives of minoritized people. The book is in two parts, part one, deconstruction and part two, reconstruction. I understand deconstruction and reconstruction as two educational strategies implemented simultaneously and continuously as part of a commitment to decolonial work in all the spaces of learning we inhabit as theological educators and students.

COMMITMENTS

This book has anticolonial commitments. It resists centering only western-oriented understandings of academic research and literature. The cooption of the academy by white and Christian hegemony has prioritized certain epistemologies while discounting others, mirroring the colonial grab of knowledge and knowledge production. Though this text refers to educational theory, it does not focus on it or recreate it in the recognition that many peoples and communities have educated generations in ways theories have historically erased, excluded, and invalidated. This book also does not ground itself on didactic teaching as the primary modality of teaching and learning. Instead, the book embraces expansive epistemologies, postures, and modes of teaching and learning.

I am a religious and interreligious theological educator who focuses on freedom, liberation, and communal understandings of identity and spiritual formation. As such, I write in a hybrid scholarly and narrative style. Freedom is a communally oriented task, dream, and goal. Likewise, there is no such thing as teaching and learning disassociated with self, others, community, and accountabilities. It is through the experience of life in its fullness that we learn and teach. Attempting to write about teaching and learning without coming from an autoethnographic place is not an authentic undertaking. Throughout the book, I emphasize the importance of connectional learning, or connection with one's history, home, and people, to enter the process of deepening intercultural and interreligious intelligence. Connectional learning is communally bound and at times intangible. This emphasis also grounds my writing throughout the book. I share much of my personal histories and stories as a Korean American Christian woman. Borne out of my experiences of teaching and learning in both intercultural and interreligious spaces, this book carries my hopes for the transformation of these very same spaces. In my commitment to intercultural and interreligious spaces, I learned that for many of us, interculturality and interreligiosity happens in theological education before we are prepared for it and before we effectively can learn to teach toward it. I have engaged this topic as a student and a teacher in theological education, in denominational leadership in the Presbyterian Church (USA), and in my personal life. As I designed courses on intercultural and interreligious learning and assisted faith communities in cultivating relationships, I reshaped how I teach and engage in the scholarship and practice of intercultural and interreligious life. I am still learning from those who have gone before me, both teachers and students, and it is my sincerest hope that this work honors their contributions and commitments. This volume is given shape by those experiences and the experiences shared with me by coteachers and colearners.

Part one of this book begins by unseating the term "competency" and how we have used it colloquially and academically. Competency is a word often used in intercultural and interreligious spaces as a measurement for success and growth, but competency is also fraught in the way it assumes that one can attain mastery in a culture or religion outside one's own. I propose the framework of interreligious and intercultural intelligence instead. For my own understanding, I consider intelligence not through the lens of social or cognitive sciences but more akin to Korean *noon-chi,* or eye-measure. The intangible way many Korean people communicate through high context understanding of the world, environment, and relationships. *Noon-chi* is a posture and a learned skill more valuable at fostering communal health and well-being than being book smart. Likewise, interreligious and intercultural intelligence does not seek to describe competency or mastery but a specific posture and expectation toward listening and understanding across difference. As theological educators, we are desirous of formational spaces defined by the people and communities one encounters. Spaces that inspire and shape the cultivation of a posture of learning for all.

If the term "intelligence" is jarring, it is because we commonly use it as a synonym for competence and mastery, not as an expression of posture. We weaponize the word "intelligence" as code for people who fall in line or reach a cognitive bar. We use it in conjunction with destructive words like civilized and cultured. We readily assume the signifier of intelligent on white and male bodies and pejoratively on Black, Indigenous, people of color, and femme presenting bodies, as if femmes and BIPOC are *surprisingly* knowledgeable. I cannot count the times white people have called me articulate for no good reason. I am meant to hear it with the silent modifier, "for a woman or for a non-white person." A person can declare on their own that they are intelligent, but it takes a community to testify to that claim! Intelligence is more than scholarship, textual knowledge, or advanced degrees. Institutions of higher and theological education have historically been the most segregationist across race, religion, and gender. Intercultural and interreligious intelligence is an embodied posture. It is connectional. Each of us can name someone in our lives who has embodied a posture of intelligence. A posture of humility, deep listening, and understanding. For me, this person was my maternal grandmother. She possessed a fourth grade education but was wiser than any of us. She was always learning and sharing what she knew with her children and grandchildren. She was the person everyone in our family approached with their concerns and spiritual questions. She possessed a well of wisdom that came from a posture of intelligence that was beyond the one-dimensional way I learned to understand it through academe. She embodied intelligence as a posture for how one navigates and uses emotional and spiritual heft, how one deepens instincts grounded in empathy and compassion, and how one fearlessly engages in the sharp critique of the powers that be as a form of resistance to dominant and oppressive structures and systems.

REFRAMING INTELLIGENCE: AN UNDEFINING PRACTICE

It is out of a framework of intelligence turned on its head that this book moves to break open other constructs unhelpful to the cultivation of the appreciation of intercultural and interreligious difference in theological education. Emphasizing the undoing of webs of oppressions in theological education, part one of the book focuses on deconstruction. Chapter 1, *Undoing Competency*, interrogates the term "competency" as the measure for excellent engagement of difference. Chapter 2, *Unbinding Liberation*, seeks to expand our understanding of the dynamics of teaching and learning, toward the model of colearning, where all participants and learning produce liberative scholarship for all learners including "traditional" teachers. I discuss how classroom facilitators might examine power and privilege in the construction of spaces of learning, and how they might help their colearners welcome other people, places, practices, and spiritualities into the room to make the traditional classroom a dynamic and connectional place, even across space and time. Chapter 3, *Upsetting the White, Christian, Patriarchy*, encourages educators to overturn the normative dynamics of scholarship, culture, and religion in their spaces of learning, the premise being, only in resisting dominant culture narratives can we model a recentering of minoritized lives and voices for one another. Chapter 4 discusses *Uncivilizing Teaching and Learning*. The academy and its institutions are in the business of domesticating, civilizing, and disciplining, the minds, bodies, theologies, spiritualities, and identities of colearners. In order to truly participate in a decolonial futuring in theological education, we must do the careful work of being strategically uncivilized in the ways we reconstruct spaces of learning together.

Part two of the book takes the concept of uncivilizing narratives of colearning and argues for a reframing of how we assess knowledge, religion, spirituality, culture, and personhood in shared spaces of learning. Chapter 5, *Reclaiming Epistemologies*, introduces the Korean concept of *woori* as a way of knowing and generating knowledge that lies outside of traditional academic and colonial models of education. The chapter emphasizes research among the complex and diverse Asian American community; an example of a group with complicated histories, identities, and conflicts that necessitates nuanced understandings of difference in our teaching and learning. The chapter discusses how the experience of immigration is the lifelong touchstone for how immigrants engage religion, self, community, and world. Chapter 6, *Retelling Histories as Story and Story Formation*, explores ways knowledge is constructed and reconstructed through oral histories and stories. Often, through the integration of religious and personal themes. The chapter discusses the significance of narratives for people and communities who are in the diaspora, exile, and displacement and cannot return to sacred lands and people. The chapter examines how stories connect generations even when language is lost and how stories give birth to new sacral realities in new lands. I argue that these narratives should be given primacy as a way of resisting the mapping of colonial understandings of self, body, community, the sacred, and land, onto the lives of colearners. Chapter 7 flows from centering stories to *Reframing Religious and Cultural Borderlands*. This chapter unpacks how minoritized communities and people cultivate new forms of spirituality, practice, and even new customs and lexicons in new lands while simultaneously struggling with internalized resistance to the messiness of fluidity. I discuss the dangers of colonial purity narratives about culture and religion in spaces of learning and how the dynamics of unbound classrooms might encourage existing fluidities to surface and thrive. Chapter 8, *Restoring Genealogies of the Intangible*, discusses the restoration of genealogies in intercultural and interreligious life and learning, the erasure and destruction of knowledge that must necessarily be put back together. The chapter re-envisions how minoritized people might trace their trajectory of learning and growth outside of the colonial machine. The chapter resists the idea that racialized and religiously minoritized people need to validate or verify the existence of alternate genealogies of epistemologies, stories, and fluidities against the dominant culture. Intercultural and interreligious intelligence is cultivated and nurtured through motherlands, mother tongues, community elders, spiritual practices, and stories. In living into the fullness of those genealogies, entire communities can flourish, including dominant culture spaces through the denial of its base need to dominate and steal. This chapter discusses how spaces of learning might honor these unearthed genealogies of intelligence in ways that both challenge colonial structures and systems and eventually, replace them.

WHAT ISN'T HERE

My hope and love of teaching and learning undergird this entire effort, and perhaps it is your hope and love of teaching that encouraged you to read this book. However, there are some things I refuse to do in this book out of anti-oppression commitments. A word about what this book is not. This book is neither a handbook on best practices in teaching and learning interculturally and interreligiously, nor is it a book that outlines basic religious literacy for world religions. Though both are important to a decolonial futuring, internalizing a new posture and approach to the intercultural and interreligious classroom comes first. This book emphasizes a posture of humble modesty, the reframing of classrooms, lives, and livelihoods for a free and liberative future. This book is also *not* a map toward intercultural, interreligious, and interracial reconciliation or restoration. The book pushes back against the problematic nature of the desire for racial and religious reconciliation. I have seen reconciliation operate as the foot of the oppressor on the neck of the oppressed. I have witnessed many pleas and demands for the type of reconciliation that requires the survivors of violence and oppression to forgive and move on so that perpetrators of violence and abuse might escape their guilt and grief. Weaponized reconciliation incites more trauma and pain among the most vulnerable. In addition, restoration is fallacy when it comes to antiracist and interreligious education. Restoration language is tied to Christian sanctification and assumes something good once existed to which we can return. The truth is we are moving away from what once was; we are not attempting restoration. What exactly are we trying to restore? The good and healthy relations between Black, Indigenous, people of color, and white folks in North America? The once equitable ways Christian institutions in the United States served both Native and white people? The language of reconciliation and restoration is fantasy. Bishop Roy I. Sano of the United Methodist Church wrote in 1982 about the nature of reconciliation and restoration as falling short of the divine promise. Many of us still do not understand him. Sano states that though "The attitudes and actions of individuals may be forgiven and changed, but it(reconciliation) has not promised any changes in the institutional racism which can override individual efforts."[10] Though we are now decades beyond when Bishop Sano wrote on the problem of racial reconciliation and restoration among Christians, many of us who seek after intercultural, interreligious, and interracial solidarity are still expressing a desire for reconciliation and restoration as the ultimate goal. The collective vision of reconciliation and restoration is a step toward the goal of dismantling systems of oppression, but it is not the goal itself. Instead, this book attempts to speak forthrightly about the existing oppressions emanating from empire, white supremacy, and Christian supremacy, as many others have already done in both theological and activist circles. No, you won't be equipped to solve the problem of racism, white supremacy, and dangerous theologies by reading this book, but my hope is that it offers the theological educator pause to reflect on what teaching and learning might look if we lived interculturally and interreligiously with embodied intelligence of the mind, heart, and spirit.

Part I

DECONSTRUCTION

Chapter 1

Undoing Competency

THE DEVASTATION OF MASTERY

What do we mean by Colonialism and Anticolonialism?

At the heart of colonialism is the desire to master everything and everyone. Colonialism possesses an insatiable hunger for ownership and control. Control over bodies and land. The theft of freedoms. Mastery over places and beings. Colonial mastery devastates. Embodied colonial mastery is power wielded to control, diminish, and erase at will. Ania Loomba, in her foundational book *Colonialism/Postcolonialism*, calls colonialism a midwife in the birth of capitalism. Loomba defines capitalist colonialism as imperialism.[1] Colonialism is both a historical period of a geographic and military takeover and the domination of entire peoples, cultures, religions, and all they create. Colonialism aided and abetted the violence of Christian mission history throughout the world. Colonization is simultaneously a swift and lengthy process. Historically, colonialism's happening might seem like the sudden conquering of land and people, but its violence propels itself forward into generations, creeping into perceptions, stories, and dreams. Colonialism makes its home among people and divides them; collusion of the outside and the inside. Loomba calls this, "a version of colonialism . . . duplicated from within."[2] Once set into motion, colonialism perpetuates itself into future generations, into diasporic rebirths, and traumatic internalizations of self-hatred.

Anticolonialism is resistance to the colonial enterprise. It is the seeding of the possibility and hope of a collective, multiversal, decolonial dream. Anticolonialism is a stance that works alongside the process of decolonization. We resist the perpetuation of all the ways colonialism seeps under our skin and into our collective lives while working toward reparations. Both anticolonialism and decolonization occur on the world stage, in and on our bodies. Decolonization is a political process between nation-states and their militaries, aided by the resistance strategies of anticolonial practices. Decolonization as a process incorporates anticolonial strategy and is also a lived reality. It begins as a process of the heart. I remember in third grade, I would be surprised that my reflection showed the face of a Korean girl when I understood myself internally as white. Whiteness was a lie of safety for a child who struggled with being bicultural, negotiating intergenerational conflict at home, and who held resentment toward her immigrant parents. I remember the jarring jolt in my body and heart as I was simultaneously shocked and disappointed by the truth reflected in the glass. Decolonization is political and individual. Anticolonial action furthers decolonial process. Both are painful and necessary. Even after the official exit of a colonial nation, colonialism's systems and ways of being are rooted in place, mixed in with the soil, language, family names, and even the food of a people. Loomba writes, "The dismantling of colonial rule did not automatically bring about changes for the better in the status of women, the working class or the peasantry in the most colonized countries."[3] What comes after colonialism is still colonialism, stealthy and internal, entwined in religion and culture. Colonialism changes language, food, practice, and worship, often forever. Resisting colonialism through anticolonialism is not the glorification of the precolonial context, but a ritualized mourning of its absence and our inability to return to it while turning a critical lens on the ways colonialism has changed the way we see and know one another and ourselves. Anticolonialism is a living practice, tradition, and activism that fights against the determination of colonial threads in our everyday lives.

Anticolonialism as a daily practice begets intercultural and interreligious intelligence as a posture for teaching and learning. The concept of mastery and its sidekick competency are illusory for the posture of intercultural and interreligious intelligence. Intelligence framed as posture does not seek mastery over knowledge in order to wield it against others but aims for openness to the new. It seeks accountability outside of personal and normative understandings. Intelligence is respectfully curious about how different peoples, cultures, and homelands understand what intelligence looks, sounds, feels, and tastes like. Again, not for the purposes of appropriation but in order to understand power and beauty that can and must exist outside of a relationship with narratives of the dominant culture and religion. Black, Indigenous, and people of color, and those who are religiously othered by a white Christian supremacy do not exist for capitalist consumption. We are not food, hunted and gathered by an apex predator. In fact, whiteness would starve if it did not constantly feed off of the vibrancy of those it envies. Our narratives do not exist to become foils to white Christianity's understanding of itself, the divine, and the world. We don't exist for whiteness and white institutions to assess for value and to comprehend. Whiteness can never truly comprehend us because it can't understand beyond itself.

The way we use competency and mastery in educational frameworks is in terms of perfecting comprehension. I once took an inventory that claimed it could assess my teaching ability. The first question was, "How would you rate your *competence* in the task of teaching?" Choose one: (a) expert, (b) mostly competent, (c) satisfactory, (d) some knowledge, (e) novice. The multiple choices puzzled me. I immediately spiraled into more questions. How are the creators of this inventory defining competence? What does it mean to be a competent theologian and a competent religious educator? I struggle with the notion of competence to describe skillful teaching. Can one ever actually claim full competency or mastery of a subject? Could I, as an instructor, ever fully possess mastery over all the knowledge available to me within a particular field of study? Mastery enough to transmit that knowledge to students, and then measure *their* competency in the subject? The question so jarred me that I don't even remember what I chose!

There are other sets of questions we might ask as we consider what it means to teach in this particular time and place. The premise of this book speaks to those of us in theological education teaching in a white supremacist, Christian centric, and religiously suspicious North America. In a time where many educators are intentionally attempting to integrate justice-oriented methods, decolonial perspectives, and anticolonial resistances into our classrooms, do we ever want to claim "mastery" and the violence it suggests? Are inventories on competency like this, useful? As educators, are we prepared to teach and learn among a growing racialized, ethnic, cultural, and religious diversity? When it comes to intercultural and interreligious intelligence, how do we assess our ability to teach and facilitate classes full of cultural and religious differences? How do we bring our own racialized, ethnic, cultural, and religious differences into an already complex mix? For educators who are aware of the reality of white supremacist and Christian hegemonic structures in theological education, how might they teach well given those glaring realities in campus climates, faculty, and student life? How might we reframe or discard "competency" toward the aim of teaching and learning anticolonially? I raise these questions and more in hopes to disrupt, dismantle, and reconstruct our intercultural and interreligious commitments to teaching anticolonially in theological education.

A Question of Competency

The use of competency as a measure in education is partly grounded within the field of competency-based education (CBE) models. These CBE models were and are used primarily with vocational contexts like health and sciences[4] where the mastery of a subject is truly life or death. Competence in the health and sciences is about modeling enough knowledge about a topic or task to constitute expertise. For example, if you are going to the hospital for emergency surgery, you are highly desirous of at the very least a competent surgeon. You hope for more than competence, but you cannot agree to less than this. Though competency has positive connotations in some fields, historically for others including in ethnic studies, religious studies, and theology, the measure of competency and any assigned value has required assimilation to white and Christian norms.

The notion of competency when it comes to people's lived experiences in culture and religion harkens back to the colonial operationalization of science and education to subjugate, control, and destroy. The colonial mindset harnesses science and education to assume dominance and control over people, cultures, and experiences via policies and education. Indigenous educator, Margaret Kovach writes, "In the colonization of Indigenous people, science (Darwin's evolutionary theory) was used to support an ideological and racist justification for subjecting Indigenous cultures and ways of knowing . . . the racism inherent in this evolutionary paradigm contributed to the genocidal polity toward Indigenous peoples in the Americas."[5] The direct result of colonialism's weaponization of science and measure of competency was the destruction of nonwhite and nonwestern ways of being.

Competency in religious education and even theological education through a dangerously colonial understanding presumes whiteness and Christianity as normative. Any difference is "other" and therefore expendable or buried in favor of white and Christian ways of knowing and being. In other words, differences exist to conquer and subjugate to a higher form of civilization and authority. Difference is valuable only as much as it is commercializable and commodifiable. Empire commodifies and capitalizes on the labor of those it dominates. Among communities of color, the social sciences, anthropology, sociology, and even practical theology with its focus on qualitative research, have moved within these domineering constructs for centuries. All have studied people of color without acknowledging them as fully human. These academic fields have explored Indigenous communities and their religious beliefs and practices, not for the sake of learning about them through the eyes of community members who are intrinsically part of the community, but to relegate them to the status of native informants, people of racial and religious difference who exist to inform outsiders about what is happening on the inside without benefit to their community of origin. The term native informant serves to define a community member's primary role in service to the research agenda, a reductionist description. The work of Indigenous social scientists and researchers like Kovach in her text *Indigenous Methodologies*,[6] helps qualitative researchers understand the detrimental effects of colonial social science on minoritized peoples and communities, particularly Native peoples. Social science, at its worst, works to lock native informants, particularly those who are already racialized and religiously minoritized, into social and racial categories of dominance and subjugation, of master and slave, of human and subhuman.[7]

Leaning on data mined only by the social sciences is it even possible for educators to claim competency or proficiency in a culture or religion not their own? As a religious studies scholar Stephen Prothero believes, "religious literacy in the abstract is an impossibility."[8] Facts and figures without embodied relationships do not teach us all we need to know to "participate in our ongoing conversation about the private and public powers of religions."[9] Mastery is a flawed approach to learning about racial, cultural, and religious difference. How can one gain mastery over the study of entire peoples and communities and teach students to do so as well?

To be sure, a level of cultural and religious literacy[10] as proficiency is necessary for theological education, but only in tandem with the understanding and critique of why and how cultures and religions change over time. For example, Prothero's book on why North Americans need religious literacy is an eye-opening look at the pervasive religious amnesia that occurs with the rise of secularism. Religious histories are not static but forgotten over time as religious practice and understandings shift. Prothero's argument is not that North Americans have forgotten religious history altogether, but with the marriage between religion and political power, even very particular theologies begin to transform and diverge from their roots.[11] The danger of this politicized shift is the threat of a growing white Christian supremacy and nationalism in the United States.

Without cultural and religious literacy and a critique of power within those constructs, people who suffer from the violence of bias, racism, and bigotry will continue to suffer. Intercultural and interreligious literacy as proficiency at its best is a beginning, an open door to deeper forms and methods of understanding. It is an invitation to engagement and relationship across differences. Proficiency at its worst is an end to learning and the assumption of mastery on colonial terms, the most basic forms of knowledge simplified, reduced, and digested for commodification and use by the newly minted "cultural and religious expert." There are elements of culture or religion in which one should gain proficiency as a starting point not as an end goal, such as language, core, and common understandings and beliefs. However, the overall tacit cultural[12] understanding of peoplehood, culture, and the personal knowledge of the individual and communal experience is not comprehensible through rote memorization and study. The academic assumption that cultural and religious competency exists and can comprehend tacit culture, or that tacit culture does not matter, is hubris.

In college, I took Korean as a foreign language. I was in a classroom of mostly second-generation Korean Americans who were taking the course to supplement the colloquial language we had learned at home and weekend Korean language schools. I was also among military servicemen and women who were taking the course before deployment to the Korean Peninsula. Almost instantly, class divisions appeared along the lines of second-generation Korean folks and those who were not Korean. Korean students had more trouble with the grammatical parsing of sentence structures and other linguistically oriented types of learning. Those who did not identify as Korean or Korean American had more difficulty understanding the meanings transmitted through careful tonal modulation, or the subtexts of high context conversations typical of Korean culture. Though a student could gain expertise in the Korean language itself, understanding the implicit contextual role of Korean language in people's everyday lives was something only a member of the community could understand. Likewise, the study of human life and experience, in particular religious, spiritual, and cultural experiences are intimate and cannot be replicated or ascertained by those outside those communities and experiences. Community insiders invite outsiders[13] to experience tacit culture themselves. However, this is a revocable invitation should the outsider overstep their bounds. Ideally, with minoritized groups, the power in the insider and outsider relationship exists with insiders.

INTERCULTURAL AND INTERRELIGIOUS INTELLIGENCE

How does the scientific understanding of competency or proficiency correlate to the humanities or theological education?[14] Theological education possesses racialized hierarchies of theologies and models of education. I have often wondered if there was better terminology to describe the deliberate process of anticolonial teaching and learning to which I am committed. I am influenced by but not bound to Howard Gardner's work on multiple intelligences; a framework for how people think and learn differently founded on eight scientific criteria.[15] In 1983, Howard Gardner impacted an entire generation of educators with his reframing of intelligence as a framework of seven intelligences.[16] In 1999, Gardner expanded the concept of multiple intelligences to include other forms of intelligences, including naturalist, experiential, moral, and spiritual intelligences. Gardner's updated definition of intelligence in his book is, "a biopsychological potential to process information that can be activated in a cultural setting to solve problems or create products that are of value in a culture."[17] Through Gardner's invitation to expand our understanding of intelligences, I lean toward the phrase, "interreligious and intercultural intelligence" as a way to mark whether or not someone is productive and effective as both a teacher and a learner in spaces of knowledge transmission.[18]

Reimagining Intelligence

Expanding on Gardner's concept of multiple intelligences as beyond what is logically quantifiable, I explore what it means to grow simultaneously in individual and communal intercultural and interreligious intelligences. Gardner's essential scientific criteria are compromised by the ways science has historically objectified and diminished nonwhite and non-Christian expressions of what has long counted for signs of intelligence. Can intelligence be a communal process and communal in the realm of the intercultural and interreligious? Intelligence is something with which all sentient beings are born into this world. Intelligence signals the potential for growth and the behavioral change depending on that growth. Gardner "suggests that intelligences are not things that can be seen or counted. Instead, they are potentials—presumably neural ones—that will or will not be activated, depending on the values of a particular culture, and the personal decision made by the individuals, and/or their families, school teachers, and others."[19] I agree with Gardner that intelligence does not mean someone is guaranteed to grow or learn but signals the potential for growth to occur. Intelligence is infinite and multifaceted. Like Gardner, I believe there is not one modality of intelligence, but a multitude of ways one can expand and exercise intelligence in one's life. Intercultural and interreligious intelligence is one framework of engaging self and the world that expands on Gardner's theory.

Intelligence in the way I describe it and use it in this book does not primarily have to do with the capacity for cognitive skills in the way Gardner linked his framework of multiple intelligences. To frame intelligence as only concerning cognitive development is ableist and denies the deep intelligence that resides within different states of neurodivergence. My paternal grandmother, who is ninety-six, has lived with dementia for the last fifteen years. One summer night, while I was visiting her, I abruptly awoke to the sound of her singing in her bedroom. I shot up and quickly swung open the door of her bedroom fully expecting to see something terrible. My grandmother was sitting up in bed, her back poker straight and arms stretched out. Her hands poised over invisible piano key, fingers feverishly playing. At the top of her lungs, she sang the hymn; *A Mighty Fortress is Our God*. Alarmed, I asked, "Grandma, what are you doing?" Continuing to play her piano, she hissed, "Be quiet! We're in worship!" Stunned by the "we," I paused and asked, "Grandma, who's here?" She listed off the names and titles of people I knew and didn't know, among them family members, people who were left behind in North Korea, and friends, all of whom had long since passed. At that moment, I knew I was on holy ground, witnessing a thin place borne from the longing and memory of my grandmother whose body was still here and now. I could not see it. I could not hear it. Yet it was real and happening outside of my understanding. My grandmother, through her experience of dementia was a time traveler and brought me with her. She epitomized a form of intelligence beyond what science could tell me and beyond what I could grasp or know. Intercultural and interreligious intelligence has to do with the ways of seeing, feeling, and being that are often beyond what is considered intelligent by western science. The framework of intercultural and interreligious intelligence harnesses several other types of intelligences including some that Gardner names such as personal and interpersonal relationships, emotional intelligence, and spiritual intelligence to name a few. Sometimes these noncognitive modalities are a much more significant indicator or growth. The value in interreligious and intercultural intelligence is its potential for integrating known forms of multiple intelligences to expand cultural and religious awareness toward more inclusive expressions and understandings.

MEASURING INTELLIGENCE

A shared goal as educators in theological education, no matter the specific field, is to help our students transform and grow in ways that positively impact our world. Yet, how do we even measure the impact of transformation and growth? We might strive to measure the reproduction of knowledge, tests, and essays which aim to demonstrate whether or not a student can retain new knowledge and recalibrate it for their contexts, but often these assessment do not measure the effects of long-term change and impact. Intercultural and interreligious intelligence can, like other forms of intelligence, undergo testing for basic literacy and knowledge retention and production, but its real impact is in many ways immeasurable in our classrooms. Intercultural and interreligious intelligence at its core is about curiosity, the desire to know and be known. Intercultural and interreligious intelligence builds upon the foundations of basic cultural and religious literacy and invests communally in relationships, conflict transformation, the cocreation of justice and the dignity of all life. If taught in specific ways students can perform the type of intelligence required for an A letter grade. A transformative moment for me as an educator was when a student in an introductory theology course wrote a final paper defending the enslavement of people. I was shocked. His paper cited resource after resource to assert his claim. The student met every criterion for critical thinking, theological inquiry, and style. The student's precise citations of academic and religious texts reminded me of the plethora of scholarship which seeks to dehumanize nonwhiteness. Were it not for a component in the assignment's requirements that asked students to consider justice and human dignity, they might have technically earned an A. At this moment, I realized that it is not enough to teach students how to excel in research and academese. It was not enough to hope that a written research assignment might measure growth in all the different aspects of a student's life. Cultivating students that are book smart, who can regurgitate information is *not enough* to change the world. Likewise, being teachers who are adept at nurturing traditional academicians and theologians is *not enough* to change the world. We need to cultivate a different posture toward the world, one another, and ourselves. Change begins with our postures of teaching and learning.

Humble Modesty

Intercultural and interreligious intelligence requires a posture of humble modesty. Though the words humility and modesty may sound redundant, they function differently and together. They work together to describe an inward perspective that naturally creates an outward response. Humility is an inward posture. When deeply internalized, humility becomes embodied in acts of modesty. Modesty is not self-deprecation. Modesty is the basic understanding that you move through this world without having figured it all out yet. At its core, the desire for interreligious and intercultural intelligence is about a posture of humble modesty. Intelligence is not the same as desiring expertise or mastery of the ins and outs of religions or cultures, as if one could possess mastery of a culture or community in the first place. Intelligence signals potential and the possibility for growth beyond what is currently known or understood. Intelligence is part curiosity and part wonder; a mode of being, not an end result. Like, the insider and outsider dynamics of qualitative research, interreligious and intercultural intelligence is measured in multiple directions. Both the person who is practicing wonder and curiosity and the communities to whom the person is accountable determines intelligence. In other words, one cannot merely claim interreligious and intercultural intelligence as a descriptor for one's practice or posture; it is an invitation modeled on accountable practices and commitments. A person is called intelligent for their constant effort to grow toward communities of difference.

Not all of us are squarely in the field of teaching, but as long as we remain committed to the posture of intercultural and interreligious intelligence, there is hope and possibility of changing existing systems and structures of oppressions and resisting the creation of new ones. In teaching and learning well, the posture of humble modesty as embodied through intercultural and interreligious intelligence is critical. Though not all educators receive pedagogical training, it is never too late to internalize the foundations of teaching well, especially the foundations of understanding interreligious and intercultural differences through the lenses of equity, power, privilege, and vulnerability.

As theological educators, we were not all necessarily trained to teach using expansive methods or epistemologies that are both intercultural and interreligious. Many of us are not prepared to attend to any cultural or religious difference at all if it does not serve a paradigm of white and Christian normativity. The role of theological education has been to condition people into ideologies of Christian supremacy and by default the glorification of a white Christianity. As theologian Jeannine Hill Fletcher describes, "It was in academic spaces of theological training that ideas of Christian supremacy were manufactured as knowledge, to be put to the project of conquest, colonization, conversion as they made their way from lecture hall, to pulpit, to legislative assemblies."[20] We are trained through academe to center the written text, usually a primary text in a primary language. In doctoral exams, we pass or fail based on our comprehensive understanding and engagement of the written word. Our doctoral language exams measure how well we can use a secondary, third, or fourth language to translate and comprehend, never mind that to truly understand there may be tacit cultural and religious understandings only accessible to insiders of a particular community. None of this prepares us directly for the postures of teaching and learning that will help us in the formation of intercultural and interreligious intelligence in the classroom. According to Fletcher, none of this was meant to do so.

Though many theological educators never encounter the theories behind teaching and learning that honor difference, they still learn how to teach by attending to how others teach. For many of us, we learn the ropes through trial and error. We learn how to teach by watching other teachers, learning from the ingenious methods that help us to learn and grow. We also mentally note the teaching tactics that fail. Each of us who have chosen teaching as vocation can bring to mind an individual whom we would call an excellent teacher. A teacher who first and foremost knew our names and made us feel seen. An imperfect but influential figure in our own education who somehow knew how to read the room and pose the right questions. A teacher who appreciated the power of silence and understood the need for learning and processing in different ways. A guide who facilitated even the most challenging classroom scenarios, who affirmed and recognized the humanity of their students, and who pushed us toward personal transformation. All of us can picture a teacher whose posture of humble modesty sparked in us the desire to emulate what we experienced for others. Most importantly, a teacher who tenaciously hoped that we would contribute to the turning of the world and the work of peace and justice.

WHY INTERCULTURAL AND INTERRELIGIOUS INTELLIGENCE IS NECESSARY: A CASE STUDY

To pursue intercultural and interreligious intelligence in our teaching and learning is to honor what communities and people who are culturally and religiously different from us consider to be postures and behaviors of intelligence. At its most intimate, intercultural and interreligious intelligence is founded on relationship, the relationship between our innermost truths revealed to one another and our interpretation and internalization of the truths we witness as a necessary part of mutual growth. Gaile Sloan Cannella interprets Édouard Glissant's concept of relationship as an anticolonial tactic. Relationship is counter to "western humanism's relentless quest to define and limit the 'other' permanently, the concept of 'Relation' sees the 'other' not only as equal but as needed precisely because of the difference."[21] Intercultural and interreligious intelligence founded on relationship means the ongoing work toward deconstructing the rigid binary of teacher and learner. Teaching and learning crisscrosses lines of difference. We need one another to teach and learn because of our differences.

We are *both* teachers *and* learners, as are our students. Deconstructing the teacher and learner binary does not mean that there are no longer any power differentials with which we assess and contend, but overall the demarcation between who holds knowledge and who does not is intentionally blurred. This relational posture of intelligence complicates the line between teacher and learner and is particularly important if the teacher is from the dominant culture or religion where systems, policies, and language all orient themselves toward privileging what and who is dominant while subjugating others. When power differentials go unaddressed in classrooms, systems, and structures, the burden of interreligious and intercultural intelligence falls on the group or person with the least amount of racial, ethnic, and religious power and privilege. When I first entered the workforce, my white boss pulled me aside and asked me to let him know if ever he said anything racist in my presence. His intention was to let his new employee know he was attending to dynamics of racial power, but he went about it by making the vulnerable person in this situation responsible for his antiracist education. Through this action, he became guilty of what he feared most. A dynamic that doesn't effectively surface and engage power and privilege usually requires the most at-risk persons to act as instructors for those who haven't got a clue. The at-risk person expends energy, not for personal flourishing, but for the burden of educating the powerful and even consoling their fragility at the vulnerable person's own expense.[22]

I've witnessed the dynamic of those most at-risk educating the powerful occurring between Korean immigrant and white congregations. In one instance, a Korean immigrant church, one of the only nonwhite congregations in the area, was asked to host monthly meetings for a regional organization. The Korean church, being a high context culture, never felt like it could say no when asked to make its building available for this purpose. Unbeknownst to the white dominant organizing body, Korean culture has a complicated relationship to hospitality. There are social cues and expectations of both host and guest. Hospitality is an intricate dance of outdoing one another in order to show mutuality and care. The host church was asked to provide only light refreshments, but instead they went out of their way to prepare a full Korean meal for their guests. Deacons and elders shopped, prepped ingredients, cooked, and served. Everyone got to work making sure the bathrooms, buildings, and landscape were pristine for the organization's arrival. What was supposed to be a regular monthly gathering became a burden of hospitality to the Korean immigrant church. They could not vocalize this to the organization because of cultural codes and their high context values. In the Korean culture, as in many other Asian cultures, the guest is responsible for reading the host's contextual cues and should reciprocate gratitude, often in corresponding value through gifts, for the generosity and effort received. The guest's reciprocating gift should show a deep appreciation of the host's gesture.[23] In this case, the organizers did not correctly read the Korean congregation's cues, nor did they know how to do so.

Month after month, the organization arrived at the meeting, ate, gave a hearty and sincere verbal thanks, and because the event was always a smashing success and all indications pointed to the Korean congregation enjoying their hosting duties, the group continued to ask the congregation to host the gatherings. After months of this back and forth, the organization's lack of cultural reciprocation was interpreted as an attempt to insult the Korean congregation's efforts. It was not enough to verbally thank the congregation and send a signed card. A grander gesture signaling mutuality was looked for and not received. The Korean congregation continued to feel used and misunderstood. Resentment grew. The mix of direct and indirect approaches to communication sent the once positive relationship between the Korean immigrant congregation and the organization into confusion and disarray.

To sum up, the burden of intercultural intelligence fell on the organization's shoulders as it was led by the racially and culturally dominant people whose role it was to serve the whole body of which the Korean church was a part. Continuing to read the situation and relationship in terms of the dominant cultures understanding of hospitality and the role of host and guest placed the relationship in jeopardy. It became up to the Korean congregation to explain and educate the dominant culture group, which would, in effect, require such significant cultural code-switching that it was deemed impossible. Eventually, the Korean congregation stopped sending its representatives and pastors to the organization's other gatherings as an outward and nonverbal signal of the increasingly complicated relationship. These cues in turn were continuously read as a lack of the Korean congregation's commitment to the greater good by the partnering organization. In this particular case, as in other high-low context relationships, the burden of code-switching[24] fell on the minoritized community and its people. To say it another way, the burden of intercultural intelligence fell upon the shoulders of the community having to enact relationship in two cultural modalities. However, the case study and situation offered *opportunities* for dominant culture people to act out of modalities of intercultural intelligence and commit to mutual relationship to resist the systemic dynamics of power. Those who are part of dominant culture groups, communities, structures, and systems needed to see intercultural relationships as opportunities to expand and cultivate intercultural intelligence.

THE INEQUITY OF FAILURE

How does one expand into a deeper commitment to intercultural and interreligious intelligence? Sometimes it means we fail while trying. Intercultural and interreligious intelligence requires a willingness to make mistakes. Have you ever watched a child learn something for the first time? A baby learns to walk by taking a brave first step. The baby is prepared to fall with their hands stretched out, but hopes they will not. They will fall and they will cry, but they always stand back up to try again. Upon falling the first time, the baby does not think, "This walking stuff isn't really for me." A child learns how things work by peppering adults with questions, sometimes the same question over and over again, asked this way and that. An adolescent learns by pushing against the boundaries set for them, testing to see which boundaries flex and which are immovable. When the opportunity presents itself, children are natural learners, leaning into the opportunity to learn something new rather than shying away from it. When did we as adults, teachers, and students learn to lean away from opportunities that cultivate growth and intelligence, instead of being willing to fail and try? Some of the reasons might be because many educators promote a culture of perfectionism, or buy into the idea that doing things correctly is how people learn rather than through a multitude of failed attempts. Perfectionism is at its core the fear of being criticized and the fear of being wrong. Being right one hundred percent of the time is not the point of learning. In the ways, we teach and learn how do we destabilize our efforts in teaching and learning through the cultivation of perfectionism? How might we instead aim to develop an appreciation of critique as a significant way through which we learn to disassemble, reassemble, and rearrange how we understand ourselves, one another, and the world?

Another reason for our fear of failing is that there exist genuine consequences for failure. When we fail, especially in our relationships with one another, people's lives are turned upside down sometimes beyond repair. Sometimes failure is straight up violence. For some, failure and moving on from failure is a luxury they possess in plentitude. For many, failures are forever and are even generational. As we grow from childhood to adolescence and adolescence to adulthood we learn that the failures of an older generation are revisited upon the younger in tangible ways. As humankind, we have made mistakes on a global scale. The word "mistake" is far too trite for some of the grievous crimes we have committed against our own kind and against our own planet. Climate change is one of the most tangible examples of the largess of human kind's irreversible and devastating failures. The climate change crisis is a justice issue, a racialized one, and one with measurable and terrifying consequences. Jonathan Franzen writes in The *New Yorker* about facing the reversible climate crisis. Franzen urges us to stop painting a rosy picture of somehow reversing our trajectory of doom and instead pleads with us to live for the small wins. For Franzen, a small and necessary win is slowing down what is inevitable.[25] Failures small and large are not without consequence, and knowing this can either make us too afraid to keep moving, to keep growing, and to keep learning, or can affirm our postures of humble modesty.

Committing to intercultural and interreligious intelligence requires the willingness to stay curious and try. Intelligence requires we not only embrace the possibility of failures but also make ourselves aware of the oft substantial consequences of those mistakes. Intercultural and interreligious intelligence recognizes that failure is a part of how we learn and grow, and part of learning and growing is making amends for how we fail. Intercultural and interreligious intelligence requires that we face head on the other less-resilient side of failure.

Failure does not impact people equally. It is a privilege to experience failure as one missed opportunity of many. Second chances are given to some not all. It is only for some that failing comes *only* with the personal rectifiable consequences of damaged pride or ego. For many people and communities, failure is a possibility and a reality with devastating consequences for the broader community and into generations. The threat of failure to communal life reminds me of Chinese American Paper Sons.[26] Chinese men who were "adopted" via forged family papers. They gave up their names and took new ones in order to immigrate to the United States as laborers with hope for a different future. These men did not have the option to fail and to try again. Their every success and failure determined the fate of others and still affects their descendants today.

Today, for immigrants and asylum seekers to the United States failing is not an option, though it may become a reality. To fail with the guarantee of another chance is not a given. Today, the children of immigrants, many of whom are our students, teach us the impact and threat of failure on their lives. Immigrant children and adolescent's roles as culture brokers for the immigrant generation, and as the embodiment of their family's hope for upward mobility through scholastic and professional achievement, is a stark reality. For them, failure is not an option, and has devastating, long-reaching consequences that are relational, social, and economical.

As early as elementary school, I remember thinking that any grade below an A was unexceptable. I wasn't a child perfectionist. I understood that As earned scholarships. Scholarships led to access to good colleges. Good colleges let to well-paying jobs. A child with a well-paying job could support her parents. Even as a child, I understood my responsibility to care for my parents as they aged. Contrary to the Asian American stereotype, my parents never demanded straight As from their children. They never told me I would have to get rich and take care of them. Filial piety was an expectation I carried on my own. I watched silently as my parents worked multiple jobs and long hours. I watched as they struggled to make ends meet and struggled to stay afloat in an America that saw them as foreign even after naturalization. "We came here for you. We wanted to give our children a better life and more opportunities." I took on the immigrant bargain. The thought of failure stung. Failure was the equivalent of belittling my parent's sacrifices. Failure was not an option.

To teach and learn well, we have to accept that making mistakes and yes, failing, is part of our journey. However, failure comes at a cost. Being a skilled teacher and learner requires that we try new things, learn new things, and sometimes fail at the things we care most about, try to learn from those mistakes, and actively engage in making right the damage our mistakes and failures create. Making mistakes and failing requires internalized humble modesty, which helps us see and mitigate the impact of the intercultural and interreligious mistakes and failures we create. Furthermore, we understand that the same mistakes and failures have different implications for different people and their communities. Even so, we do our utmost to understand the proclivity for perfectionism, the genuine contextual realities, and push forward to keep learning. Ultimately, the best sorts of teachers and learners, actively release their yearning for perfection, competency, or mastery and instead welcome the efficacy of learning from mistakes. The anticolonial, decolonial, intercultural, and interreligious teacher and learner does not seek to erase failure but seeks to learn from it, lessen its impact, and ask for forgiveness, even when refused.

Commitment to intercultural and interreligious intelligence garners us scrapes and scuffs on our minds and hearts. Approaches to cultivating intelligent constructs of teaching and learning remembers that first and foremost those scrapes and scuffs are in relational accountability with people. Intercultural and interreligious intelligence understands that the mistakes we make affect actual bodies, lives, and entire communities. Our mistakes are integral to our learning as teachers but require us to recognize their ripple effect. Our mistakes may not hurt us, but they can and will hurt others, sometimes in ways invisible to us. Understanding how we reconstruct anticolonial spaces of teaching and learning does not diminish the problem of power differentials between instructors and students. Part two of this book focused on reconstruction will unpack the concept of power differentials between teachers and students more fully.

Teaching and learning interculturally and interreligiously requires instructors to model humble modesty for students and requires the unceasing work of learning with and from our students when it comes to intercultural and interreligious understanding. Even if learning means we make mistakes and have to do the work of making things right. How teachers go about the work of acknowledging and mitigating the impact of their mistakes in expanding intelligence is determined by their social location. How we approach intercultural and interreligious mistakes and failures for minoritized teachers and dominant culture teachers is different. For example, for teachers who carry white and Christian privilege, making mistakes and failing looks very different than for teachers who are Black, Indigenous, people of color, and/or religiously minoritized. Depending on differences in power, privilege, and vulnerability, there are varying impacts when teachers make mistakes as they expand into intercultural and interreligious intelligence. Teachers from places of privilege and power might only see the impact of an error created immediately around them, and count on their power and privilege to exonerate them, or worse, have their mistakes and failures go unchallenged. Different standards exist for others who are not white and not Christian. Mistakes and failures are expected because of our presumed incompetence and functions as confirmation bias in white and Christian serving institutions. People might say, "Well, they failed because they are/are not_____" fill in the blank with any minoritizations that fit. To succeed as a racially and religiously minoritized person means rising to a performance of dominance to ensure one's safety, something that is a grave betrayal of self and community. A failing in and of itself.

Regardless of our social location, for all teachers, understanding and facing the reality of classroom power dynamics, and the efficacy and harm of our failures and mistakes is an important part of the commitment to intercultural and interreligious intelligence. It is at the foundation of a teaching posture formed in humble modesty toward anticolonial intercultural and interreligious teaching and learning and a shared decolonial future. However, because it requires such a powerful commitment from us and changes the way we fundamentally operate as teachers and learners, intercultural and interreligious intelligence necessitates daily intentionality and practice. Dominant culture teachers, in particular, are at risk of buying into the white supremacist narrative of perfection without understanding that the narrative of perfection is deceptive. Because of the power of the perfection narrative, for many dominant culture teachers, the reaction to making a mistake or failing means suffering from immobilization. I can recall countless times when white faculty persons or other persons in positions of influence become excited about antiracism and interreligious commitments for the first time. Usually, this person expends all their newfound energy focused on getting everything right and calling everything and everyone out. In the end, they tire quickly and quit as soon as they make a faux pas, or offend the people with whom they are attempting to ally.

Call-out culture gets exhausting quickly. For dominant culture people, who are learning just how much daily energy it takes to fight systemic and structural oppression, fatigue happens almost instantly. When fatigue occurs, so do mistakes. In intending to use an antiracist framework, something racist is said or done. In practicing religious inclusivity, something exclusionary makes its way in. Sometimes the gravity of the mistakes dominant culture people make cuts them to the quick and they should. They might hurt and feel defensive when they are shown that they have injured others, especially those for whom they care deeply. At that moment, it seems like the easiest way to cease creating more harm is to stop doing anything at all, including never acknowledging the hurt and damage they caused. The fear of snowballing mistakes causes dominant culture people to conjecture. "Why draw continued attention to something so terrible? Can't everyone move on and stop talking about what happened? Can't our community start over? How do we spin a bad incident into something good?" The propensity to smooth things over and go on instead of facing the pain inflicted on others, directly inhibits the learning process in an anticolonial classroom and community. Inaction for the sake of self-preservation is in its very nature an act of power and privilege. Such acts reify the power differentials between people, diminishing the impact on minoritized people while giving narrative primacy to those in power.

Recognizing our intercultural and interreligious faux pas and the violence they cause require profound humility on the part of persons in power. Owning up to mistakes and their impact, lives into the commitment to cultivate a practice of anticolonial resistance in spaces of teaching and learning. Quickly acknowledging harm and admitting failures in the ongoing process of teaching and learning works to actively reverse the instructor and learner roles in the classroom, facilitating creative spaces for the nurturing of intelligence in both individuals and the community. Undoing the myth of competency or unseating the role of the perfect teacher, the perfect learner, or the expert, makes room for a cohabitated space of unlearning and learning. Letting go of our expectation to achieve competency and mastery is an act of modest humility and decolonial futuring, which directly disrupts and destabilizes systems of oppression. The capacity for a teacher to say, "I'm sorry" and "I was wrong" is an act of solidarity with the most vulnerable in spaces of teaching and learning. It is the very mark of an intelligent pedagogue with anticolonial commitments.

CHRISTIANITY AND THE RELIGIONS

Christian Dominance

As theological education is still predominantly related to Christian traditions, albeit very loosely for some institutions, one can argue that Christian dominance still exists as both a culture and religious practice of dominance. The reality of the dominant Christian perspective means Christian-centric language, practice, sacred days, sacred texts, and especially white Christian scholarship, become normative to theological education. For racially and religiously minoritized teachers and students, choosing to become part of such an institution means having to double down on knowledge of a tradition that might not be your own. Jewish, Muslim, and Buddhist teachers and students are expected to possess some level of familiarity with Christian scriptures and theologies. A Christian-centric lexicon with words like "grace" and "call" is part of the colloquial language in Christian theological education. Christian-centric traditioning and practice also becomes the normative mode of life together. I once witnessed a Christian colleague ask a Jewish colleague to "say grace" over dinner. When the surprised Jewish colleague declined, the Christian colleague kept pushing, suggesting a mealtime prayer or "grace" was something all religious people practiced. Except, it most certainly is not. Christians look forward to an Easter break, but many make no note of when the Jewish High Holy Days or Eid fall in the academic calendar. What are the provisions in place that allow for the ritualized celebration of religious holy days other than Christian ones? Even if Jewish or Islamic holy days are honored with time off for a student, they still have to make up for missed coursework and catch up somehow, while Christian students attend classes and receive information firsthand. Instead of the impetus being on the institution, the burden falls on the religiously minoritized student to find ways to make up for the time they have spent in the practice of their faith.

One might argue that for a religiously minoritized person to choose to participate in a predominantly Christian institution of theological education, it is within reason to expect they should learn Christian expression in these lived ways. However, if one pays attention to the larger narrative of Christian political heft and the global history of colonial Christian imperialism directly facilitated by institutions of theological education, it only makes sense for historically Christian institutions who acknowledge this reality and history to want to implement more expansive and hospitable interreligious practices rather than demand assimilation. Additionally, including nonwhite Christians in our institutions and classrooms and decentering white Christian histories and theologies is a must out of the acknowledgment of the power and privilege of white Christians and Christianity in North America. As institutions of theological education become increasingly interreligious and intercultural, the design of how we practice life together must also change. Though some predominantly Christian schools and teachers might say that they will wait to make those changes when interreligiosity and interculturality appear, this is too late. The longer institutions wait, the longer change is facilitated through the labor of minoritized people. Instead, how might institutions begin processes of inclusion and belonging now? Thereby actively subverting power and privilege to initiate intercultural and interreligious inclusion in anticipation of a hospitable environment toward a decolonial futuring? Intercultural and interreligious intelligence as a posture is a humble and modest curiosity of difference, the anticipation, and implementations of changes necessary as a commitment to anti-oppression.

Christian Mastery

Part of undoing competency as a concept of mastery and making way for intercultural and interreligious intelligence is to recognize how dominant Christian frameworks of culture and religion operate. Christian dominant understandings of culture and religion are carefully constructed to establish hierarchies, subjugation, and supremacy. Theological educators enter the classroom bearing personal definitions of religion and culture, whether or not we do so intentionally. We each carry assumptions about what beliefs and practices fit into the categories of culture and religion. Unpacking these assumptions tells us about ourselves and the lenses we use to engage the world. One of the first things I ask students to do at the start of a new course is to try and define culture and religion for themselves. Usually, student's answers define culture as nationality, race, and ethnicity, while religion is defined as the worship of a divine being. How do we come to our personal and academic understandings of culture and religion? How the academy understands what culture and religion are and what they are not, stems from the origins of Christianity's encounter with religious diversity and its relationship people and cultures it deemed "other."

Interreligious educator Judith Berling points to how the Christian colonial world understood world religions and cultures through the lens of exclusivist Christian theologies. According to Berling, religious diversity was not something Christians always celebrated, instead, the exclusionary understanding of *extra ecclesia nulla salus* or outside of the church there is no salvation, framed non-Christian religions and their adherents as in need salvation through Christ and therefore Christianity.[27] This approach also influenced early anthropology. Christianity's qualities of monotheism, morality, and sacred texts became the standard by which all other religious traditions were measured. Traditions that did not fall neatly into the category of world religions were demoted to the status of spiritualities or folk traditions.[28] Vine Deloria Jr. calls this the Christian intervention in the history and lives of Indigenous peoples saying, "They(Native people) were regarded as not having ownership of their lands, but as merely existing on them at the pleasure of the Christian God . . . Upon encountering a tribe . . . the Spanish used to read their Requirement, which basically recited the Christian interpretation of history beginning with the Garden of Eden and ending with the pope enthroned in Rome."[29] Religion and culture and how researchers have attempted to define both underwent the same categorizing that prioritized North American and European cultures, their values, languages, philosophies, family dynamics, clothing, literature, and so forth.[30] Being "cultured" through this colonial gaze was associated with civilization, or literary and scientific advancement as understood by Europeans and white North Americans. Everything outside of these parameters was deemed uncivilized and ripe for colonial consumption. Native environmental activist and scholar Winona LaDuke describes the process of colonization as a colon, digesting and disappearing everything and everyone it consumes, killing many so that some might live.[31] Intercultural and interreligious intelligence in theological education classrooms recognizes the death-dealing of colonialism and its patterns in teaching and learning and strives to resist and undo it. The chapter on uncivilizing narratives in the classroom will explore these related concepts further for understanding in intercultural and interreligious classrooms.

THE INVITATION TO EXPERIENCE RELIGION AND CULTURE

How we understand what religion and culture are and what they are not are also in many ways, through a white, Christian, colonial gaze. Speaking specifically of culture, every once in a while, I will hear someone call something or someone "cultured." I also hear people talk of culture as if it is something we should categorically seek in order to pursue advancement.

This understanding of culture as "leveling up" within a hierarchy of knowledge is imperial. Culture is everywhere and is both tangible and intangible. Language, dialects, geographies, and systems of beliefs, both religious and nonreligious are embedded within cultures. Michelle LeBaron defines culture in the most common sense as, "The way things are done around here."[32] Culture is not just someone's food or clothing though these are essential examples of a culture that should not be appropriated or taken out of context. Culture is as personal as one's nuclear family and as immeasurable as part of one's entire community. Culture is not limited to ethnicity. To ask someone, "What is your ethnicity?" is not the same as asking them about their culture. People can claim ethnic heritage without claiming cultural affinity or commitments. Culture is more expansive than ethnicity, nationality, or religion. Culture is and can be what flourishes between those intersections of life with all its identities, nationalities, ethnicities, beliefs, embodiments of religion and spiritualities, and everything else that makes us who we are. Culture, like religion, is always in formation and transition. Culture cannot be pinned down. It is produced, reproduced, preserved, and transformed as we embody it in all the ways we engage with ourselves, our communities, and the world at large. Culture lives in the center and on the periphery. Culture cannot be relegated to a particular way of life or as only belonging to dominant groups.

Culture functions invitationally. People across different communities communicate cultural meaning with one another through stories about personal experience that bear insight into language, belief, interpersonal dynamics, and practice. LeBaron calls this shared intercultural space, cultural fluency.[33] Though we might receive invitations into different cultural spaces to observe and participate with others, we engage with the distinct understanding that we are still outsiders. We can learn about different cultures in the classroom, what constitutes culture for others and ourselves, but we cannot fully participate in someone else's culture unless invited and accepted into the spaces where culture is lived out. This is different from the colonial mindset that all cultural representations are up for grabs and that mimicry and appropriation are at heart appreciation, not theft. For example, natural Black hairstyles including afros, locs, cornrows, and box braids are discriminated against in the workplace. The discrimination against natural Black hairstyles disproportionately affects Black people. In January 2020, the state of California became the first state to legally protect people with natural Black hairstyles from discrimination. Governor Gavin Newsom signed the bill into law after a December 2019 incident where a high school wrestler was forced to either cut off his hair or forfeit a competition. Newsom called it a choice that forced the Black athlete to "lose an athletic competition or lose his identity."[34] Let's be clear, it was not this white governor who singlehandedly protected Black hair. Countless Black people: including scholars, activists, and community organizers have fought for the protection of Black hair and Black people. Though this law partially protects Black hair and Black people from discrimination, it also reveals how natural Black hairstyles are only criminalized when worn by Black people. The new law surfaces a broader awareness of the racist criminalization of natural Black hair. Meanwhile, white people who chose to appropriate Black hairstyles are grossly celebrated as individuals and as fashionable.

This abhorrent appropriation does not stop at hairstyles. Every day, every hour, Blackness is stolen and appropriated by both white and other people of color who have no love for Black people, who do not amplify or advocate for the flourishing of Black people, and who actively practice anti-Blackness. Even in the hallowed halls of academe, we have once celebrated scholars like Jessica A. Krug who attempted to inhabit Blackness as a white Jewish woman from Kansas, while simultaneously cutting down Black and Afro-Latinx women, and stealing funding from Black academics through fellowships meant for them.[35] As academics, we possess the ability to either appreciate or appropriate culture in big and small ways. In our research and teaching, we borrow or share knowledge from people and places that do not claim us and that we do not claim. How we choose to navigate our use of cultural awareness, theologies, and practices models for our students whether or not we are expanding our own intercultural and interreligious intelligences? When we teach source material or use examples from different cultures and peoples, how are we giving back to the communities from whence we borrow?

One consistent and straightforward way, we model this for our students is through compensating people for their work and time. When we invite people from different cultural locations or religious affiliations to help students expand their horizons in our classes, whether as guest lecturers or religious and cultural guides, we must financially compensate them without exception. Another way is by sharing classrooms with people who are invited as experts on their own experiences, not as experts on entire religious and racialized communities. We perpetuate the colonial mindset when we believe that the haphazard inclusion of religious and racialized difference means we are inclusive and anticolonial. Tokenism is never the answer. The anticolonial pedagogical question is, a teachers moving toward intercultural and interreligious intelligence, how do we honor people who lend us their incisive thoughts, words, and tools in ways that elevate their visibility rather than contribute to their invisibility?

Religion and Culture Entwined

Religion and culture are deeply entwined. It is an imperial assumption to believe religion and culture exist separately. For instance, the separation of church and state works in theory but not in reality. The way we experience and live our many religions, spiritualities, and cultures are intrinsically woven together in belief and practice. Understanding this means that we cannot assume that outsiders to religio cultural communities can come to full knowledge of how the lived experience of that particular religion and culture. However, this doesn't mean people haven't tried. Qualitative researchers who study religion and culture's intersections across different communities have developed the process of participant-observer as a way of studying religion and culture and making both more knowable. However, the flaw in this colonial model of understanding and exploring people's embodied ways of life is the researcher's very presence, which causes a dynamic shift in how people behave. Even if the researcher remains a wallflower, participating minimally, their very presence is like a small stone cast into a still pond. As the stone lands in the water, calm is shattered sending small vibrations that appear like ripples on the once glass-like surface. Therefore, embodied religion and culture are only knowable to those inside communities who create and transform them.

In classrooms, it is only through an invitational glimpse that we are privy to how religion and culture work together, and how they are embodied and engaged in their fullness. To claim we can understand the inner workings of the relationship between religion and culture primarily through disembodiment, through the sole use of textbooks or media, without the participation of those who call these religions and cultures home, is a false claim and a deeply colonial one. As teachers and learners who desire the creation of more anticolonial spaces, we must rise to the challenge of undoing how we think of and understand what religion, culture, and intelligence are, to think more expansively about how we engage them in our teaching and learning. What follows in the next eight chapters is the unraveling of the biases, prejudices, and assumptions involved in teaching interculturally and interreligiously.

Chapter 2

Unbinding Liberation

BINDING AND UNBINDING TOGETHER

Liberation *is* whether we want it or not. Those threatened by liberation and its wildly expansive qualities, seek to bind it up and lock it away. Systems, structures, and people who hoard power seek to limit the possibility of liberation because it requires the sharing of power and the flourishing of all. When we cannot see, hear, touch, or taste liberation, it is not because it is snuffed out, but because it is bound up or obscured from those seeking it. Liberation is bigger than how we might understand it. Liberation needs to get free from the systems and structures that obscure it from those who need it.

Unbinding liberation co-occurs with the continual binding up of oppressions. The need for the continual binding up of oppressions exists because oppressions are always systemic and structural. Oppressions are always with us. Even those who actively oppress, need liberation from oppressive ways of being in the world. Until the complete dismantling of systems and structures occurs, the continual perpetuation of oppressions continues to exist. For now, oppressive systems and structures necessitate disruption or bindingin order for all of us to know liberation and freedom.

Unbinding and binding requires the joint participation and commitment of all colearners and coteachers in spaces of teaching and learning. In my decolonial imagination, I envision an anticolonial classroom that incorporates resistance and resilience in the face of supremacist powers. A space that weaves the hope of liberation into every aspect of teaching and learning. In order to make this vision a reality, there are systems, perspectives, biases, and other impediments to liberations that first need acknowledgment and binding up. Binding up as resistance to the colonial mindset is the direct disruption and destabilization of systems and structures of oppression. Binding up what is harmful to the human dignity of all, along with anticolonial teaching and learning requires teachers and learners to recognize how deeply entrenched white supremacy and Christian supremacy cloaked as hegemony are in North American theological education. These oppressive structures and systems of dominance are nearly impossible to escape. Binding up requires the recognition of how supremacist ideology bleeds into classroom design through teaching and learning. Teaching and learning with anti-oppression commitments require classrooms to become living and active spaces where decolonization is in process through anticolonial actions despite the presence of colonialism and its patterns.

The anti-oppression classroom is not a space where colonialism is over or absent. Our classrooms are not quite postcolonial in that way. Maori scholar Linda Tuhiwai Smith, calls postcolonial affinity a continual danger to Native and Indigenous communities because of its implicit assumption that colonialism is over when, in fact, it is still at work in the everyday.[1] Smith is correct. We are not postcolonial in the most authentic sense. I believe we can still embrace the dream of postcoloniality through anticolonial commitments to disruption. Anticolonialism is different from postcoloniality in that it is a committed process of engagement on our way to a shared postcolonial and decolonial reality. We cannot wait for the demise of colonialism to commit to anticolonial life. We cannot wait because the power of colonial oppression is, in many ways, the entirety of theological education. It suffocates us all. Instead, anticolonial perspectives and direct action create spaces to breathe, the facilitation of spaces which assist teachers and students make strides toward mutual and unbound liberation amid oppressive structures and systems.

BINDING UP WHITE AND CHRISTIAN SUPREMACY

White supremacy as a structure and a system needs binding up in order to make liberation possible. The goal is for teachers and learners to flourish and thrive together. However, white supremacy will viciously fight any attempt at its binding. White supremacy partners with other systems of power, privilege, and dominance like patriarchy and Christian hegemony functioning out of supremacist ideologies, to stay rooted in place.

Every spring, I do a clean-up of my yard and green spaces. Since moving to the southern United States, I learned that the ivy plant, though attractive, lush, and green is a threat to even well-established trees and at times my home itself. The ivy's sinuous roots crawl along the ground and up walls like a rope, sticking to any surface with tiny hair-like barbs. Ivy climbs over, under, and around other plants and walls, strips paint from exteriors, clogs pipes, and worst of all silently asphyxiates mature trees. A stormy and windy day might topple those ivy-covered trees altogether. The dark green ivy plant is beautiful to behold, but it is stealthy. If I do not pay ivy constant attention, it quickly takes over large swaths of my yard. If I am not swift at pulling the ivy up as soon as I see it, it will become far too strong to remove on my own, and I will need to call a professional to come and destroy it before it can claim anything else. Most of all, neglecting ivy hurts my pocketbook! White supremacy and its partner, Christian hegemony is like the ivy in my yard. It necessitates uprooting on sight and requires careful removal, or it will eventually mangle every living thing in its path, even the strongest of us.

Khyati Y. Joshi in her book *White Christian Privilege: The Illusion of Religious Equality in America*, examines the intricate interdependence between structures and systems of white supremacy and Christianity. She writes, "For those who imagine an American 'blood purity' that interweaves Christianity and Whiteness, current immigration trends represent not just demographic change but a loss of national identity."[2] The threat to a white Christian nation is the racially and religiously minoritized person and their refusal or inability to assimilate to the toxicity of a white Christianity that requires their literal and figurative death. For many in the North American context, everyday lived experience reveals the joint power and presence of white supremacy and Christianity supremacy through hegemony. Growing up in Los Angeles, one of the first things I remember about attending a Christian kindergarten was dutifully standing and reciting the pledge of allegiance every morning at 8:00 a.m., hand over heart. I remember the American flag in a place of prominence at the front of the classroom. Next to it was the Christian flag, emblazoned with the same red, white, and blue of the American flag. The cross in red, nestled between the blue and white folds of cloth, jumped out at me from where I stood. We saluted the American flag but also were to infer that the auspices of the United States and Christianity, represented by these two flags, operated hand in hand in ways that supported one other. There are Christian churches all over the United States with the same two flags decorating the sanctuary, many also with a cross hanging poignantly above and between them. We are indoctrinated from a young age in the United States that the United States and Christianity are not mutually exclusive and in fact function together for good or for ill. For those who belong to different faith communities or are not adherents of religious communities, how are they to internalize these Christian, United States, and North American dynamics? The subtext is exclusion and dominion: patriarchy, cisgender, ableist, white supremacy, and Christian supremacist ideology disguised as hegemony working hand in hand.

We can witness the tandem function of white and Christian supremacy in U.S. politics and policies. The current pro-life political climate in the United States as a challenge to Roe V. Wade is an example of this. Lack of access to reproductive rights for women disproportionately affects communities of color and immigrant communities. Though billed as anti-abortion, pro-choice is much more than about the right to abortion; it is about the right women have to their bodies and reproductive justice; the right of women to make decisions about their bodies without oversight by men and the government. As of writing this chapter, the anti-choice stance has created near bans on abortion and choice in six states. I am a constituent of one of those states, Georgia. In Georgia, even the description of the anti-choice bill as "The Heartbeat Bill," intentionally called to mind anti-choice Christian teachings. Such teachings make equivalencies between aborting a fetus and killing a human being. In the meantime, Latinx children and their families, many of whom claim Christian faith, lawfully cross the U.S.-Mexico border to claim asylum and are wrongfully interned in concentration camps. As I write this chapter, six migrant children have died at the hands of ICE in these camps. Here we see the inner workings of white supremacy and death-dealing Christian theology that steals the human rights of people to their bodies and their own lives. Laws like The Heartbeat Bill, claim pro-life stances, but in reality, are only "pro" the lives of white Christian elite. Supremacist logic identifies Christianity with whiteness and together claims narratives that rely on the destruction of nonwhite people and other minoritized groups for its very existence.

As a child growing up in Los Angeles, California, I was constantly reminded of my nonwhiteness and through socialization and was prodded to strive for the emulation of whiteness and the societal and systemic protections whiteness bought. As Korean American immigrants, my parents fought to move us out of the Koreatown enclave in Los Angeles, they fought tooth and nail to move us to areas with access to better and whiter schools with resources. Sociologists Derald Wing Sue and David Sue in their studies on behavior and development theory, discuss how racism, white supremacy, and white adjacency work in the development of minoritized children and adolescents. They introduced how part of the way racially minoritized children and adolescents develop is at one point to yearn for whiteness or at least strive for kinship with whiteness. In my own family's case, the cost of being next door to whiteness cost us almost everything. My parents sacrificed so much, including their futures to make it possible for their children to one day have access to whiteness and everything it symbolized in society even if it meant internalizing racist tropes like the Model Minority Myth and abandoning Korean culture and identity altogether.

Part of this socialization toward eventual whiteness was a recommitment to Christianity on U.S. soil, a religion that they perceived synonymous with being and becoming American. In the United States, the separation of church and state as experienced by people in minoritized communities is nonexistent. Though there have been dramatic shifts in racial-ethnic and religious representation in U.S. government, it is still the case that the majority of elected officials in state and national politics still identify as religiously Christian, at least for the public gaze.[3] My parents, who were nominally Christian in the homeland of Korea, became hyper religious post immigration as a way of finding a community within a hostile environment toward immigrants. They raised my brother and me in the arms of the Korean American church, a place where we found acceptance among other Korean American children and youth who were asking the same questions about biculturalism and belonging in both a white-dominant Christian U.S. society and a fossilized Confucian Korean Christian culture at home.

White supremacy and Christian supremacy through hegemony are also interlocutors in the theological classroom. Added to this partnership of oppressions are patriarchy, cisgendered heteronormative privilege, ableism, and American exceptionalism. These oppressions are both visible and invisible in the ways we teach and learn as teachers and students in larger structures of theological education. The sad truth is, we cannot fully escape these structures and systems because we are intricately beholden to them in the largess of the institutions to which we belong. Most of us in theological education teach at historically white institutions built on racial and religious exclusion, which still exist on stolen Indigenous land. Most of us in theological education, also teach at institutions built on the lives and labor of enslaved people, through the trafficking of stolen men, women, and children, the destruction of entire cultural and religious communities, and the evisceration of families and entire genealogies. Most of us in theological education, teach at institutions that have no intention of ever admitting to this historical fact, or of offering reparations for these atrocities and the benefit their endowments still reap from crimes against humanity. Most of us work at institutions that still seek to enroll and admit students from racially and religiously minoritized communities for the sake of diversifying the institution without the intention of offering them the level of access and support white students receive daily. The anticolonial move for educators in white and Christian supremacist systems and structures is to acknowledge that we are complicit in this exclusionary and supremacist agenda. The bottom line: if you take a paycheck from an institution that behaves in white and Christian supremacist ways, you are complicit. All of us who teach at these institutions are complicit in upholding and reifying oppressive systems and structures and benefiting from them. As a Reformed Christian, I understand this as an institutional and individual confession. Only in admitting to the systems and structures in which we too are entrapped can we begin to disrupt them effectively.

UNBINDING BINARIES

What Are Binaries?

In teaching and learning, white and Christian supremacy are revealed in classrooms through the lenses we use and the binaries we construct, confirm, and reaffirm. Binaries are understood as polar opposites: good and evil, rich and poor, Black and white, pass and fail. While teaching in theological institutions based in the southern United States, I noticed two significant binaries at play. The binaries of Christian and other and white and Black are everyday realities for students, teachers, and for the lives of institutions. Since much of theological education is built on the constructs of white and Christian empire, both which support the dominance of heteronormative patriarchy, these realities are inescapable. These are realities based on the histories of oppressions that pit dominant groups against minoritized ones and minoritized groups against each another. In a binary, systems of good and evil, Christian and other, white and Black, oppression olympics is the name of the game. Meanwhile, white-dominant institutions are happy to exonerate and extricate themselves, sit back, and watch minoritized people fight for every scrap of so-called "liberation." In progressive schools of theological education, there is an inherent tension between how we continue to live into binaries that create invisibilities and erasures of entire peoples, and how we are committed to teach justice and liberation.

The Binary of Belonging and Unbelonging in Education

As scholars, in our own education and formation, how do we reify the limiting binaries of Christian and other, Black and white, in explicit, implicit, and null ways?[4] How has our time in education shaped our understanding of who belongs and who does not? How have those of us in minoritized bodies taught ourselves to perform belonging? How have we attended to education and formation that subverts and disrupts the problem of binaries? We are products of broken systems of belonging and unbelonging. Graduate programs discipline theological educators and their scholarship into conforming to colonial modalities of teaching and learning. Through our education, we internalize western modalities of research and writing.[5] We cannot belong to the academy unless we prove our belonging, even if it means we enter into a painful *un*belonging from our most sacred communities to do so. Most of us do not instinctively know how to resist the colonial binary hold on our education through anticolonial pedagogy. We are taught to reinforce the very tools of teaching that create binaries and thus impossible conditions for educational equity and difference. Worse, unless we are specifically in the field of education, many educators are not taught about teaching at all, let alone teaching toward the complex, nonbinary realities of human narratives. The process of a doctoral program does not naturally guide theological educators into learning liberative pedagogy and research that serves the needs of our distinct communities. Instead, most doctoral programs condition students, especially minoritized students, to seek and assert the ineffective banking model of education that relies on binaries and erasures. A model despised by liberative educators like Paulo Freire and bell hooks.[6]

Part of admitting our complicity as educators in spaces of oppression, white supremacy and Christian supremacy as hegemony, includes conscious deprograming from the belonging and unbelonging binary. Educators committed to decolonial futures through anticolonial pedagogy need to intentionally undo much of what we internalized about effective teaching and learning in colonial spaces. We cannot establish hospitably intercultural and interreligious classrooms without first interrogating the oppressive conditions in which we as educators, have also found comfort and power. That is to say, we find different modalities of comfort and power in "traditional" classroom spaces depending on who we are and our social locations. For teachers and students who are white, cisgendered, hetero, male, neurotypical, and documented, classrooms are spaces of privilege that reward how one exists in the world. For BIPOC, non-gender conforming, queer, women, neurodivergent, undocumented, and international folx, classrooms are spaces where we code-switch to survive. We work on invisibilizing the most at-risk parts of our identities in order to purchase a small bit of safety. We agree to a death pact of tokenization: reductionist and essentialized pictures of ourselves and our communities. At times we have to defend our very right to belong and share space with dominant culture people.

For those in the dominant culture, unlearning and unbinding white supremacy culture and its binaries is a necessary part of the decolonization process and anticolonial commitments. Dominant culture people unbinding themselves from white supremacy culture recognizes the necessity of mutual liberation and the creation of new spaces where truths are taught and learned by all. White supremacy culture in theological education steals from the dream of what bell hooks calls democratic settings "where everyone feels a responsibility to contribute,"[7] or what I imagine as liberative classrooms where everybody feels not only a responsibility to contribute but also where everyone is honored for their particular form of contribution, especially when it deviates from white and Christian normativity. For instance, white supremacist academic culture in theological education includes the privileging of the written word and speaking over other forms of communication. English is the primary language used while white and European theologies are normed as canon, classical, and foundational theologies. A singular white, colonial, missional, world Christianity is the lens through we study world religions, and world history. Overall, there exists an expectation of assimilation to white and western epistemologies for nonwhite students.[8] Students are expected to find a way to belong to this western, colonial narrative or risk unbelonging and the invalidation of their very lives.

BINDING UP AMERICAN EXCEPTIONALISM

American exceptionalism[9] as a lens and culture goes hand in hand with the lenses of white supremacy and Christian supremacy. American exceptionalism is a narrative of divine chosen-ness over and against difference. It functions as the narrative around which all other bodies and stories orbit. Theologian and activist, Kelly Brown Douglas calls American exceptionalism "the grand narrative of American identity . . . responsible for the culture that has determined the history of particular peoples in America, notably black people."[10] For many, when hearing the word "America," they visualize predominantly white and Christian spaces. Douglas believes the foundations of American exceptionalism lie in the glorification of the Anglo-Saxon myth of racial purity. The Anglo-Saxon myth not only glorified racial purity but also its institutions and form of governance.[11] Both the history of Anglo-Saxon Protestantism and the resulting white supremacist lens influences the way people see and interact with one another. The white and Christian supremacist lens is everywhere and infects everything. No one is immune, not even those who are new to the land. I always found it puzzling how my parents and their Korean immigrant contemporaries, always referred to white people and only white people, as *mi-guk sah-rahm*, or Americans. The white supremacist lens invades even the way new immigrants think about who can claim the identity of American and who cannot. American exceptionalism must be rooted out as part of anticolonial theological education. It is ever-present in our classrooms and also in us. The auspices of U.S. empire continue to infect our lives, ultimately dictating how borders and boundaries function in classrooms and between people.

Spaces of teaching and learning in theological education are reflective of borderlands and border crossings. Borderlands and border crossings are increasingly representative of transnational and religiously fluid identities and natures. Teaching and learning toward interreligious and intercultural intelligence should reflect the transnational and religiously fluid people and communities represented in the classroom and theological education at large. Gloria Anzaldúa considered borderlands anywhere two or more cultures touch and places where different racialized people coexist. Borderlands are not places of tranquility. Borderlands are contested and sticky places where disorder prevails.[12] bell hooks describes all acts of border crossing as contributions to a cultural climate where biases are challenged and changed.[13]

Both teachers and students cross borderlands daily, whether in their embodiments as BIPOC, immigrants,[14] religious practitioners, spiritualists or through the auspices of media. Transnationalism is understood not only as multiple national identities but also as a borderland and border crossing practice that is unresolved and contested. Transnationalism as a borderland and border crossing practice is a way of life for people not only within an immigrant generation but also for those in consecutive generations as well. The connections that borderland and border crossing families possess to different religions, nations, and lands does not end with the first generation and can through language, ritual, practice, stories, and technology, effectively transmit to the next generation. The stickiness of peoplehood and place remains even as generations take root across diasporas.

Transnationalism as a growing identity of both/and national identities is also now more possible due to accessible technology. Growing up, I watched my parents go months between any personal news or contact with their family from Korea. Long-distance phone calls cost a small fortune, and there was no such thing as the Internet. Handwritten letters were the only form of communication that avoided the exorbitant cost of international long-distance calls. Now with access to instant and free video calling, international news across what seems like infinite platforms, the world feels smaller and more connected than ever. In many U.S. classrooms, there is a temptation to assume the mode of being and engaging with the world is one that centers the news, politics, and social concerns of the United States, but this is not true. Students and teachers are thinking much more broadly about the world. At any given moment, I can obtain a global news stream through my mobile device in several different languages. In theological education, student bodies are more transnational than ever. Students are seeking skills, training, and knowledge that takes into consideration that the United States is not, in fact, the center of the world and its affairs. When we teach only toward the dynamics of race and religion in the U.S. contexts, we neglect, erase, and flatten the complexities of race and religion worldwide. We force students who sit squarely in globalized contexts to center a United States context that does not necessarily serve their needs. We assume what they need instead of listening to what they are asking for from their educational experience.

At interreligious dialogue tables, which are in many ways an extension of classroom spaces in theological education, this penchant for preferential treatment for American narratives of power, privilege, race, and religious experience is troublesome. As a litmus test, take a look at your syllabi. Does your course incorporate knowledge from around the world or predominantly from United States, North American, European based sources? If global resources are incorporated, are they utilized on their own merit or as a foil against U.S. sources and experiences? Are your U.S. sources primarily white and

Christian? Do your sources incorporate racially, culturally, and religiously diverse representations, especially transnational ones? Think about ways you might decenter the white, Christian, and American exceptionalist narrative in your course construction. Think of ways that supporting American exceptionalism might function to invisibilize the transnational, Indigenous, and religiously rich narratives that might expand and deepen the teaching and learning in your courses.

There is no such things as a singular American or U.S. experience or narrative. One summer, I co-convened the interreligious dialogue table for a national Christian organization and witnessed the way blanket American narratives can damage and diminish cultural and religious complexity. A precursor to the national gathering was a sharp rise in Anti-Muslim bigotry and rhetoric both at the community level and in national U.S. politics. As a part of scheduled announcements, a clergy person from a mainline denomination shared that there would be a moment of solidarity for American Muslims later that day. A banner bearing the phrase, "We stand with American Muslims" would be displayed with members from the organization invited to stand behind it for a photo op. The photo would then be shared with member ecclesial bodies and interreligious partners. As the announcement was made, a palpable tension grew in the room. As discussion ensued, representatives from the Coptic and Orthodox churches stood together and shared their dismay. They shared how the churches and clergy persons they represented throughout the world were terrified. Christians were the demographic minority in some of these places. Coptic leaders feared abduction. Some had been disappeared and later found beaten and murdered. The Coptic and Orthodox representatives voiced their growing fear that the organization was too focused on the well-being of ecclesial and interreligious bodies in the United States. They named how choosing to lift up narratives of concerns for racism and Christian power and privilege in the United States was not actually a collective concern. The Coptic and Orthodox Bishops urged the group to keep in mind the violence minoritized Christians in other parts of the world experienced on a daily basis. These events rarely made the U.S. news cycle but impacted their communities in terrifying ways. Though the conversation could have easily drifted into either/or territory, the group began to understand that both the U.S. representative advocating for solidarity with American Muslims and the Coptic and Orthodox representatives advocating for minoritized Christians on a global scale were right. Both concerns were urgent and valid and not in competition with one another. In this particular situation, the way U.S. concerns and narratives for interreligious advocacy cast a shadow on the concerns of

Christians undergoing persecution in other parts of the world, put the two in unnecessary competition..

A white supremacist and Christian centric paradigm is desirous of pitting central concerns of minoritized communities against one other. An American exceptionalist paradigm pits the concerns of minoritized people in the United States against minoritized people across the world. A primary tool of the white and Christian supremacist culture within American exceptionalism is the false theology that confesses a scarcity of justice for all. A theology of scarcity sells suffering communities the lie that liberations can only occur in pockets, only one group at a time, sowing seeds of animosity and discord between those who struggle. A question we might ask in situations where oppression olympics is the name of the game, is one I first heard from interreligious educator and activist, Najeeba Syeed. When faced with a conflict or crisis, Syeed asks, "Who benefits from this conflict?" In this particular situation, neither the U.S.-based Christians nor the Coptic and Orthodox Christians benefited. Instead, they suffered from the false notion of division among Christian ecclesial bodies. In situations where minoritized voices battle for primacy, recognition, and advocacy, it is only the systems and structures of white and Christian supremacy and American exceptionalism that become reified and reconfirmed through conflict. At the end of the day, the body count includes minoritized people who fight with one another for scraps of justice. Instead of building coalitions to target the dismantling and disruption of systems and structures holding everyone hostage, they instead believe the lie that justice is doled out first to those who can prove the enormity of their suffering through the diminishment of others.

STRATEGIES FOR UNBINDING

Positive change or transformation of the teacher and learner is a noble goal, but change requires strategic and procedural implementation. Lasting communal and personal change does not suddenly occur without effort. For the work of anticolonial teaching and learning and the furthering of intercultural and interreligious intelligence, strategy is essential. Crucial strategic questions to ask when planning courses are, "What am I hoping will change or transform in students and my teaching as the result of this course?" and "How will I resource the path toward that change and transformation?" When working on transformative pedagogy, part of the answer to these questions includes the unbinding of oppressive frameworks that think unimaginatively about conflict. An anticolonial strategy of unbinding, the disrupting and dismantling amid competing narratives of suffering, is to acknowledge the presence and power of conflict and conflict transformation, to work to build caucuses and to build coalitions of those caucuses toward freedom and liberation for all. Working toward freedom and liberation requires all participants and stakeholders to commit to being present and engaged at all times,[15] even as the systems and structures of oppression continue to attempt to separate and bind people up. Teachers, students, and the various communities they represent are immediate stakeholders in a classroom. There are stakeholders present in the room even if they are not physically present or visible. As stakeholders, representing other stakeholder communities, students bring different perspectives and levels of power and privilege to the presenting conditions of oppression in their institutions and classrooms.

Students, regardless of their different racial, cultural, and religious dynamics of power and privilege, when met with different situations of oppressions and hardships, are thinking about the communities they come from, the places they find themselves rooted, and the places where they imagine themselves going as part of their journey. Some students might struggle with how to bring together those disparate people, communities, and causes in ways that collectively work toward the liberative models teachers are desirous of sharing with them. . For instance, after the election of Donald Trump in November 2016, my white Christian students, many who were from the midwestern and southern United States, spoke of their concern about going home to their more politically conservative communities over the upcoming winter break. Could they resume relationships with people who voted against their better interests and those of communities of color? How were they to navigate relationships with people whom they loved but who also held prejudice and bias against Jews, Muslims, and immigrants? At the same time, my students of color, who were mostly African American, responded to these frantic questions by their white colleagues saying, "It's Wednesday. What's new?" Racially and religiously minoritized students were expressing their frustration with the disbelief of their white and liberal colleagues. The sentiment that the election of Donald Trump was so unbelievable even though he was accused of sexual assault, defrauded the public, and incited racism, Islamophobia, Anti-Semitism, and xenophobia as part of his presidential campaign, was abhorrent to them. This public grief and lament came from a place of significant power and privilege. The majority of white students had never contended with the bowels of racism and xenophobia until that moment. Students of color, particularly Black students in this southern midwestern culture lived these destructive and racist dynamics daily, even during the oft romanticized Obama-era. In this instance, the election of Donald Trump as president of the United States threatened all the students in the room, but how and when they began to feel threatened were different. The stakes were different for students of color, religiously minoritized students, and their communities. These are the nuanced differences for which educators committed to teaching into decolonial futures must make room.

UNBINDING CONFLICT TOWARD TRANSFORMATION

Eboo Patel, in his 2013 commencement speech at the Claremont School of Theology said, "When you find yourself at a cocktail party of like-minded people, you are in a toxic situation."[16] What Patel referred to is the danger of flattening human experience to the binary of theologically and politically progressive or conservative and staying in the political lane we are comfortable with in order to avoid conflict. Our students come to theological education from varied religio cultural theological homes that do not neatly separate along lines of conservative or liberal. In some of my classes, I have had politically, and theologically liberal white Christians who are LGBTQIA+ affirming but deny the Palestinian plight. I have heard from students who are African American Muslims who are on the front lines of fighting for the visibility of Palestinian human rights but are still in dialogue with one another about affirming queer folx. The lines of who is liberal and who is conservative are not cut and dry. Teaching toward intercultural and interreligious intelligence should heed the complexities of theological and political commitments that do not always align with a universal definition of who is liberal and who is conservative.

Complexifying Conflict

As Patel suggests, sometimes we enter classrooms where students seek to categorize identities into liberal and conservative. Students and even teachers reach for categorized narratives over complex ones because they are frightened by what conflict might bring into the classroom. In some cases, conflict, whether latent or visible, is considered the enemy of progress and learning. We might think, how will students learn about (fill in the blank) if all we do is argue about this or that? We also avoid conflict through assumptions about our shared commitments. Students and teachers alike fall into assumptions about collective commitments to power, privilege, vulnerability, white supremacy, Christian supersessionism, and American exceptionalism. It is easy for a teacher like myself who has what are considered "liberal" opinions, to teach toward others with similar experiences and understandings. Teaching only toward people who think and feel like me invokes a power dynamic that silences students with opinions different from mine. Those students, especially when they come from cultures and religious traditions that avoid confrontation, can endanger themselves by speaking up against what I have established as my position. In fact, by teaching toward only students who think like me or will agree with me, I create heightened tension in the room for those who do not agree with me by making them choose whether or not they will surface conflict in the classroom. bell hooks writes about the commitment to transformative pedagogy being intentional about conflict awareness and engagement and how it affects teachers. She writes, "The presence of tension—and at times even conflict—often meant that students did not enjoy my classes or love me, as their professor, as I secretly wanted them to."[17] hooks acknowledges that the intentional avoidance of conflict is to some degree the acknowledgment of both an unwillingness to let go of one's ego and the discomfort it causes both students and teachers to work toward transformation.

I've been privileged to teach with womanist ethicist Marcia Y. Riggs, the creator of Religious Ethical Mediation, a conflict transformation method. I learned from her that the potential for conflict exists in every space. It takes what Riggs calls moral courage to engage in the acknowledgment of a potential conflict and work collectively toward conflict transformation.[18] Teaching and facilitating conflict-laden issues in classrooms of difference, requires the same moral courage Riggs teaches us via her REM method. When we lack moral courage, we cater our teaching only toward like-minded perspectives and theologies and run the risk of invisiblizing the many communities attached via accountability to our students. These include communities of color and threatened religious communities in North America for whom some conflict-laden issues are dealt with differently from white Christian norms. When we teach toward a like-minded audience, we neglect people's connection to communities and the understanding that those communities are also stakeholders in conflict and dialogue. If we are not careful, divergent opinion holders and their entire communities are villainized and even dehumanized. We need vigilance to different modalities of oppressions, or to the intersections of religion, race, and culture that sustain political or theological differences.

Disproportionate Risk in Conflict

As teachers lean into conflict transformation, they must also become aware of how different risks are associated with different embodiments. Students might choose to engage, aware of these disproportionate risks, but we must not force them into circumstances that would perpetuate violence. For instance, I would not ask a queer identifying student to enter into relationship and dialogue with a family member who outrightly dehumanizes them. I would never ask a Black student to engage a student who is anti-Black.

Bottom line, it is not the work of the person who is dehumanized to convince an oppressor of their humanity and right to exist.

Teaching toward conflict transformation is not about recreating conditions and cycles of violence for the most vulnerable in our classrooms. Frank B. Wilderson III also helps us understand the disproportionate violence experienced by different minoritized people, especially Black people. In his book *Afropessimism*, Wilderson discusses the impact of anti-Black violence in the realm of other gendered, racialized, and religious violence suffered by women, Jewish, and Indigenous peoples. He states, "Anti-Black violence murders, *destroys* subjectively (eviscerates the capacity for relationality), whereas misogynistic and anti-Semitic violence, along with the genocide of Indigenous people, exploits and alienates subjectivity *without* obliterating relational capacity . . . the difference between some*one* dying and some-*thing* dying cannot be analogized."[19] Wilderson is not upholding the system of oppression olympics. He simply states the facts. All violence is bad. Violence against humankind is especially bad. However, do we even register the impact of violence against people who have already been dehumanized? Wilderson helps us understand what is at stake for Black people is different. For Black folx who engage their dehumanizations over and over again in all corners of a white supremacist society starting at birth, engagement in conflict can bear incredible risk and pain. Sure, students may choose to take up the risk of engaging conflict that might jeopardize them, but it is up to us as teachers to help them weigh the risk of violence to their human dignity. Students need tools and resources to shore up their opinions and to live and dialogue with people of varied political, cultural, racial, and religious difference in their communities while *also* retaining their sense of self in the face of potential violence.

Violence in classroom conflict can come from any side and any position. Politically and religiously liberal people and institutions can also wield racial and religious violence in their avoidance of conflict and truth telling. I have had progressive-minded students tell me they are preparing to serve progressive white communities, without the careful analysis of why those progressive-minded communities are still so Christian and white and how those people and communities still facilitate the everyday oppressions of Black and brown people. The student's assumption that they are joining progressive communities assumes that the conflict is "out there" and not inside the community itself. Students need tools and resources to help them reframe their conflict avoidance and tap into the potential of conflict transformation or conflict that stirs up the potential for positive change. Conflict transformation is central to intercultural and interreligious intelligence. Conflict transformation holds power to imagine what liberations are possible across difference.[20]

UNBINDING GRADING AND ASSESSMENT

I have rarely met a teacher who says they love to grade and assess. I once co-presented a workshop on assessment to a group of theological educators, and the anxiety in the room was thick! The perspective that assessment and grading was a chore; something that does not add to our teaching life or to student learning, was common. Teaching with intercultural and interreligious intelligence begins with the acceptance that yes, grading and assessment often feel like the enemy of teaching and learning. There is something about having to evaluate someone's growth that smacks of the measurement of mastery we try to avoid. We might even feel suspicious of colleagues who enjoy the assessment process! It is true; student classroom engagement does not always present itself in ways that make it possible to evaluate, assess, or grade effectively. This is because we are beholden to institutions that require specific metrics. We must become creative and subversive in the ways we think about constructing syllabi, assignments, and in assessing and grading our students.

The culturally different ways students engage teaching and learning can frustrate teachers who require students to present as learners in ways that give primacy to text-centered learning. Common ways of grading and assessment in North American and European oriented classrooms prize literacy, verbal engagement, and a particular hermeneutic. Gaile Sloan Canella in her text *Postcolonial Education* discusses the history of western and imperial educational frameworks whose primary objective is to seek to undo Indigenous ways of being, thinking, and knowing in order to domesticate and civilize student's minds toward an imperial mindset. When teachers emphasize literacy in their syllabi or emphasize verbal and written interaction in the classroom, they emphasize North American and European ways of learning. When teachers emphasize verbal or written interaction only through a hermeneutic of critique without appreciation, it diminishes the cultural and even religious commitments of students who do not hail from eurocentric models of education.[21] Therefore, when teachers approach teaching and learning by recreating imperial methods of education, they might notice that international students or students grounded in Indigenous communities remain silent or obscure their perspectives in the classroom. Canella refers to this deliberate obscurity as opacity. Opacity comes from a place of resisting dominant culture modalities of teaching and learning. By choosing to decline the invitation to transparency and vulnerability, minoritized students continue to be the sole bearers of their community's truth and experiences. The forced sharing of these truths and vulnerabilities becomes what both Gaile Sloan Canella and Linda Tuhiwai Smith consider the theft of knowledge.[22] When dominant culture people hear the truth from the mouths of minoritized people, it is doubted, devalued, and erased, or it is stolen and operationalized for the benefit of those in power, and ultimately disembodied from whence it originated. The negation of truth is the whitewashing of communal memory, process, and thought. How might teachers facilitate educational spaces where students are honored for strategic disengagement as a form of resistance to the norming of dominant culture modalities of participation and learning? How do we resist punishing minoritized students through assessment and grading for their commitments to strategic resistance? What might we do instead that makes space for many different forms of commitment to resistance as a part of holistic theological education?

UNBINDING COMPLEXITIES AND BINDING UP PURITY NARRATIVES IN INSTITUTIONAL LIFE

Interculturally and interreligiously intelligent teaching and learning embraces complexities and resists the lure of binaries and purity narratives. Binaries and purity narratives are attractive because they dangle the possibility of distinct good and bad categorizations, which intercultural and interreligious complexity and experience refutes. We must relinquish and bind up binaries and purity narratives to resist a falsified competition between various oppressions, histories, religions, spiritualities, and cultures. Colonial narratives embrace binary and purity narratives which allow for partial liberation or the liberation of a few, not all. Binaries or dualisms falsify and invisiblize the vulnerable truths revealed in spaces of teaching and learning. The damage done by embracing binaries and purity narratives goes hand in hand. Both binaries and purity narratives make the claims that human and communal narratives are flat, either/or, and support stereotyping and tokenism.

My seminary graduating class was international and racially diverse. This ideally should have encouraged the institution to cultivate a space where we were invited in spaces of teaching and learning to dive into the complex nature of the national, transnational, and racial differences we embodied, yet over and over again, I witnessed my international and BIPOC classmates, including myself, reduced and essentialized to flattened narratives of self and community. Disdain met any attempt to complexify a flattened narrative. Two particular instances come to mind. In a core class, a Kenyan classmate was frequently asked by the professor what Africans thought about this or that. The professor assumed that the totality of the continent of Africa had a singular narrative. This one assumption harbored other dangerous assumptions about shared languages, cultures, and histories. In short, a flattened colonial, and American exceptionalist narrative. In response, my classmate would always qualify that he was Kenyan and was approaching the question from that specific experience and that he in no way could know the totality of the breadth and depth of the continental African experience.

Another instance was my own. I received a request from an office on campus that dealt with media. I was asked to come to the quad to participate in photos about campus life. The request included a suggestion that I come dressed in cultural clothing. The suggestion was curious, and I was not sure what they meant until I showed up and the photographer was visibly upset with my appearance. He asked me why I had decided not to wear my cultural clothing as that would have made for a better photo. I told him that I did not have *hanbok* with me and that as someone who identified as Korean American, my cultural clothing included what I had chosen to wear that day. Frustrated, he threw his hands up in the air and rolled his eyes. When classrooms and institutions of theological education do not take into account the complexities borne by those who participate in those spaces, we limit potential learning and worse, we erase the fullness of human beauty and complexity.

White supremacy is a trickster. It tricks institutions and teachers into believing and perpetuating the lies of intercultural and interreligious accomplishment. White supremacy will point to the faces of a racially and religiously diverse faculty and student body and say, "Look how far we've come! See how much less racist and bigoted we are now?" White supremacy feeds us the lie that institutions have achieved diversity or that institutions love diversity and difference. At the same time, they work to essentialize narratives, people, and communities into subjects wielded for the benefit of the institution. On the surface, an institution can appear racially and religiously diverse, but in actuality, power ultimately lies with white, cisgendered people, even if they are in the numeric minority. While demographic racial and religious diversity might exist, the support systems and structures for these minoritized groups usually do not. Support systems and structures that genuinely support minoritized people in theological education would directly undercut the power and privilege of the racial and religious majority.

Complexity within difference is the bane of white-dominant institutions because complexities within difference work against the colonial and imperial model of dealing with the problem of difference through the flattening of narratives. Institutions work hard to recruit diverse faces, people across various differences: racial, religious, gender, human sexuality, and nationality. Once "diversity" arrives on campus and becomes a part of institutional life, they quickly find that the institution has done little to nothing to establish support for the differences and complexities embodied within the community. In order to offer institutional support that would help people flourish across differences, an institution would have to learn deeply about the complexities people carry daily. An institution would have to learn that though it recruited students across several Asian countries, it cannot assume these students fall under the imagined cultural category of Asian, or that they possess solidarities with one another. An institution would have to learn that gender, sexuality, and generational complexities can cause conflicts within a community that appears monolithic. It would have to acknowledge that there are complex histories between different communities of color and nations, including histories of violence and colonization. As my colleague Jonathan Freund says when he teaches about the Shoah, history is always on the table no matter how long ago events seem to outsiders or how often outsiders conveniently forget those histories.[23]

Institutions that aspire toward intercultural and interreligious intelligence should not seek to recruit and bring faculty or students of racial or religious difference to their white and Christian dominant communities unless they also attempt to learn about the complexities and conflicts that will most certainly arise upon the new person's arrival. Institutions must internalize and learn these complexities from the perspectives of different groups of minoritized people. There is not a singular, minoritized perspective. The needs of African American students are different from the needs of students from different African nations. The needs and histories of Asian American students differ from the needs and histories of students from nations throughout greater Asia. In fact, these Asian students may not even identify as Asian until they arrive in the North American context! The needs and experiences of white coded Native and Latinx folx will differ and even conflict from the needs and experiences of Black and brown coded Native and Latinx folx. The needs and experiences of Muslim Americans are vastly divergent as the term Muslim American includes people from all over the world. All this to say, there is no healthy version of the one-size-fits-all approach that many white-dominant institutions have so eagerly adopted. Models that flatten diversity to skin color, continental, or Orientalized understandings only serve the institution's commercialized narrative of inclusivity, they do not foster visibility or communal belonging.[24]

The urge to do away with complexity and difference, to tame both to a standard narrative, and to utilize both without giving anything back, is imperial. This modus operandi harkens back to the scientific undertaking of colonization as a method of attempting to learn and understand others to steal knowledge, appropriate it for personal gain, and for dominating it, all of which are different models of destruction. These models are at their core, white supremacist, though on the surface they seem to live into commitments of honoring difference. Institutions and the teaching and learning that occurs within an institution's walls must work on authentic support for the communities and people called to dwell in their midst. The labor of creating spaces where flourishing can occur should come from the institution and the classrooms that inhabit it, not on the backs of the most minoritized students and teachers. At a minimum, flourishing requires the institution to examine the ways it benefits from the diversity and difference it touts. Does the institution use images of culturally, racially, and religiously diverse people in its media? How does it then give back to those individuals and the communities they represent? Does the institution sit on stolen Native land? How then does it recognize this and give back to the Native people from whom it has stolen? Does the institution have a history of economically benefiting from the enslavement of Black people? How, then will it commit to reparations on Black people's terms? It is one thing for institutions to offer lip service to the ideas diversity and inclusion among culturally, racially, and religiously different people and their communities, but it is another thing entirely for institutions to commit to the profound labor of liberation; the liberation of minoritized people and also of itself as the bearer of the structures and systems that perpetuates the oppression of histories, people, and communities via the imperial tactic of appropriation and capitalism.

Institutions of theological education need to understand the danger of purity narratives or the story that there is one pure form of this culture, that culture, this religion, or that religion. Purity narratives, like binaries, are falsehoods. In interreligious and intercultural spaces, purity narratives claim that religions are ex nihilo, or come from nothing, and arrive as they are, in their complete form. Purity narratives claim no transformation has occurred over time, place, and space, instead, adhering to the story that immutability is perfection. Under this premise, any culture or religion that appears to have shifted dynamically or incrementally is perceived as flawed, inferior, and insufficient. Every culture and religion has experienced alterations over time, changes to practices, traditions, language, and even central doctrines of belief. As part of racialization and racism, purity narratives tied to whiteness are what gives birth to globalized anti-Blackness. In North American classrooms, Christianity is also a primary culprit in the practices and edification of purity narratives. Christians, particularly white Christians who claim the superiority of Christianity over other religions also claim that Jesus was a white man. In theological education and dominant Christian spaces of teaching and learning, it is especially important to dismantle and disrupt the narrative of Christian purity, whether this is represented as doctrinal purity, theological purity, or historical purity. Resistance to interreligious and intercultural expressions that include the Christian narrative often come from the place of wanting to claim a Christian purity narrative which then naturally plays into a narrative of supremacy over other religions and in the case of white Christianity, over other cultural and religiously fluid expressions of Christianity.

Purity narratives and their relationship to binaries are unhelpful and even damaging to the possibilities of intercultural and interreligious exchange in the classroom. However, rather than ignore or dismiss the urge to claim purity narratives and binaries, it is better to interrogate the need for them, whether those needs arise in students, the teacher, or from the topic at hand. Interrogation of the assumptions we claim can help participants witness decolonial framing which seeks not to redefine—which might duplicate a colonial move—but to express complexity and attend to the histories and narratives brought into classroom discourse by students and the communities they represent.

Unbinding liberation in our classrooms requires the binding up of the many modalities of colonial education from American exceptionalism, white and Christian supremacy, to overarching binaries and purity narratives. The process of unbinding and binding are simultaneous in decolonial theological education. The tension between the two form and shape our questions and create space for answers, even if they are a long time in coming to us. When committing to intercultural and interreligious teaching and learning, we commit to the decentering of what we have been conditioned to see and understand as normative: U.S. centric narratives, whiteness, Christianity, and forms of religious and cultural purity. The dream of the anticolonial intercultural and interreligious classroom is to imagine what we might become as we inhabit spaces that no longer possess centers and margins, borders, and boundaries. The dream is the existence of spaces where liberation is unnecessary because oppression does not exist. We are not there yet, but until then we do the slow and careful work of binding up and unbinding together.

Chapter 3

Upsetting the White, Christian, Patriarchy

THE LION

Theological education swims in an ocean of white, Christian, patriarchy. How do we escape? As educators, we are domesticated and civilized into frameworks of being, thinking, and moving beholden to the white, Christian, patriarchy. Racially and religiously minoritized theological educators find ourselves perpetually waiting for the other shoe to drop. We wait for institutional structures and systems to dole out punishment for resisting oppressions, fighting back, or living into joy and creativity. There is nothing a white serving institution despises more than Black, Indigenous, Latinx, and APIDA people and people of religious difference living into their joy without the constant, grating weight of institutional antiracism and antibias labor.

When I think about what it feels like to be a woman of color in a white and Christian serving institution, I picture myself sitting in an enclosed room with a lion. The lion is wild, but not hungry. I am not in imminent danger. The lion lays on the opposite side of the room, eyeing me without malice, only interest. Do I notice a tinge of acceptance in its eye? Does it know that I am an inhabitant of its space and not food? I say, "its space," because without a doubt, the room belongs to the lion who for now is not looking to devour me. I am assured by those who brought me into the room, the lion is tame. The lion was fed. I am told that the lion will not feel hunger pangs while I am here. Just in case, they advise me to try and befriend the lion. I will do all I can to befriend this full and tame lion knowing that while it is full, it will accept my advances. I also know it is only a matter of time before the lion feels hungry again. At first, the lion might reason through its hunger, its stomach growling only a bit. It will not hurt me yet. The lion might deign to wait, even though it will start to salivate when it looks at me, the glimmer of acceptance gone.

I must remain calm and speak to the lion soothingly. I must not let my voice shake. I must not sweat or smell of fear. I will remind the lion we once shared a bond. In the end, it won't matter what I do. In a blink of an eye, the lion will become ravenous, and it will no longer see *me*, only a meal. Nothing I could say or do in this moment will help me. The lion will devour me, wholly and completely. The lion will return to its satisfied and tame nature, until the next time someone is ushered into its room.

The lion of white and Christian-dominant institutions is always in the room for racially and religiously minoritized folx, for both teachers and students. The lion is always present in institutional spaces not created for us to enjoy and thrive. The lion is present for one reason and one reason only, to devour us and consume what we work for, what we create, what we love, and what gives us joy. The lion is a constant threat to our survival and our flourishing. You see, in white and Christian-dominant spaces, racially and religiously minoritized people are not meant to survive. We are food. When we trick ourselves into thinking, we have finally tamed the lion or have befriended it; it is because the lion has already devoured our kin. We survive for that day, not on our merit or because we have successfully tamed the wild creature, but because the lion has consumed one of our own. We are always waiting and hoping not to be next.

Black, Indigenous, other people of color, and religiously minoritized folx who teach in white and Christian-dominant institutions understand that unless the systems and structures of oppression which created the lion are dismantled, they will eventually be consumed. The anticolonial work of teaching and learning toward joy and liberation from white, Christian patriarchy begins with how we frame and construct our classrooms, goals, and the expectations therein. This chapter will discuss teaching and classroom dynamics, including, code words, trauma and pain, performativity, stereotypes, white guilt, accountability, imagination, and co-conspiring together toward imaginative liberation.

CODE WORDS, STEREOTYPES, AND BIASES

Whether we know it or not, we code our language daily. Helpful and unhelpful euphemisms litter our engagement with one another and our teaching. Coded words, sayings, and stereotypes are neither neutral nor simply good or bad. Code words hold power. In the classroom, teachers can wield the power of coded words in ways that edify students and their learning or hinder it. At worst, the harmful use of codewords can negate human dignity, do violence, and destroy the capacity to teach and learn. At best, code words create space for reflection, space or cultural difference, and ultimately, attitudinal shifts.

Code words are not always negative. Code words can sometimes strategically teach while preserving the dignity of the hearer. In some cultures, direct communication is shaming, while indirect communication saves face. My fourth-grade teacher, Mr. Seymour, was an expert in using indirect code words to couch a reprimand while preserving someone's dignity. While other teachers disciplined by sending students out of the classroom to the vice principal's office or by keeping them restricted from socializing with other students, Mr. Seymour would call the student by name and kindly ask if they would not mind staying behind to help him tidy up the room. His tone was gentle and inviting but firm. The coded message was that the student needed time to process their actions and was to use their time cleaning up the room for personal reflection. Mr. Seymour was legendary among students at our school for his kindness. No student ever turned down his invitation to "help." Something about the way he framed his words and request made it sound as if the student was doing him a favor. Mr. Seymour's tactic both preserved the dignity of students in front of their peers and drove home the message that specific behaviors needed to change. Mr. Seymour could have used other tactics instead of the one he chose. He could have gone with the more direct tactics of his colleagues, refused to address the problem altogether, or angrily shamed the student, and made clear that this was a punishment, not a restorative practice. Instead, Mr. Seymour put the dignity of his students first. When students know they are acknowledged and seen in their full dignity as people who also make mistakes, they are more likely to acknowledge what went wrong, accept the invitation to make amends, and find a way to return to the community without experiencing debilitating shame.

Not everyone is Mr. Seymour. Many code words used in the classroom carry negative connotations which function as colonial strongholds in teaching and learning. When we enter classroom spaces with unchecked biases, we use code words to mask the lenses we use to see others. It may seem as easy as unlearning our biases to avoid using code words, but we must first understand where and how we obtain and cultivate our racial and religious biases. Jessica Vazquez Torres, a leading national antiracism trainer with Crossroads Antiracism Organizing and Training, teaches institutional leaders how white supremacy and whiteness infiltrates the way we encounter one another. Vazquez Torres, reminds people living into antiracist commitments that whiteness is the lens through which we *all* perceive and experience people of racial and religious difference.[1] Racism and bias kick in because white and Christianity lenses facilitate all our interactions. The white supremacist lens filters economics, news, pop culture, publications, and media.[2] For instance, U.S. produced movies and media scrutinize and demonize Black, Native, Brown, and Asian people[3] and people of different religions, while white people are glorified as saviors. Have you ever wondered why Hollywood has a fascination with the "last" of a nonwhite people portrayed as a white person adopted and accepted into exoticized communities? *The Last of the Mohicans*, *The Last Samurai*, and *Dances with Wolves*, are three Hollywood fantasies that imagine white men as the penultimate example of a people western conquest destroys. Countless images of Black, Indigenous, and other people of color in the United States and European media both historically and in current times reveal these damaging caricatures. Popular classic movies like *Holiday Inn* with Bing Crosby include blackface, while *Breakfast at Tiffany's* with Audrey Hepburn includes Mickey Rooney in yellowface. My friends and I used to play a game whenever we watched a new movie. We would take bets on when the person of color in a white-led film would die or disappear. We usually did not have to wait long. We also do not often see a broad representation of BIPOC and religious diversity in media unless they are expendable or the comedic sidekick. Popular television shows like Homeland and Jack Reacher, perpetuate the Orientalist image of the evil brown or yellow men from the Middle and Far East.

Growing up, I remember looking for people who looked like me in movies only to see Long Duk Dong and Short Round staring back at me from the big screen. I learned early on that this is how people saw me and other Asian Americans. We were ridiculous, goofy outsiders who existed as the butt of white people's jokes. It is only in recent years that we have seen the rise in film and television centering Black, Latinx, and APIDA people and their experiences. Though this newfound representation is terrific, it is still slow. The current trend of representation only makes a dent in the already pervasive and harmful narrative that Black, Indigenous, people of color, and religious diversity are dangerous, unintelligent, evil, and expendable.

Even those of us who are racially and religiously minoritized see one another through white supremacy's inescapable lens. Even within minoritized communities, we believe the white supremacist lies about one another, lies that only serve to reify white supremacy and Christian supremacy cloaked as hegemony. When minoritized communities buy into white supremacist biases and engage one another through them, only whiteness is served at the end of the day having proven even to minoritized people that white supremacy is correct.

Whiteness codes our interactions with one another at every step, and anti-colonial commitments require our recognition and acknowledgment of our biases before we can begin to undo the damage in spaces of teaching and learning. Whiteness also codes the way we read into one another's responses to us and interactions with us. Think about how you might read the classroom on your first day of teaching an unfamiliar group of students. You do not know the students well enough to know their social locations, how they might approach your class, or why they are there. Without realizing it, you might jump to assumptions about how students are presenting in your classroom. For example, when students choose to show or not show emotion in classes, we code the way we understand and react to their emotional visibility. We even police who is allowed to show certain emotions and who is not. Gender studies scholar and activist Brittney Cooper, in her book *Eloquent Rage*, discusses how the weaponized and racist trope of the angry Black woman affects her as a teacher and a scholar. The stereotype of Black women's anger assumes that there is no justification for her anger. Her anger is unreasonable and out of order. Cooper discusses how she has worked to mitigate or downplay the rage that she felt in response to racist systems and structures for the comfort of others. Cooper goes on to say that she has instead worked to claim her eloquent rage as a way to emphasize the strategic place of rage in systemic injustice. "Black women know what it means to love ourselves in a world that hates us. We know what it means to do a whole lot with very little . . . we know what it means to snatch dignity from the jaws of power and come out standing."[4] It doesn't have to be this way. In what ways do our biases as educators squash the real and honest reactions to oppressions our students live and feel? In what ways do the politics of niceness, force colleagues of color to swallow their pain because it is not fit for public consumption at our institutions?

While we might unfairly discount the justified anger students surface in our classrooms as out of order, we also discount the intentional silence of others as uninvolved and uninterested. Students of Asian and Pacific Islander descent may speak less in class, not due to disinterest, but out of acknowledging the power differentials between teachers and students. Though I was not born in Korea, as a Korean American, I grew up in a household with those same dynamics of respectful silence. These dynamics transferred to the classroom, and each year my teachers wrote home to my parents about their growing concern that I was not paying attention or interested in learning. I eventually learned extroversion as a way to signal engagement to dominant culture teachers. Sometimes it would take all my strength and courage to ask a question in class, my face turning beet red as I did so and my hands clenched together so they would not shake. My body was psychosomatically responding to what my culture had conditioned me to think and feel was negative behavior.

Many high context cultures have long used code words and phrases to cover up what people are mean. Even those in low context cultures code words every day. I first heard the phrase, "Bless your heart" when I moved to Louisville, KY, from Los Angeles, CA, several years ago. The first few times I heard "Bless your heart," I responded with, "Thank you!" It seemed a natural response to a blessing. Later, someone kindly informed me that "Bless your heart" was not a blessing at all, but at its best an expression of sympathy and at its worst insinuated a person was dim-witted. I certainly felt dim-witted when I finally figured it out! Likewise, in Korean households, we might say to someone that they appear "healthy" or in Korean, *uhl-goohl joh-ah bo-ihn-dah* or "Your face looks well." The saying could mean they look refreshed and healthy, or it might mean they have noticeably gained weight. This greeting is not to say gaining weight is in any way unhealthy or undesirable, but merely that there is a coded way of letting someone know you noticed. The greeting comes from an era where food insecurity was a reality for most Korean people and mentioning someone looked well enough to have gained weight was a good thing. Likewise, a running joke between my childhood friends was when we asked our parent's permission to go somewhere or do something they didn't condone, they would say *mah-um dae-roh-hae* or, make up your own mind. They did not actually mean we should decide anything for ourselves. They were warning us that if we made up our own minds, there would be severe consequences! Our job was to read the subtext of what they were saying. Our parents wanted us to access the communal wisdom instilled in us to know better. The message was that if we made decisions on our own without communal consensus, it wasn't a decision worth making.

There are subtexts, code words, and phrases used throughout history in North America that reveal our biases and carry racist and xenophobic connotations. These saying are so deeply internalized that we no longer realize how they might sound to others who hear themselves described this way. Code words and phrases can function to support dangerous binaries. One of the codified binaries I long stopped using in and out of the classroom is the dichotomy of dark and light as a stand-in for good and evil. Sayings like "he has so much darkness" or "she finally came out of the darkness to the light" comes from a history of anti-Blackness wed to white Christian supremacy. Hymns or contemporary praise songs speak of being "washed in the blood of Jesus, white as snow" carry vestiges of times when in the U.S. media one could find household soap ads that claimed their product could wash away the blackness of someone's skin and that whiteness was desirable.[5] A Pears' Soap advertisement from the 1800s pictures a before and after of a white child bathing a Black child with Pears' soap. After the bath, the Black child's skin has become white. This is only one such racist advertisement of many in the soap market alone. These images and phraseologies carry connotations of Christian theology that presupposes Black personhood as sinful while whiteness is a symbol of purity and holiness.

In my teaching, there was a particular moment when I recognized that these white and Christian supremacist code words and phrases also worked to bury and erase the complexity of meaning grounded in other ways of cultural and religious being. During an exercise in scriptural reasoning on the sacred creation narratives among the Abrahamic faiths in an interreligious class, a Muslim student spoke of the importance of the night/dark or *layl* as being holy and beautiful. This struck me because the way Christians understand or hear the creation story is first to say there was void and darkness until G_d spoke light into existence. The void and the darkness are seen as emptiness and nothingness awaiting abolishment via the creation of light. The student's story attested to a different theological perspective, wherein the darkness did not merely exist to be banished by the light but was also, like the light itself, called forward to be part of the creation story. Darkness was not equivalent to void. Darkness held gravitas, significance, beauty, and meaning. The purpose of darkness was not as a foil to the light but to be unto itself, singular, and good. What nuances and complexities might we miss in our classrooms when we weaponize words? What message are we sending students when we do not take into consideration how they hear the words we choose to describe them or their commitments? What might we lose when we assume our language is uncoded or when we do not commit to the work of uncovering our biases?

Some code words are blatantly racist and discriminatory. Words like thug bring to mind anti-Black and brown images and sentiment.[6] In rapidly gentrifying neighborhoods, phrases like "up and coming," "low-crime rate," and "good schools" have become real estate code for anti-immigrant and anti-Black sentiments. In education, some language may seem innocuous to dominant culture people but are understood as coded to minoritized peoples. These words include minority, diversity and inclusion, equality, communication, assimilation, racially tinged, and racially charged, among others. These days, in higher education and theological education, it seems everyone is hungry for diversity, equity, and inclusion. BIPOC know that this hunger translates into an institutional desire for diverse racial representation and even international representation, but primarily for the sake of optics. Once the long-sought-after diversity is present, there is rarely equity in the level of resources allocated to care for and support those groups. Sometimes, those budget lines and other resources, once there for white faculty, staff, and students, disappear into thin air! There are rarely avenues or plans for sharing power with the diverse people the institution collects.

There are also institutional codes that signal racism and religious discrimination for minoritized people. In many institutions, specific administrative offices handle equity, diversity, and inclusion. Black, Indigenous, people of color run many of these EDI offices. These administrators are people with the most to lose and are the most at risk. They speak to the "community," often a word that solely refers to communities of color, within white-dominant spaces attempting the work of inclusivity.[7] EDI is code for the labor of minoritized people. In other words, EDI is code for the antiracist and anti-bigoted education of white people through the labor of BIPOC, the world religions education for Christians by religiously minoritized people, LGBTQIA+ affirming education for cis/het people, and dis/ability education for non-disabled people. When there is a minoritized administrator heading up an EDI effort, this administrator, is often seen as suspicious by other minoritized people whose quality of life their office oversees. This suspicion arises from the administrator's perceived power and kinship to white, Christian, cis/het, ableist, American exceptionalist, patriarchal power. Sometimes, the administrator succeeds in the eyes of the institution by implementing policies and cultures that utilize the continuous invisible labor of Black, Indigenous, people of color, and religiously minoritized people. A reality which further works to isolate the diversity officer, eventually undermining the efficacy of their work as well as inherently working against issues of diversity, equity, and inclusion by silo-ing them away from support. In the classroom, the code words, diversity, equity, and inclusion carry the underlying assumption that it is the job of students and teachers of color to name, mitigate, and fix institutional racism as part of their course of study. Code words are wielded *against* people, not for them, by white serving institutions which have the power to wound if people do not comply.

Additionally, words like "minority," which refers to a racialized demographic status, rings false in an era where Black, Indigenous, and other people of color outnumber white people in major metropolitan areas. Minority is really code for someone's minoritized social status. The term "minoritized" serves its purpose better by naming that people considered "minorities" are in actuality directly *minoritized* by dominant culture people, systems, and structures through policies, rules, regulation, and bias. The problem lies systemically outside of them, not with their identity or with themselves. Assimilation, likewise, is codified to mean that minoritized people should seek assimilation, not toward a particular nation or culture but to whiteness and systems of whiteness. Codified terms like "racially tinged" or "racially charged" function as weak euphemisms for racism itself, created to pander to what Robin DeAngelo calls white fragility.[8]

In teaching, think carefully about the words chosen to represent some but not others. Why do some words like racism make some teachers and students uncomfortable while words like racially tinged feel safe? A way to disrupt the use of code words in teaching is to learn how people prefer to identify themselves. Ask people, and keep asking. My identity as a Korean American and an Asian American developed for me at different times in my life. At one point, I rejected one for the other. I now claim both, but it was a journey, a journey I'm still on. I appreciate it and feel seen when colleagues and students ask about my racial and ethnic identity without operating out of assumptions. Code words and questions like, "Are you Chinese?" teach me about the asker's assumptions, biases, and narrow understanding of the world. The assumption is outlined in the question; there is no room for my complex identity to present itself. The question is merely a vehicle for me to confirm or deny the asker's suspicion about my race and nationality. The question tells me the asker believes I am a foreigner and has assessed my presentation as nonwhite and therefore, un-American. Such questions tell me to keep my guard up and instigate fatigue and anger in me. They are not innocent questions, but a sugar-coated bias that strips me of the right to share myself out of personal choice, but instead to share out of the need to correct someone's assumption about me.

Not all my students want to identify as Asian American. Some identify as Burmese, Vietnamese, or Sri Lanken. Not all of my Pacific Islander students want to identify as Asian, Asian American, or Pacific Islander. Some identify solely as Tongan or Native Hawaiian. Not all of my Filipino students want to identify as Asian or Asian American.[9] Some of my students prefer not to identify as international but as transnational, or neither. Some of my international students want to claim the word "American" as a modifier to their racial or ethnic identity in resistance to the systemic ill of dehumanizing undocumented peoples. Why do you need papers to identify with the place where you live? The terms "Hispanic," "Latinx," "Latin@," and "Chicano," are not interchangeable but refer to specific identities, communities, and belongings. Queer is not always a catch-all community or phrase depending on how someone identifies and where they feel inclusion or exclusion. Muslim is not a catch-all for all brown people who wear articles of faith. Not all Muslim women wear hijab. Not every head covering is a hijab. Not every person wearing a head covering is Muslim. Code words can exist for comfort of privilege, for the preservation of our innocence and denial of our racism, biases, and prejudice. It is time to stop weaponizing our words.

TRAUMA AND PAIN

The white, Christian, patriarchy invests in the weaponization of histories of trauma and pain against minoritized people. These supremacist systems and structures created these histories of trauma and pain but want racially and religiously minoritized people to explain how and why. Systems and structures of whiteness utilize trauma, pain, and its embodiments to educate itself without conditional accountability to the people providing the education. Accountability to the folx providing the labor of anticolonial education in white-dominant spaces looks like proactive work against whiteness as a system and structure in daily life. Without this reciprocity, the performative nature of minoritized trauma and pain in white, Christian, male-dominated spaces only furthers the fatigue of minoritized people. Racially and religiously minoritized people such as Sikhs and Muslims are brought into white and Christian-dominant spaces to tell their stories of trauma and pain, without the acknowledgment that this labor is viscerally painful. The practice of weaponized trauma narratives against minoritized people forcibly exhumes the bodies of ancestors, causes restlessness in their spirits, and leaves their bones exposed to the bleaching of the hot sun. Their bones are left unburied, dishonored, and are eventually ground back into the earth by the frequent passage of colonizer's feet, persistently making trails and paths through sacred ground. Being witness to these stories and histories is a privilege, not a right. It requires a blood pact of accountability. These stories require those who hear them from places of power to participate fruitfully in the decolonial uprising.

The presence of trauma and pain is tangible and powerful in every classroom, even in courses that have no intention of exploring trauma and pain explicitly. Trauma and pain are latent, visible, and invisible because classrooms are made up of personal and communal experiences and histories. Experiences and histories that are more complicated than a linear past, present, and future. Both teachers and students carry trauma and pain into classrooms, setting the stage for potential conflict and conflict transformation, including the reliving and revisiting of those traumas and the revealing of buried pain. Communities that have witnessed and borne trauma through inflicted violence and pain, carry them for generations. This generational trauma has been the subject of epigenetic studies, in particular of people belonging to Native, Indigenous, Black, and Jewish communities. The simplest epigenetic explanation is that the behaviors and the malformations produced via the traumatic experiences create cyclical patterns within the next generation exposed to those behaviors. The necessity to survive trauma, violence, and bear up under pain, etches much onto our worldviews and behaviors and those of consecutive generations.

I remember asking my parents why my paternal grandmother had peculiar habits. When we would bring her Korean sweets, she would hide them around her home. I would find carefully wrapped *gyul* (Korean clementine) in dresser drawers and other nooks and crannies in her home. Once my father brought back her favorite caramels from a trip to Japan and shared them with us at our grandmother's apartment. He placed them on the kitchen table. One by one, those caramels disappeared while we were milling about the apartment. When we were about to leave, my grandmother stood up and a dozen caramels fell out of her pantlegs! My mother quickly pinched my side as my mouth dropped open in astonishment—a silent plea for me to ignore what I had just seen and preserve my grandmother's dignity. As someone who survived the Japanese Occupation as a child and the

Korean War as a woman, my grandmother grew up in tremendous poverty. It was only by immigrating to the United States after her husband's death, leaving her two children behind, she was able to find a way forward out of her complicated and painful history. In southern California, she built businesses from the ground up and sent for her children and their spouses through immigration pathways. Remnants of her war-torn life still governed many of her interactions with her family and the world. Her traumatic experiences impacted and altered the way she moved about the world forever. As a second-generation Korean American, sometimes I find myself unconsciously mimicking the things I have seen both my grandparents and even my parents do out of the desire to survive both poverty and traumatic pasts. Korean Americans sometimes talk about the post-war generation's proclivity to hoard free material items such as napkins, ketchup packets, and plasticware. To this day, I mentally remind myself only to take a few napkins instead of reaching for a handful. In the classroom, these behaviors and patterns, which are keys to our human formations, reveal the relationships we have to intergenerational, transcultural, and border crossing that occurs in full visibility of one another as witnesses to the annals of history across space and time. Generational trauma is more than about extra cutlery and napkins; it is about pain inflicted that is too great to bear alone, sorrow that is too heavy for one pair of shoulders. Pain that is shared and communal in the most profound sense.

Performative Trauma and Pain

Dear reader, I want to explicitly note that I did not have to share any of the above with you, but I often engage in this type of intentional narrative performativity of pain and trauma because I am regularly presumed incompetent in white-dominant spaces. BIPOC, especially those who are not Christian in the United States and North America are consistently urged to display their narratives of pain and trauma while being pitted against one another by white supremacist systems and structures. Racially and religiously minoritized people are expected to teach others out of their pain. As a non-Black person of color whose East Asian and Asian American community is complicit in anti-Black racism through white junior partnership, I strategically reveal these narratives in the classroom to disaggregate the data and narrative of what the experiences of Asian Americans are like. This act bears the potential for creating solidarities across lines of racial and religious divisions created by systemic oppressions. Both BIPOC and religiously minoritized educators need to keep in mind that the strategic use of trauma narratives in classrooms may be defined as performativity, but can also help us connect with one another and those of our students who hail from similar backgrounds and stories of pain and trauma. As people with power in the classroom, we can visibilize the narratives of our students (if they are willing) by making our stories and experiences accessible to them. This practice models personal risk and trust-building and inherently has the potential to create space that holds stories of trauma and pain in accountability to one another.

Educators who are religiously and racially from dominant cultures can take a different position. Instead, of prioritizing and giving platforms to their own stories of pain and trauma, which are categorically different from the pain and trauma of racially and religiously minoritized folx, they can invite students to first consider the work of scholars from minoritized communities and the choice of opacity from minoritized people in classroom dialogue and discourse. This practice both affirms the choices of minoritized students to keep their histories of trauma and pain to themselves, if they so choose, as an anticolonial mechanism against structures of inequity. The practice of honoring opacity rather than delving into trauma and pain stories helps students consider the value of silence. It reframes silence as opacity and reclaimed power, the valid and intentional space holding for trauma and pain that resists vocalization.

THE DIALOGIC SPIRAL FOR HARD CONVERSATIONS

The teacher does not have to reveal their own stories of pain or trauma if such revelation is not helpful to the creation of spaces of mutuality. Depending on the situation and the classroom, sometimes, decentering the teacher's narrative and centering student's narratives are necessary. A powerful tool for creating the conditions for dialogue across painful and traumatic subjects like white supremacy and its impacts is through the dialogic spiral.[10] I have practiced the dialogic spiral[11] in classrooms where the conversation on religious and racial difference was potentially virulent because of all the radically different racialized and intergenerational stories present. I begin the process with pre-work ahead of using the dialogic spiral by inviting students to do word association with the phrase, "white supremacy." I invite students to say out loud anything that comes to mind and write everything they say down on either the whiteboard or in a visible document. I then ask them to spend a moment to take in the words and phrases that they have spoken out loud. After a few minutes, I ask students to vocalize their gut feelings while gazing at these words. Students might say things like, "sad," "angry," "grief," or "shock." I acknowledge their contributions through nonverbal signals like nodding or with solemn eye contact. I make sure to turn my body toward them, when and if possible, to connote attentiveness to what students are expressing. Then, I invite students to pair up with their colleagues, facing one another, sitting knee to knee, but not touching. The process of the spiral requires that the teacher set up framing questions about the topic at hand, in my case, the personal impact of white supremacy. Framing questions I have used in the past include, "How and when did you become aware of racism?" I do not regulate whether these stories are about encounters with racism in which students have been targets, observers, or perpetrators. Leave the decision about how much detail to share up to the students. Before beginning the dialogic spiral, I ask for student agreement on the questions. If students request tweaking of the questions, I do my best to oblige.

The dialogic spiral is an exercise in telling and listening to hard stories. It is an exercise in mindfulness to the present moment of accompanying someone as they tell their story even if the story conflicts with your own. Kinlock et al. describe the dialogic spiral as, "the construction of a conversation between two or more people whereby the dialogic process of listening and speaking co-creates an area of trust between speakers—the space between."[12] When used to discuss experiences of racism and religious bigotry, the dialogic spiral is also an exercise in becoming aware of how telling and hearing stories of racism affects the mind, body, and heart. In two rounds of ten minutes for each round, one student will share while the other student listens. The listening student listens with their full being. They pay attention and signal attentiveness with their gaze and their body by facing the speaker. Students who are listeners are asked to listen but not to interrupt by speaking back or using distracting nonverbal cues. For instance, a listening student might gaze at the speaking student but will be careful to remain aware of their nonverbal cues that might detract or distract from the sharing and listening. Staring into someone's face is difficult! We are conditioned in conversation and dialogue to mirror what we see, to continuously communicate as the speaker is speaking. However, doing this can alter the story and shift communication—both verbal and nonverbal—to the listener. The dialogic spiral emphasizes processing what one hears before taking time to speak back. It deliberately slows down the process of speaking and listening. As the facilitator, the teacher will signal when the first speaker's five minutes are up.

Before moving on to the second speaker, invite students to turn their chairs, and face you for a moment. Lead them in a moment of mindful breathing, one or two breathes in and out, and if they are willing, with their eyes closed. With their eyes still closed, ask participants to do a body scan. I usually phrase this invitation this way, "With your eyes closed, as you are able, do a body scan. Check-in on yourself from the top of your head to the bottoms of your feet. Where are you holding tension and pain? As you find pockets of tension and pain, acknowledge them, then release them." Facilitators should take their time with this step in order to give participants time for processing the internalization of what they have heard and felt. I am always surprised when I engage in dialogic spiral work, at how much tension the body holds when we listen to stories of pain and trauma. When I am teaching, the muscles on the right side of my neck and shoulder remain clenched, even causing headaches. In practicing body scans, I attend to the ways teaching affects my physical well-being or causes me physical pain. Anticolonial pedagogy attends to the effects of trauma on the body as much as possible by deconstructing the falsehood that the power of colonialism is only a mindset. Colonialism and white supremacy are perpetual and embodied realities. When we are doing work with pain and trauma attending to how it affects us physically as well as mentally is part of the holistic task that imperial modalities of teaching and learning have broken off from us. After a time of body scans, ask students to switch roles in the same pairs, and begin the process again, entering the second stage of the dialogic spiral. After the second spiral, invite participants to do a second body scan.

The third and fourth stage of the spiral initiates a time of speaking back to what students have heard from one another. Remember, at this point, all students have shared their story but have not responded to one another. Students will reenter the spiral process, but this time use their five minutes to speak to the other person about how they felt listening to their partner's narrative. As a facilitator, I do not place conditions on what students share concerning their experiences of hearing one another's narratives other than time and the invitational question of, "What did you feel and what came to mind in hearing one another's story? What else do you want to convey to your dialogical partner?" Within these broad parameters, I leave it up to the students to share more or less intimately as they are willing, to make room for students to practice the opacity necessary for the preservation of their dignity, putting participants in control of minimizing their risk-taking. As before, the listening participant only listens. After each five-minute session of sharing the facilitator leads participants in body scans. If doing this for the first time with a particular class, the facilitator should debrief the entire process and experience with students as a practice of transparency and feedback,[13] important steps in just pedagogical practice.

UPSETTING CHRISTIAN AND WHITE RAGE AND GUILT

When upsetting the white, Christian, patriarchy, one can expect the presence of Christian and white rage and guilt. These classroom encounters with guilt and particularly rage can cause further violence, trauma, and pain, the effects of which follow people outside of the classroom and into their private and communal lives. I remember one such example from my own teaching that still haunts me. A white male student openly challenged whether or not I should be teaching about white supremacy as a nonwhite person. This challenge resulted in a thinly veiled threat to my physical safety. I needed over a year to process the event. Reentering that same classroom the following year, I experienced a resurgence of post-traumatic whiplash, which caused me to approach the triggering session differently for self-preservation. Those of us who are BIPOC and are religiously minoritized in the North American context understand how teaching on white and Christian supremacy in environs, where students have both internalized oppressions and exist in systemic and structural systems, work together to undermine the progress of interculturally and interreligiously hospitable spaces. When we teach on white and Christian supremacy, we are immediately disbelieved, disregarded, or challenged. Christianity argues to reassert itself over and against different religious traditions and experiences. When coupled with white fragility and white tears Christianity and whiteness as systems and structures work in tandem to fight for recognition, coopting precious time and sidelining other voices and experiences. All of this works to further establish the hold of white Christian supremacy in the classroom. The reverberations of this Christian, white-lash, are violent, painful, traumatic, and often invisible, as we do not have time in inhospitable places of learning to process what is happening to us as teachers in our classrooms. Only after we leave our classrooms the deep grief, anger, and all the other effects of Christian white-lash confront us in force.

In my classes, I intentionally take the time to teach postcolonialism, decolonialism, anticolonialism, white supremacy, Christian supremacy through hegemony, and other aspects of systemic and structural oppression as par for the course and as a framework for how we think about and how we define cultures and religions. I have found that there is not one classroom that is not fully possessed by the specters of oppression, visible or not. Even subjects that seem disconnected from white and Christian supremacy are intricately affected because they are squarely a part of the academic and theological gaze. Both students and teachers walk into the classroom racialized, bearing bias, and bearing the biased gaze of others. Framing subjects or courses by being inclusive of teaching on white and Christian supremacy in intercultural and interreligious spaces allows students and teachers to enter into a conversation that needs to be revealed in order to be exorcised. If nothing else, unveiling the ugliness of historic and present day white and Christian supremacy visibilizes minoritized students, their communities, and the daily and unforgiving encounters with systems and structures that are meant to diminish them in every respect. An educator's sacred role is to loudly recognize and honor students in their fullness in the presence of that which desires their erasure.

SETTING LOOSE LIBERATION AND THEOLOGICAL IMAGINATION

Classroom constructions in spaces of theological education, lean heavily on paradigms of oppression and liberation. These are theological and social justice constructions that have bearing on one another. In becoming mindful of interreligious and intercultural life in classroom contexts and beyond, we learn to hold these concepts more loosely, letting them breathe outside of dominant Christian understandings of the theologies of liberation and imagination. Holding concepts loose help us exist beyond the binaries of oppressor and oppressed, liberated and captive, especially when it comes to unhelpful and dangerous constructs of power differentials between students and teachers. Teachers might be tempted within colonial Christian constructs of liberation to see themselves as the liberator and their students in need of liberation, particularly students of color and students of different religions. White feminist educators might see their female-identified students of color in need of rescue or saving from their seemingly patriarchal cultures or religions without regard or understanding of how feminism is embodied and thriving among different people and places without white feminisms.

Liberation and imagination are concepts and lived realities that are not owned by one group or another. The way we speak of them and encounter them must, therefore, be through an ever anticipated expansion. Like the infiniteness of the universe itself, we finite human beings can never fully grasp how all people experience or do not experience liberation and imagination. When we speak of liberation and imagination in theological education, do we only conceive of them as flowing out of Christian understandings, histories, and spaces? If you are a Christian educator and your students are Christian, how do you both honor how Christians frame liberation and imagination as part of their lived experiences without setting their particular experiences and understanding on a pedestal of absolutism, under the gaze of Christian and white supremacy? Or how do you honor liberation as experienced among world Christianities rather than one Christianity?

The danger of framing liberation and imagination in Christian and white-centric terms creates false narratives that work to diminish the self-hood of already minoritized peoples. There seem an infinite number of false narratives having to do with racially and religiously minoritized people and communities in North American spaces. In classes, I've encountered Christian students, white students, sometimes both, mapping their assumptions about both cultural and religious oppressions onto the lives and experiences of racially and religiously minoritized students. Racialized stereotypes and biases co-opt personal and cultural embodiments which were never for public consumption into alternative narratives that then must be publicly cast off by those they affect the most. For instance, the narrative of oppression around the hijab or women in the Islamic tradition covering their heads is a constant source of narrative cooption in interreligious and Christian-dominant classrooms. North American students outside of Muslim communities, some who have never even personally met a Muslim woman, might speak about the hijab as a symbol of oppression to women. This type of mapping over someone else's tradition presupposes the value of a damaging colonial and white feminist epistemology over that of the Muslim women who choose to wear hijab. This assumption, though it might come from a place of desiring liberation of some kind, prioritizes the Christian and white feminist critique and understanding of the female body, religious symbols, and their meanings, serving only to erase and undercut the actual meaning behind a women's personal and religious choice to wear hijab. This mapping over is in itself a colonial enterprise that echoes the remapping of the entire world through the lenses of Euro-American conquest.

Rewriting narratives, like remapping landscapes, can enter our classrooms in racialized, sexist, homophobic, and Christianized ways, all in the name of particular forms of liberation and justice. Even when dominant culture people have the best of intentions regarding the mutual liberation of all, the temptation is to put themselves, their agenda, their pain, their grief, and their celebrations ahead of what minoritized people say they need and want. I believe this reification of white and Christian centric stories and experiences is due to performative ally-ship anxiety. White and Christian allies feel a need to make explicit their experiences as allies in the struggle for the vocal affirmation of minoritized people. In other words, what antiracist activists colloquially call, needing a cookie.

The anticolonial antidote to the cooption of liberation is to let loose a wild imagination in spaces of teaching and learning. Franz Fanon describes decolonization as chaos. Breaking away from the colonial enterprise and the trap of one's colonial mind is to unbind oneself from all of the ordering one knows. Wild imagination is unbounded and chaotic in just this way. As teachers, what might we do to facilitate a wilderness of imagination in our classrooms? I do not speak of a romantic wilderness. The wilderness is a daunting and terrifying place. It is unknown, unmapped, and resists the taming and domestication of those that seek to own it. The wilderness has secrets to which we are not privy. The wilderness also possesses tremendous and terrible beauty, a beauty that we may have never considered beautiful via a civilizing lens.

Every year when spring arrives, and the grass turns green and begins to grow again, I am surprised by its bloom. The grass behind my home blooms with cream colored clover, tiny wild strawberries, and deep purple blossoms carpet fresh blades of grass. The bloom is wild and lovely. It attracts wild things. Butterflies and honeybees swarm to harvest pollen. Rabbits come to nibble on the sweet flowers. I discover the occasional turtle hidden between tall blades of grass underneath tree canopies. In spite of this, the first thing most people itch to do when the grass grows too tall is to mow it down to the uniform length and color. We worry our neighbors will think we are messy and unkempt.

I remember a time of drought in California when our neighbors resorted to spray painting their brown lawns green in response to water conservation ordinances prohibiting watering the grass. Better a faux-green lawn, seeping toxic chemicals into the soil than an unattractive brown piece of land. Contrary to bad Christian theologies of stewardship, the wilderness does not exist for us to control and mow it down. Dominant cultures and Christianity have made the wilderness an evil thing, anthromoporphizing it as evil and even reducing human beings and entire cultures and civilization to savage and barbaric so that they might have the excuse to have dominion over them, remaking them into their image. How is this tragic worldview and philosophy any different when we squash the imagination that bursts forth in our classrooms? When we cut down new ideas, and desecrate alternative paths to knowing and knowledge, and distrust difference in general? The white, Christian patriarchy does not need rescue or preservation, only disruption, and dismantling. The liberation of all will not look the way we imagine. It will be more fantastic and whole than we could ever dream. Thank goodness.

To teach in a way to allows differences to flourish even when differences challenge the way each person might think about the world is a tenuous and wild thing. I have in my classrooms both people who believe in the clerical and official ministry of women and those who do not. I have in my classroom students who affirm the rights of LGBTQIA+ folx, students who struggle with affirmation, and those who might never do so. I have my classrooms students who profess color blindness and students who profess the celebration of difference. I have in my classroom those for whom Christian evangelization is the sincerest form of living out one's faith, those who have suffered historically and presently from evangelism, and those who want to eviscerate evangelism completely. One thing is sure in classrooms that gather such differences together. Life together is messy, chaotic, wild, and beautiful. One begins to live into the imagination and truth that the world itself must indeed look and feel like this. In encountering our stark differences together, the classroom becomes, not a place where the wilderness of differences is tamed or cultivated, but where change is possible and where the relationship of genuinely seeing one another without the desire to map over one another can be born between each person across chasms difference. It is in this way with the flourishing of wild imagination as the first step in mutual liberation, that we upset the white, Christian, patriarchy. There is nothing the white, Christian, patriarchy detests more than being decentered so that something wild and free might emerge.

Chapter 4

Uncivilizing Teaching and Learning

THE AUDACITY OF CIVILIZATION

Chapter 3 introduced the concept of wilderness and the wild imagination necessary for anticolonial intercultural and interreligious teaching and learning. Wilderness and wild imagination are deeply connected to the anticolonial concept of uncivilizing spaces of teaching and learning. Wild imagination is dangerous precisely because it is chaotic. Chaos cannot be controlled, dictated, or cultivated into something useful for powers that want to overtake it. In fact, over time chaotic wilderness can take over the footprint of civilization. In New York City, there is a popular park called The Highline. It sits above the city as a prime example of the work of wilderness in spaces that seek to push it back. The Highline is now an industrial green space. It used to function as an elevated railway used to deliver good around the city. As the railway fell into disuse, greenery started to inch its way across it, covering the steel and wooden structures with moss, wildflowers, and weeds. Mayor Rudy Giuliani signed a demolition order for the dilapidated structure and many called it an eyesore until locals began a movement to convert it into a walkable green space.[1] Today, when walking along The Highline, you can still observe the steel and wood tracks that coexist with the wild greenery which has retaken the space. Wilderness will creep back in and overcome, even incrementally.

Similar to the misused Christian theology of stewardship as domination or the idea that human beings can and should subdue the wilderness, the concept of western civilization itself is colonial. Western civilization is built on the paradigms of subjugation and dominance. Western forms of civilization are forced upon people and land. Civilization at its worst is about the dirty business of control and domination, the trafficking of indigeneity. The commercialization and commodification of what existed prior to the arrival of "civility." We may think civilization is about advancement and culture, and it certainly can include these, but civilization is also about the advancement and cultures of the *dominant* culture and the outright end of everyone and everything in its way. This should not come as a surprise to anyone who has attended schools in the United States. Our textbooks and curriculum are akin to swiss cheese in the way they are void of information about what we might call the underside of history or the narratives of those who were conquered. The lacuna of stories from those who suffered under enslavement, setter/colonialism, and genocide speaks volumes about what and whom we consider to be the epitome of civilization.

In high school, I remember a required history course called Western Civilizations that studied the founding, growth, and destruction of Hellenistic civilizations, other European nations, North America, and their places of conquest. The only time we learned about nonwhite peoples and nations was via the colonial gaze, as subjects of Christian mission and political conquest. Even growing up in the Pacific Northwest, where Indigenous peoples and cultures are an imbedded part of local history and reality, the school curriculum did not reflect the rich and deep history of Native peoples. Natives were often erased completely from the pages of history except as people of the past, relegating them, their lives, languages, religions, and cultures, extinct for all intents and purposes. When I was living in Kentucky, I remember a child asking me if Indigenous people still existed while the church and we were sitting in a public space called Cherokee Park. Civilization for many racially and religiously minoritized folx means that there is always a dichotomy of dominance and subjugation, a struggle and striving for assimilation to dominance, and when one fails to assimilate, death and erasure. Civilization is violent in the way colonial and religious powers, such as that of Euro-American Christianity, have historically exercised it. By naming this violence, we begin to see colonial civility as the actual face of barbarism. When we can see and name western civilization as barbarism as an anticolonial practice, we can enter the conversation about decolonial futuring. Through this new lens, we are able to reframe syllabi, relinquish text only classrooms, disrupt the binary between teacher and learner, and think beyond writing and research as the primary modes of epistemology.[2]

In pursuit of anticolonial teaching through intercultural and interreligious intelligence that resists supremacist understandings of civilization, I use art as a medium in place of text. I will speak more about this as a specific anticolonial pedagogical strategy in part two of this book. Using different mediums for learning disrupts the idea that text is the primary place where truth and knowledge lives. One of the pieces I go back to time and time again is John

Gast's *American Progress* (Figure 4.1), a painting commissioned by George Crofutt in 1872 for a travel guide to the western United States.[3]

In the center of the painting, a blonde-haired white woman floats above settlers moving westward, fulfilling Manifest Destiny. She wears a long white tunic and a peaceful smile across her face. In one hand is a schoolbook and in the other hand is a telephone wire. She is seen stringing the wire on telephone poles. On her forehead she wears the Star of Empire. The landscape and sky behind the unnamed woman is bright and light. The environment ahead of her and the settlers remains dark and foreboding. Native people and Indigenous wildlife like bears and bison flee in her wake. White settlers plow fields, drive stage coaches, and herd cattle safely under her watch as they move steadily west. A train with half-laid tracks chugs behind her as a boats sails down the river, no doubt bearing even more settlers and westward expansion of all kinds.

At first glance, one only sees the woman, shining out at you from the center of the painting. Then one begins to notice the settlers working the land, basked in the light she emanates. It is only later, after some time spent with the painting, that one notices the Native people and wildlife at the periphery of the painting. They are cast in shadow, escaping into darkness and away from the light. Gast's work almost instinctively invisiblizes anyone and anything that is not a settler or a form of western expansion as

Figure 4.1 John Gast, American American Progress, 1872. *Source*: Cromolithograph published by George A Crofutt. Library of Congress, prints and photographs division.

a stark representation of what must occur in order for progress, technology, and literacy to take hold in the land. Gast's painting sends the message that diminishment and obliteration meets those who try and resist the march of progress and civilization.

Though created in 1872, the symbolism in Gast's painting bears a striking resemblance to what our classrooms look and feel like today. The concept of civilization is audacious in its desire to remake the world in its image. Like Gast's painting, civilization, as it is upheld in classrooms, requires both teachers and students to live in binaries of good and evil, to negate and ignore complexities, and to bury the slightest hint of desiring anything other than academic success as it is defined by colonial understanding, and to push forward into the wilderness to conquer it, not to witness it or exist as part of it. Wilderness is seen and understood as a detestable thing, rather than a gift.

How we frame our classrooms in terms of success, failure, progress, and regression is telling. How might we as teachers cocreate spaces with our students that are not about civilized discourse, a term that speaks to assimilative thinking, but the *uncivilization* of spaces and places, of teaching and learning? If you had a negative reaction to the word uncivilization, where did that arise from? Is there something that has taught us that the uncivilization of things is only related to things without good and conditions without merit? In fact, uncivilization is not even an official word! In order to resist the colonial enterprise along with white supremacy and Christian hegemony, we must *uncivilize*, meaning intentionally undo the things that seek to give primacy to a particular hierarchies and sets of rights and wrongs, regarding people, cultures, religions, and spirituality in classrooms.

The religious education classroom is guilty of perpetuating the damage of western civilization through forced assimilation upon nonwhite minds and bodies. Western civilization on no uncertain terms meant assimilation to a culture of white supremacy and conversion to Christianity. One of the most devastating examples of this was the North American Indian residential schools. The Carlisle Industrial Boarding School in Carlisle, Pennsylvania, was the epitome of genocide under the thinly veiled guise of religious education as civilization.[4] Founded in 1879 by General Richard Henry Pratt, the boarding school was a federally funded endeavor. When the Carlisle Industrial Boarding School[5] opened, "Pratt and white Christian reformers, who called themselves, 'Friends of the Indian,' presented the policy of education and assimilation as a more enlightened and humane way to solve the nation's intractable 'Indian Problem.' Yet the purpose of the educational campaign matched previous policies: dispossessing Native peoples of their land and extinguishing their existence as distinct groups that threatened the nation-building project of the United States."[6] Entire generations of children were stolen from Native families, tribes, and nations and relocated to Carlisle.

Pratt's infamous saying "Kill the Indian and save the man" was the fundamental ideology behind the school.

His objective "was to prepare Native youth for assimilation and American citizenship."[7] Native nations with the most number of children at Carlisle included, Ojibwe, Lakota, Cherokee, Seneca, Oneida, Alaskan native, Cheyenne, and Apache. Native children were stolen from their families and forced to enter the school. They were systematically stripped of their families, names, languages, spiritualities, and cultural practices. N. Scott Momaday, Kiowa artist, and Pulitzer prize winning writer discusses the significance of the names stolen from Native children at Carlisle. Momaday writes, "Names and being are thought to be indivisible. His name stands for him; it is his shield . . . at Carlisle we are talking about the crime of neglect and negation. We are talking not only about the theft of identity, but indeed the theft of essential being."[8] A haunting photo of the Carlisle school student body from 1884 (Figure 4.2) shows stolen Native children sitting en masse in front of the school. They are dressed in uniforms and have their hair cut the same way. The only barbarism in the photo what has and is happening itself. The photo is a single snapshot into to trauma forced upon an entire generation of people and one might say the consecutive generations of people

Figure 4.2 The Carlisle Indian School Student Body in 1884. *Source*: Cumberland County Historical Society. Carlisle Indian School Students, "Photograph," *The Sentinal*, https://cumberlink.com/news/local/indian-school-new-research-puts-carlisle-indian-school-enrollment-closer-to-8-000-students/article_82f8fbdc-db62-5191-bc92-5fc37d9d661e.html.

thereafter. Entire generations of Native nations and people were wiped out in religious education classrooms which purported to desire the furthering of Euro-American modes of knowledge, Christianity, and progress. The violent heritage that is the theological education classroom necessitates an anticolonial stance, a position that does not seek to bury history, but uncover it, helping the settler-colonial academy and the church face their complicity in genocidal and epistemic violence; setting loose newly imagined spaces of teaching and learning.

THE VIOLENCE OF CIVILITY

We might understand the concept of civility as a particular set of behaviors that stem from members of civilization. Civility consistently appears as part of colonial discourse, setting up and re-ifying binaries of good and evil, of intelligent and unintelligent, of dominant and subjugated. Civility is a loaded term that carries with it histories of violence and erasures visited upon entire peoples in its name. In classrooms, we experience the cry for civility in the urge to avoid and squash conflict. In interreligious and intercultural spaces, civility is a call for common ground as the ending point instead of the entry point of relationships and dialogue. For civility's sake, we push aside and bury grief, pain, and trauma that occurs naturally within and outside of ourselves. All in order to align to an ideal form of teaching and learning that normalizes one way of engaging one another. There are certainly aspects of how we understand civility that we might generally appreciate. Civility associated with polite encounters between people in the midst of disagreement, for instance, is not necessarily negative. Civility as decorum and empathy can prevent the reoccurrence of dehumanizing violence and meanness. However, civility is weaponized when the call for civility is used as code for making dominant, white, Christian cultures, theologies, and ways of being normative and all others aberrant. Anticolonial classrooms and pedagogies make efforts to confront the civility mythos introduced to us through Homi Bhahba's "Sly Civility"[9] head on, moving past the benevolent intentions and exposing the impact of civilizing as a concept which visits erasures on people and places.

These days, the term "civility" is the battle cry of North American political liberals and progressives. Civility, like civilization is a polarizing term, inviting the creation of unhelpful binaries that work against the antiracist and religiously inclusive narratives that emphasize difference. The press for civility in political and religious dialogue, out of binary thinking, demonizes the political and the Christian right,[10] making them seem backward and unintelligent in comparison to those on the political and religious left, creating another unhelpful binary that works to dehumanize entire groups of people. I say this is not to exonerate the complicity of the Christian right, for they have allowed incredible violence to occur in the name of their G–d. The religious and political right do their share of demonizing religious traditions and their adherents outside of Christianity, immigrants, and queer people, among others, further establishing the existence of good and evil narratives and binaries. The call for civility in this Trump era of U.S. politics[11] is in response to the degradation of these code words and phrases which those in political and religious realms enjoy using. The fascinating thing about Donald Trump and his contemporaries is that codes like civility have been abandoned. People that think and act out of despising cultural and religious difference say so and mean it. For racially, culturally, and religiously minoritized people, this is not new or surprising. Nothing has changed. It is only the veil that has been cast off in such a fashion that now the privileged can also hear and see what minoritized people have known and understood all along. Civility, therefore, is privilege in the deepest sense. Civility is the fluff of Christian and white privilege. It is called upon and called for to comfort the fragility of a white supremacist Christianity that cannot bear to face the truth of its complicity laid bare: the truth that would reveal the colonial nature of civilization and civility itself as uncouth and barbarous.

Civility mythos is part and parcel with racial and religious stereotypes. It forces people, even minoritized people, to see one another through the lens of white supremacy's gaze. Students and teachers who identify as Black or brown, immigrants, Muslim, or Jewish, have civility weaponized against them. In North American media, particularly in the United States, the reality of unarmed Black folx being murdered by police is spun to reflect "threatening" Black men and women being shot by police out of self-defense. A bag of skittles in Trayvon Martin's hoodie pocket becomes a weapon through the dehumanizing and violent lens of white supremacy. Whenever there is an act of domestic terrorism, the likelihood that the actor is a white male holds the highest probability, but since 9/11 the suspicion instantly falls on the Muslim American community. Ironically, is the Muslim American community that remains on high alert for the bigotry and violence targeting them through violent white supremacists. White men who mass murder are labeled lone wolves or mentally ill, while Muslim Americans are perceived as threats for simply existing.[12]

Classrooms also carry the weight of these civility and incivility binaries and biases. It is our role as facilitators to parse out in the open, on whom the expectations of civility lie and why. In intentionally exposing the impact of civility narrative's assumptions, we help ourselves and our students understand the heaviness of the histories in regards to the narratives of civility and incivility and we begin to uncivilize spaces of teaching and learning. A basic way of starting the civility and incivility conversation is to facilitate an exercise about cultural and religious bias. In smaller classes, I will ask students to name the assumptions others have made about them in the past. I start out by naming the assumptions others have made about me. If students know one another well enough and are mutually willing, toward the end of a course I will ask them to name some of the assumptions they had about one another upon their first meeting. Though simple, it is an eye-opening exercise that helps everyone realize that assumptions and bias abounds. Working together as a class to expose different types of assumptions and biases points to the false equivalencies between them. The impact of someone assuming that a white man is athletic because he is tall is not the same as someone assuming a Black man is hostile because he is tall or simply because he is Black. The logic and impact of those two assumptions are not the same. The assumption about the tall, white man will not get him killed. The assumption about the tall, Black man could very well get him killed. Complexities are also part of the conversation about assumptions. The model minority assumption that I am good at math because I am Asian may not directly negatively affect me other than my being a disappointment to people who hold that expectation, but it becomes a wedge issue, negatively affecting other minoritized groups who are set up in comparison with the model minority stereotype. It also works to negatively affect my relationship with other BIPOC because the model minority stereotype works to pit Asian Americans against Black, Indigenous, and other people of color.

UNCIVILIZING COLONIAL EDUCATION

Uncivilizing spaces of teaching and learning for the sake of anticoloniality also includes the process of unpacking the twisted nature of colonialism. We have to understand colonialism and our complicity to it in order to stand against it. Part of the binary loving civility narrative is that the "civilizers" were and are only European and North American nations and peoples. Anyone who has ever had an international presence in their classroom or is a transnational person themselves would know this is untrue. Colonial histories of violence exist between many different peoples and nations. When we teach out of only the binary of "Euro-American and other" assumptions about colonialism we neglect the many other colonial histories that are present in the lives of people in our classrooms. In doing so, we run the risk of conflating the complex histories of different nations and people into a flat singular narrative that is again rooted in the white supremacist gaze. We run the risk of buying into the Orientalist narrative that all people and nations in Asia are homogenous, while the rich and varied histories of different African nations and people become one African narrative.

I was once invited to a Hiroshima and Nagasaki memorial event in Louisville, Kentucky, where I was asked to say a prayer as an Asian representative. Never mind that I participated as a Korean American at a memorial for a tragedy in Japan, a nation that prior to those events had annexed Korea. I was also asked to say a Christian prayer at a function where most people were not religious and in the name of memorial for a nation that is nominally Christian. At the same time, there were celebratory Chinese dragon dancers and Chinese lanterns set afloat on the lake behind the event. The event was culturally and religiously confusing. The underlying assumption made by the organizers of this interfaith group was that one could lump all of Asia into a single culture and people without the acknowledgment that the nations represented at the event via only appropriated cultural symbols had colonized one another and been at war with one another across centuries. Instead of a memorial, the organizers ended up creating a spectacle of pieced together a strange tour of Asia cultural and religious buffet for white and Christian consumption.

As another example, I notice in many theological institutions that when Asian student groups are mentioned in passing that people are really only thinking about East Asian people and identities. South Asians, Southeast Asians, Desi Americans, and Pacific Islanders all get systematically left out of conversations and gatherings meant for all who identify as belonging to Asian kind. In doing so, not only are people erased but also are the religions and cultures that they hold dear. White supremacy works to flatten how institutions, communities, and people see one another without the integration of different and complex realities. Uncivilizing classrooms requires that we redefine the histories and complexities that have been systematically flattened or erased through the gaze of white supremacy, even if it means conflicts will become unburied and embodied in new ways. Just as colonization is a destructive and systematic endeavor, anticolonial commitments are creative and chaotic ones. In order to attend to anticolonial actions, we ready ourselves to live on the edges of both creativity and chaos as we work on surfacing the stories, people, and histories that have gone unheard and unacknowledged. Civilizing and civility are concepts and narratives that we throughout the world have thrust upon one another at varying points and places. I bring this to bear not to exonerate European and North American nations and people which have disproportionately colonized other parts of the world and their peoples, but to disrupt and dismantle the false and damaging narrative that the work toward solidarity is unnecessary between communities of color.

UNCIVILIZING UNDERSTANDINGS OF POWER, PRIVILEGE, AND VULNERABILITY

Complexities

Uncovering and wrestling with the complexity of power dynamics in the classroom is part of the practice of uncivilizing. Complexifying power dynamics resists flattened narratives and histories. Power dynamics are not either/or but both/and. There is not a binary of people with power and those without; it is usually far more complex and intersectional. Each classroom possesses different types of power dynamics. There are power dynamics between white students of different backgrounds, between white students and students of color, between different groups of racially minoritized students, between represented religious traditions and their adherents, and between teachers and students. These dynamics are further complicated by gender, sexuality, age, dis/ability, explicit and implicit expectations, explicit and implicit assumptions, generational understanding, and among immigrants, points of arrival to name only a few. The thing to understand about power dynamics is that they resist resolution in the way that one might solve a puzzle or riddle. Power dynamics are seismic, they constantly shift like tectonic plates, causing ripple effects as life happens and even as a course goes on, and we must reassess, come to fresh understandings, and raise new questions at every turn.

What works to mitigate the impact of power dynamics at one point in a classroom will not always work as we continue to interrogate how we experience, see, and understand one another in our deep differences. I have learned that even the most creative and eye-opening ways of teaching power and privilege need to be continuously reexamined, redesigned, and even put away as students continue to teach me about how such exercises impact their experiences in the classroom. One of the earliest exercises that taught me about power and privilege was the privilege walk. I first encountered the exercise in graduate school. I learned to appreciate it and use it in my own classrooms. After reassessing its impact, I no longer use it. The privilege walk requires all participants to begin by lining up at the back of the room. As the facilitator makes statements that resonate with one's life experiences, each participant takes steps forward. The facilitator states things like, "If you've ever had a private office with your name on the door, take a step forward" or "If you had access to nonloan financial assistance, take a step forward." The privilege walk and variants of this same exercise have been popular among educators because it quickly and visibly reveals the intersectional dynamics of power, privilege, and vulnerability. In my experience, the exercise reveals the common invisibility of students who have racial privilege but come from economically poor backgrounds and male privilege coupled with racialized experiences. The privilege walk can even break down assumptions about people by revealing the impact of chronic illness and other personal struggles that impact people's daily lives. For all its good, I stopped using the privilege walk because in the North American context I noticed one consistent result, Indigenous, Black and African diasporic, and undocumented students who already experience such tremendous systemic racism from the government, institutions of higher education, and in classrooms are constantly made to embody those experiences in front of their more privileged peers. Often, when asking questions related to race and religion in particular, I noticed that most of my racially and religiously minoritized students stood at the middle to back of the classroom, while most white and Christian identifying students stood middle to front. Though this certainly was educational for dominant culture students for whom comparative understandings of power, privilege, and vulnerability might be new realities, for already minoritized students, this was daily life. Using the experiences and physical embodiments of minoritized students in the classroom as teaching tools for dominant culture folx is something I am unwilling to do. Though some might argue that the privilege walk exercise along with others like it centers the experiences of minoritized people by visiblizing them, the exercise is really only news for dominant culture people who are sheltered from these realities. We must find fresh ways of teaching dynamics of power, privilege, and vulnerability that do not further exploit and exacerbate the impacts of white supremacy and Christian supremacy on the most minoritized participants.

The Card Exercise

As I moved away from exercises like the privilege walk to complexify dynamics of power, privilege, and vulnerability, I developed some of my own. I sometimes teach a strategy game to my students that they can use with one another during the course of a class. It is a game that teaches the dynamics of power through speaking, not speaking, sharing of power, and choice. I teach students the game at the beginning of the course and ask students to facilitate it among themselves during the semester. At the beginning of each class session, I hand out five cards to each student. You can use more or less. I use index cards that have a different color on each side so that the card can be flipped over when used.

The rules of the game are as follows: each student can use their five cards to say or share something during the course of each class, either as part of a discussion or small groups. It is up to each student if, when, and how they will use their cards. Students should place their cards on their desk or a place where they are visible to their peers. When a student decides to speak, they flip their card to show the bright colored side and place it on their desk so that their peers can see that they have used their card. Students who value speaking as a means of participation run out of their cards quickly, while students who value listening, silent reflection, and rhetorical questions will hold onto theirs much longer, sometimes never using them at all. Students who run out of cards may ask to use their peer's cards. Their peers may or may not grant the request for sharing cards. Sometimes students who resort to borrowing cards from others have been over speaking or taking up too much space and are therefore denied. Students who choose not to use all their cards can also choose to give their cards to others as a way of encouraging them to speak up. I sometimes see students at the end of class with a pile of cards shared with them by peers but who still exercise their power *not* to speak into the space. This image is a powerful one that teaches us how silence is a particular kind of engagement and power that can transform space. The Card Exercise teaches students and teachers about the dynamics of their class. On the one hand, it teaches students who are prone to speaking as a way to take up space, to critically reflect on their vocal participation. On the other hand, it makes visible the engagement and participation of students who choose to participate nonverbally.

The Card Exercise is also a game about individual and collective power. Sometimes students will work together to collectively silence a student who will use all their cards quickly by speaking out of turn. There is collective agreement that no one will share their cards with this person. In fact, I have seen classes choose to participate silently rather than share cards with the one person who keeps speaking. The game also teaches us about the assumptions we make about those who choose to participate nonverbally. It shows teachers that those who are silent are indeed engaged in the dynamics of colearning in the class and in terms of assessment gave teachers a way to assess participation outside of the boundaries of verbal participation.

Power Dynamics between Minoritized People

Power dynamics between different Black, Indigenous, and other people of color exist and like all power dynamics, are always tenuous and complicated. Narratives of solidarity can be operationalized between minoritized people to flatten the complex narratives and histories between minoritized people. Though I am a woman of color, I am also a non-Black person who comes from East Asian, Korean, and Korean American communities complicit in anti-Blackness. East Asian communities also do harm across larger Asian American communities through practices of erasure. East Asian narratives commonly dominate the wider Asian American story, contributing to the increased invisibility of South Asians, Southeast Asians, and Pacific Islander communities. I am a non-Indigenous person who is a settler-colonizer on

Indigenous land. I am also a Christian teaching at an institution that privileges my religious commitments. My racialization as an Asian American in the United States vacillates between people's perception of me as white adjacent, a white junior partner, and as perilously foreign. Solidarity needs to exist in all its complications, pointing out complicity and working toward the mitigation of those complicities.

The intersectional dynamics between Black, Indigenous, and other people of color (BIPOC) also cuts across religion, gender, sexuality, and dis/ability. In terms of histories of power, there are histories of settler-colonization, racial and religious dominance between different communities of color, contested terms and language that invisibilizes some while visiblizing others, all the while systems and structures pit minoritized people against one another in an oppression olympics, scattering any efforts to organize and build coalitions. It takes much practice and time to create and sustain interracial and interethnic solidarity. Those efforts and the absence of those efforts make their way into our classrooms and affect the way students interact with one another and their teachers. Uncivilizing requires that we continuously work at assessing and reorganizing power as a strategy for anticolonial teaching and learning.

As previously mentioned, not all histories of colonial violence directly occurred through the auspices of European and North American imperial powers, though militarization of other nations through the United States does enable these realities. There are histories and current realities of colonization and violence between and within nations and people across what we call "Asia." Today, the existence of ethnically and religiously minoritized people in China such as "Uighurs, Kazakhs, and other chiefly Muslim ethnic minorities in northwest China" laboring in concentration camps and undergoing genocide is widely ignored and unknown by the U.S. public.[13] Currently, there are ethnic and religious genocides occurring in China and Myanmar that escape the notice of people who refuse to see the entangled histories of difference, ethnic, and religious violence between Asian nations and their people. What does this have to do with classrooms? When all APIDA[14] folx get lumped together under one flattened assumption of origin and experience, the result recenters white normativity and the lenses of white Christian supremacy. When South Asians and Southeast Asians are lumped under white-gazed caricatures of "East Asian-ness," the distinctive ethnic, cultural, and religious markers of South and Southeast Asian people are subsumed under stereotyped, cartoonish, and racist East Asian identity markers invented by white supremacy culture. A racist and Orientalist legacy originating back to the earliest days of Asian immigration and the exploitation of Chinese and Punjabi Sikh immigrant labor for agriculture and building railroads.

Movements of interethnic solidarity are powerful and necessary throughout North American history, but were brought together for the purposes of interracial solidarity movements and in order to dialogue with power. When we forget that those interethnic narratives of solidarity are not actually supposed to negate experiences of difference within racialized and religiously minoritized communities, we lean into the type of power and privilege that works to diminish some narratives, nullify others, and assimilate all.

There are politics of belonging and unbelonging even among people that one might easily assume are homogenous. One year, a Korean exchange student came to meet with me during office hours. One of the first questions she asked me was, "How do you identify?" When I told her that I identified as both Asian American and Korean American she looked at me incredulously. "How? How can you identify as Korean at all? You were born in the U.S.! To me, you aren't Korean at all, really just American. You look Korean but you think and sound American." Understanding belonging and unbelonging even within my Korean and Korean American community are complex because of borders, boundaries, immigration, and the colonization of bodies and minds. Linda Tuhiwai Smith also writes about the dissonance and conversations she experienced in the Maori community of whether she was an insider because of her Maori heritage or an outsider because of her western academic indoctrination.[15] These are conversations and arguments our communities will continue to have as long as there are arguments about different epistemologies, national borders, immigration, and diasporas. We cannot be afraid of the conversations that help us mark broker and traverse our bordered way of understanding ourselves and others.

When I have Korean and Korean North American people in a classroom, students outside of the Korean culture often assume that all Koreans, regardless of where we root ourselves, will agree on issues considered divisive. They are surprised to discover that even those identifying with the same ethnic group, have deep political and cultural differences between just a few generations. Issues of women's ordination and acceptance and affirmation of LGBTQIA folx among Korean Christian clergy, for example, are rife with controversy. Even within a culture and people that seem homogenous, there are differences that divide people from within. In the face of this complexity, how can we assume that solidarity across racialized communities are present in spaces of teaching and learning? Sometimes those interracial and interethnic solidarities are still in the burgeoning stages of formation and acknowledgment. The anticolonial task is to do what we can to make space for this creative and complex coconstruction of solidarities and understandings in classrooms that resists the flattening of narratives and histories.

Even terminologies about communities, racial, ethnic, religious, or otherwise are hotly contested and evolving. The act of defining, labeling, and naming is one of the first acts of dominance. In the Christian and Jewish scriptural tradition, one of Adam's first tasks is naming creation. I always find it interesting that Adam is told to name instead of asking for names! To question the process of defining, naming, and resisting concretizing definitions is in itself a resistance to the impulse of categorization and dominance. Our classrooms therefore should become spaces where terminology, names, and naming are debated and negotiated as a commitment to uncivilizing. One of the terms that constantly evolves in spaces of religious diversity are the terms interreligious, interfaith, and multireligious. To someone who is unfamiliar, all three of these terms might signal the same thing, but for those whom religiously diverse spaces require hefty negotiations for visibility, each term is vastly different. The term "interreligious" is more fulsome in its meaning for creating dialogical interlocutors between religious traditions but may leave out those traditions for whom the term "religion" might not quite fit. The term "interfaith" has an early history of being used in Christian ecumenical circles to refer to ecumenical partners. Later, it was used to describe members of Abrahamic faiths who think of their traditions as related faith-based systems of belief and common texts. Use of the term "interfaith" among some religious and spiritual traditions might not quite fit when historically it was the lack of a faith-based system of religion that relegated them to philosophies and folk traditions, rather than religious traditions on their own merit. The term "multireligious" is used as a way of reflecting on the equanimity that should exist between different religious traditions. I have heard multifaith described as if religions were islands unto themselves, all of equal shape and size. However, the reality is that religions are not truly perceived or experienced that way in the real world. The reality of Christian dominance in North America, in particular white Christianity, is undeniable and does not quite fit with the multifaith or multireligious narrative. All of these terms have served some purpose or another in different iterations of different religious and spiritual traditions working and living together, and none of these terms are completely satisfactory in their attempt at inclusivity. All of them leave out humanists and atheists though both of these groups are significant to the interreligious, interfaith, and mulitreligious efforts of many organizations and life together.

Even terms that describe racialized groups have shifted and changed over the decades and years. Today, the term "people of color" is the most commonly used identifier for communities that would otherwise be described as nonwhite. The term "people of color" has come into use for academics, activists, and social justice advocates alike in an effort to use an identifier that does not fall into a Black and white racial binary. The term is meant to signal interracial solidarity and to resist descriptions of people as nonwhite. However, even the term "people of color" has its limits.[16] In 2019, writer and activist Nadra Widatalla wrote an op-ed in the Los Angeles Times called, *The Term People of Color Erases Black People. Let's Stop Using It.* In her article, Widatalla describes the way the term "people of color" has been used to include all people of color except Black people.[17] She describes the term as coopted by the white narrative to do its shallow diversity due diligence, all the while excusing institutions and media from directly including Black people and their stories. I agree with Widatalla that there is need for a term that describes all racialized people of color communities, without the diminishment or erasure of Black communities and Muslim communities[18] and their experiences. Like Widatalla, I find that some non-Black people use the term "people of color" to avoid using the word Black or to avoid identifying people as Black when they are talking explicitly about Black people. As if Blackness and Black people and communities can't be acknowledged. If you have a problem saying Black or have an issue naming Blackness, you've probably been using the terms pejoratively this whole time.

Widatalla brings to our attention the twofold operationalization of the categorization of racialized people into one group, one, so that racialized people might organize against white supremacist structures and systems and two, so that white supremacist systems and structures, might define people into groups for their own use and manipulations. Widatalla's invitation to consider the use and misuses of the phrase, "people of color," does not come with a suggestion for another name to take its place, instead leaving the reader in a liminal space where we might see the need for something more and still witness its effectiveness in some places. She invites us to the anticolonial work of uncivilizing narratives of collective and individual power by resisting the urge to reify the very norming of terminology that reinstates the violence of erasure.

Some scholars and activists have begun using the term "BIPOC" to mark the Black and Indigenous experience as distinct and different from the experiences of Latinx and Asian people of color, resisting assumptions of shared narratives and solidarities. It is helpful to nuance everything we can when we group people together. Especially when we are grouping for the purpose refining positionalities and solidarities.

Power Dynamics in the Classroom

In addition to power dynamics between students, there are also power dynamics at play between teachers and students. These dynamics also need uncivilization. One significant way to do this is to disrupt the binaries between teacher and learner. The posture of humble modesty helps us access ways in which we enter the classroom, not as experts, but as people still on the journey to expand our intercultural and interreligious intelligence. Our students are always teachers. As you are reading this, pause for a moment and recall a time where something a student said or did in class pushed you to a deeper understanding of yourself; a time where they took part in your formation as a person, a community member, a teacher, and a learner. We can disrupt dysfunctional power dynamics between students and teachers by remembering that the posture of teaching is also a posture for learning and vice versa. They are two sides of the same coin. In this way, we engage the disruptive and anticolonial work of sharing power, of uncivilizing the creation of binaries between our students and ourselves.

There are many ways to deploy anticolonial strategies to disrupt power dynamics between students and teachers and to transform teaching and learning in the classroom. Which strategies are deployed depend on how we assess power dynamics between teachers and students. As I mentioned in earlier chapters, there are endless combinations of teacher-student power dynamics and one must remain acutely aware of the differences present in the classroom in order correctly assess. For instance, the dynamics of power when the teacher is a woman, a Black, Indigenous or person of color, queer, religiously garbed, or is in other ways minoritized while the students are mostly white are different than if the teacher is a Christian white male in that same space. Likewise, if the teacher is a Christian white woman, there are additional differences in dynamics. Student demographics and social locations also shift these power dynamics.

Some students and teachers are presumed incompetent based on their embodiments, while others are automatically given authority for their presenting race, religion, and gender. Some teachers and students enter classrooms and automatically disrupt spaces designed for civility through their very embodiments. Religious educator and theologian, Lynne Westfield, writes about this experience in her article on *Personal Practice and Austere Reality* saying, "To never be at home is to contend with the accusations that we cannot do 'classical' scholarship while at the same time reeling from the critique that our ethnic/cultural approaches are quaint, interesting . . . exotic. Our work and scholarship is othered along with our personhood. This constant confusion sends firm messages that we are not safe, not welcomed to be authentic or real."[19] This disproportionate allotment of power is most noticeable when there is a difficult conversation at hand or when there is less energy in the room to acknowledge and manage emotions. When I teach on the subject of white supremacy in my classroom, even in politically liberal spaces, I am strategic about how I do so in ways that students will best hear and consider what I have to say. I walk into those spaces fully aware that my physical embodiment reads as much younger than I am and that stereotypes about Asian women as both submissive and dragon ladies are present. In some spaces, I am fully able to lecture or facilitate exercises that work toward the unfolding of white supremacy and white fragility in our midst, but in others, some students remain caught up in the fact that a nonwhite body is teaching about white fragility, rather than hearing the message of what I am trying to teach. There are times where I choose to show informative video clips on whiteness or white supremacy and white fragility, rather than lecture on it myself. I instead, show the video clip of white men teaching via webinar and facilitate a discussion afterward. I also work to think about where my student's energy levels are in order to gauge whether or not there is capacity in the classroom for speaking about difficult subjects. When talking about white supremacy, doing so at the beginning of a course when people feel more energized to tackle difficult topics feels more worthwhile and productive. I realize that I have to think about these strategies when others who have different embodiments do not. I do so as a mode of self-care as well as for the well-being of my racially and religiously minoritized students. As teachers, as we attend to the different presenting dynamics of power in our classrooms by listening, watching, and asking key questions, we will find the strategies of facilitating transformation and shifting the balance of power for the sake of teaching and learning toward the uncivilizing of shared spaces.

CONCLUSION

Reconstruction does not occur linearly after deconstruction in the interculturally and interreligiously intelligent classroom. The work of uncivilizing and justice is not linear. We simultaneously reconstruct as we work to deconstruct the rigid and unhelpful colonial templates through which we have learned to teach and learn. Uncivilizing spaces of teaching and learning often means leaning into wilderness and imagination, something that Native scholars in their work of imagining decolonial futures and anticolonial practice, call indigeneity. The practice of indigeneity as anticoloniality originates from and is held by Native scholars who do the work of indigeneity in their own communities, much of it, simply by living and thriving as their resistance against narratives of violent erasure. For those of us who are not Native peoples, uncivilizing means teachers and students work together to cast off the labels and expectations of oppressive systems which benefit from the civilizing of what and who is considered savage and civil. Uncivilizing is related to the practice of cultivating anticolonial spaces where knowledge is produced. We reclaim the knowledge and the production of new knowledge akin to the ways racially and religiously minoritized people have always practiced. We begin by acknowledging them, reclaiming them, then reintegrating them into spaces of teaching and learning. In part two of this book, we will explore different ways in which anticolonial, intercultural, and interreligious intelligence is possible and already present in classroom communities.

Part II

RECONSTRUCTION

Chapter 5

Reclaiming Epistemologies

TEACHING AND LEARNING BORDERS AND BOUNDARIES

There are borders we cross, borders that cross us, and borders mapped onto our lives and bodies. Visible and invisible borders and boundaries shape us inside and out. "Where are you from?" This seemingly innocuous question about origin is one asked of Latinx, Asian American people, and religiously garbed people so that others might locate us and fix our image as something other, inscrutable, and foreign. For many racially and religiously minoritized people in the United States, especially people who choose to wear religious dress, this question feels hostile and akin to an interrogation. The interrogator seeks to shape and reshape racial and religious identity, a formation marked not only by personal knowledge but also out of fear and assumption. Even though my children are third-generation citizens of the United States, I know because of their Asian racialization, people will pepper them with the "Where are you from?" question throughout their lives. As a parent of Asian American children I do not wonder *if* my children will be assumed "other," I wonder *when* they will be assumed "other" and if I will be prepared to help them understand the racism and miscognition taking place.[1]

At first glance, this "Where are you from?" question is about location and identity. The question seems friendly, but it is not. When I answer Los Angeles or Seattle, there is usually a quizzical reaction, a furrowed brow, or a widening of the eyes. Then my conversation partner will either silently accept my response or push back with "No, I mean, where are you *really* from?" My answer is usually unsatisfactory because I have not obliged and identified why I look "foreign" to the person asking this question. My self-identified location within the binary borders of a Black-and-white United States is not a good answer. My answer is incorrect. A better answer, a more correct answer, would have been, "Oh, I'm from Korea." The question, "Where are you from?" comes from a place of bias. The person guilty of asking the triggering question is not always a white person, but they are always a person for whom the white supremacist lens for perceiving the place of yellow bodies in their world is foreign and other. In their eyes, it is not enough for me to answer that I was born on North American soil. As Indigenous people everywhere will tell you, birthplace is not enough to actually belong in the eyes of others. So I find myself looking for other places I might call home that people cannot steal from me with their confused and furrowed brows. Poet Nayyirah Waheed writes, "My mother was my first country, the first place I ever lived."[2] I love this poem because it reminds me that, yes, though land is significant, for racially and religiously minoritized people land is not always where we find our homes and identities. Land is stolen, pillaged, occupied, colonized, and divided with borders. There is nostalgia with land and a grief at its loss, its disconnection with self and peoplehood but people that look like me are forever being told we have never belonged to the land that knows us. Therefore, the feeling of home is established in our connection with people and peoplehood and the formation that occurs within those connective tissues, sometimes even body within body. Sometimes stories become our motherlands, our homes, and the ground of our being. For our students of color and religiously minoritized students, their homes are not only tied to place but to people, nurturers, caregivers, and lovers. Those relationships are the wombs that continue to form and shape their identities and selfhood in a world that wants to reorder their identities and narratives to operationalizable ones. These relationships are cultural, spiritual, and religious all at once. The knowledge produced and reproduced in these womb like relationships and communities is a pivotal epistemology in classrooms and other spaces of learning. As educators committed to decolonial and anticolonial ways of teaching and learning, we task ourselves with making generous and hospitable space for the oldest epistemologies. The classroom itself transforms into a womb where identities are formed, shaped, remade, seen, heard, and affirmed, a space where knowing and belonging are a possibility for the most minoritized among us.

Teaching Woori

The borderlands which continue to shape me and the womb that continues to nurture me are the ones my parents crossed when they immigrated to the United States. They are also the borders of relative safety and sanctuary set up by the Korean American churches in my childhood and adolescent years. It is and was through the experience of hearing and learning the stories and experiences of my family and the cultivation of my culturally tied faith and spiritual practices through the Korean immigrant church that I began to seek the reclamation of the epistemologies, or ways of knowing for which I hungered. As a child of Korean immigrants growing up in Southern California and Seattle, the Korean American church was a place where I found comfort in my skin and my spirit, even when the world at large was less than hospitable. In church, no one pointed out my physical differences, the features that made me a "nonwhite" person in society.[3] No one defined me by what I was not, but by who I knew I was. For me, my experiences in the Korean American church world and in larger American society were always juxtaposed. The church world was communally centered, and the outside world was individually focused. At church, the way in which we talked about one another was through the Korean word *woori*, or us. It was always, *woori kyo-hwe* (our church), *woori ah-e-duhl* (our children), *woori seng-myung* (our life), and even *woori nah-rah* (our nation). *Woori* is far more than a word that connotes togetherness or possession, it is a word embedded with theological significance of a singular peoplehood. *Woori* encompasses what it means to cultivate a communal theology that gives birth to a theology of selfhood, not the other way around.[4] A theological selfhood shaped and defined by the community of which you are a member. The concept of *woori* is one we might carefully consider in our teaching and learning practices of theological education but first we explore its conditions within its Indigenous Korean roots.[5]

The shaping power of *woori* in my life is both cultural and religious. For some people, over time, for those that cross borders, it becomes extremely difficult to parse out what is solely cultural and what is solely religious. The process of immigration does the work of melding together what might have once existed separately in someone's mind as their spiritual practices and religious beliefs and cultural identity. The experience of crossing borders tangles up the commitments to cultures, religions, people, and communities, just as it multiples and complicates the definition of home. As the complex image of self and community mirrored back to immigrants is flattened by the media, government, and neighbors, either that image of self as a racialized religious person undergoes self-erasure and covering up in an attempt to assimilate to the dominant culture, or it becomes sharper and more visible in resistance to the caricature mapped over it.

Teachers and students possess similar understandings of *woori* or the collective we in their experience that continues to teach them about their personal and communal identities and histories. These formations are not neutral but carry a mix of positive and negative power. For example, in the formation of people in the Korean American community the concept of *woori* is double-edged. The connectional quality of *woori* anchors Korean American

Christians to and within shared coethnic structures and histories of religious community and spiritual practice, but *woori* also has the potential to require a denial of the aspects of personhood that develop counter to the theological leanings of the *woori* community. Divergence from what is normative to *woori* is risky and isolating. I will discuss this challenging attribute of *woori* later in this chapter. In sum, the Korean American diaspora and church are *woori* in the eyes of G_d and one another, sometimes even to the detriment of authentic individual and communal life. As a Korean person in diaspora, being able to reclaim *woori* as part of my understanding of self, community, culture, spirituality, and religion is tempered with the critical hermeneutical lens of interpreting for myself which parts of the *woori* feed and add to my flourishing and which challenge it. In the classroom, it is a good goal to help students understand that they must continue to keep a critical eye toward the dynamics of power within different epistemological structures so that power and therefore the narratives of people are never flattened but continually complicated and deepened.

Teaching Dissonance across and between Borders and Boundaries

Students enter the classroom already connected and tied to place, community, language, and people in their lives. Students who come from cultures that are communally oriented rather than individual, or are high-context cultures, rather than low context,[6] arrive with a sense of "us-ness" or *woori* already as part of the very fabric of their identities. How they engage the course, the teacher, and their student colleagues is determined by the shaping they received and still receive from these locations of community and how they operate in the student's life. We might see one student in the classroom, but we are actually witnessing ancestors, families, cities, villages, temples, mosques, and/or churches coexisting in one body. For example, in the Korean American community, there is an understanding across generations that each of us belongs to a tapestry that is still growing, a tapestry that is far larger than our individual selves. Our actions simultaneously echo forwards and backward into time. How one person behaves, lives, and embodies faith, whether well or poorly, reflects on that person's family and even their larger community. This communal or corporate identity formation begins in childhood and adolescence and is part of a preconstructed identity[7] that is mapped onto each person as they enter into and move in community.[8] How might we honor the way students come to classrooms with their internal and external expressions of borders and boundaries? How do teachers continue to cultivate the *woori-ness* already a part of our student's experiences, rather than striving to reorient them to the individuality so potently a part of western education?

We begin by becoming aware of the lenses that tell us who can learn and who cannot, who should learn and who should not. We help deconstruct the colonial understanding of the engaged student who leads with thinking out loud and writing within western academic frameworks and help them reconstruct an anticolonial awareness of the different ways knowledge is produced and reproduced in communities of learning. In this way, we surface and engage the connection and the dissonance between who students are and how they locate themselves and community, between the information we aim to share with them and how we assess their learning.

Religiously and racially minoritized students are familiar with feelings of constant dissonance. A DuBoisian double consciousness. Students come into the classroom to experience dissonance between how they see themselves and how the outside world sees them. In my early childhood, when I learned what people meant by asking me where I was from, I also learned to navigate the dissonance between the biases of the asker and what I understood as my own identity. For racially and religiously minoritized students, they arrive at spaces of teaching and learning with borders and boundaries already drawn up, for some students, on their bodies. Students are told that the ways their womb-communities have taught them to see themselves are wrong, and they are reoriented to see themselves in new ways. These untethered new ways of seeing sometimes disconnect students from the places and people who have nurtured them.

As an adolescent, teachers used to ask me to imagine what I would be when I grew up. They wanted me to understand that I could do anything I set my mind to do if I only tried. They wanted me to embrace a type of independence that may very well take me from outside my natal family and community to bigger and better things. This perspective was deemed a natural progression of adulthood and leaving the nest. Never mind that this Horatio Alger-ian belief that one only needs to work hard to achieve one's dreams is already trite in the face of a white supremacist society that seeks to destabilize and demolish any such dreaming from minoritized communities and people. In addition, these types of individualistic understandings of self, requiring separation from the community, rather than growing out of it, never made sense to me in the face of what I was learning explicitly and implicitly at my Korean American church about our connection as a people and as spiritual beings.[9] Knowing this, how might we operate through humble modesty in ways that invite the cultivation of intercultural and interreligious self-understanding and understanding across difference, particularly when differences are embodied within one person? How do we help students connect to the dissonant locations of selfhood in their own embodiments and discover a positive connectional *woori* that produces connectional knowledge of self, community, and world between borders and boundaries?

Some of our students face dissonance because they are between places and cultures, both externally and internally, but it is not always a dissonance necessitating resolution. If teachers have the impulse to tame dissonance in the classroom, particularly in the presenting identities of students, they must ask themselves what it is they fear in what is presented. Spoken word poet Leah Anderson's poem, *You ask me what I am so you may know how to fear me*, unpacks the way she engages the question, "What are you?" A question she often gets due to the way strangers cannot neatly racialize her multiracial phenotype. In the poem Anderson's in-betweenness is called out, and she responds by tracing and casting her ancestral net wide. She describes her Indigenous, Asian, and European ancestry and in doing so, names the xenophobic fear of a white supremacist society that needs to know *what* she is in order to know how to guard itself against her.[10] Dissonance exists as a way some students navigate and flourish between two or more epistemological ways of being. This dissonance is a colonial construct of miscognition. Homi Bhabha's discussion on civility considers the construct of the dissonant self. Bhabha writes, "Both colonizer and colonized are in a process of miscognition where each point of identification is always a partial and double repetition of the *otherness* of the self-democrat and despot, individual and servant . . . It is around the 'and'—that conjunction of infinite repetition—that the ambivalence of civil authority circulates as a 'colonial' signifier that is *less than one and double*."[11] For the minoritized person, living, existing within the struggle of miscognition and dissonance meant to break you, is a form of colonial resistance. The dissonance created between identities can be a map between multiple internal spaces of being and belonging, a map that deconstructs borders and tells of something new that the colonial, and white Christian supremacist mind fears.

In my bicultural childhood and adolescence, the narratives I internalized from the two worlds I inherited and inhabited did not always align and were often in tension with one another. There was not always a way to make peace between the Korean and American worlds, within me. The two worlds coexisted unbordered, sometimes amicably and sometimes in fierce competition. To choose individuality meant I chose myself over the *woori-ness* of my family's cultural and religious expectations. Choosing individuality meant a severing of self from community in a way that felt like the betrayal of both cultural, familial, and religious ties. To choose *woori-ness* meant that the parts of myself that defied communal understandings of self would need to go into hiding. Like many children and adolescents of immigrant parents, I walked in the space between two worlds without being able to reconcile them to one another and without desire to do so. Yet, religion, faith, and theology was constructed differently in both worlds, and I had to learn how to function in both, to code-switch back and forth as necessary, and compartmentalize questions and pain in order to survive in both places.[12]

During a time in my life, where I was still in the throes of understanding who I was and who I wanted to become, and as an adolescent with limited social power in both worlds, this labor of learning to move between two cultures and ways of trying to authentically embody myself in both places was exhausting. I wish desperately that someone had told me that the dissonance between worlds was rife with possibility. Where something new might be born and where creative space could be found, where I might locate myself fully. As a teacher, I strive to bring about hospitable spaces for the dissonance in students to surface, be seen and met with courage as part of my commitment to anticolonial teaching and learning. I consider dissonance not something in need of reconciliation, but in need of recognition and cultivation so something new and precious might form.

Bicultural and religiously fluid students who straddle two or more worlds are formed in those in-between spaces, through the experience of religion, faith, and spirituality interpreted differently and even possessing different and contrasting values in different places. Studies of bicultural people reveal the experience of traversing multiple cultural and religious identities at once. An attempt at the reconciliation of two or more disparate worlds, perspectives, and multiple theologies, often without help. These people are often told that true safety lies in claiming the socially dominant identity and place. Particularly among immigrant families, parents often do not acculturate as quickly as their children and are unable to help them navigate across cultural differences and the claiming of the dominant, acculturated identity is a way to mitigate personal and familial pain that intercultural dissonance can cause. In adulthood, this formational experience can leave bicultural and religiously fluid students feeling that they cannot bring their complexities into the classroom as part of a shared process of learning. Just as students have had to construct complex identities and ways of being on their own, they can also continue to do so in the classroom while remaining their most authentic selves.

TEACHING WOORI ACROSS TIME AND SPACE AS FORMATIONAL DISSONANCE

As a response to what can be the disconnected quality of a colonial and supremacist-oriented individualistic theological education, *woori-ness* as a concept can become the connective tissue between space, time, and in between cultures and religions. In my childhood and adolescence, *woori* described all the storied people and places that had been lost through war, time, and immigration. They were all tied to us and to me through communal and familial imagination, memory, and pain. Children of immigrants are shaped and formed by the tides of human movement, sometimes forced upon them by immigration. They are affected even more acutely because they understand what it is to long for a particular place, through the shared family narratives to which they are privy, often without ever having seen the places or people their families are describing. These feelings of connectivity are still very much alive as the children of immigrants grow up, and as they become students in our classrooms, bringing with them the feelings of grief and loss that affect the way minoritized people engage the world.

Even though I was born in Los Angeles, I yearn for the homeland of the Korean Peninsula. This yearning is cultivated and passed down from my parents and my grandparents who immigrated post 1965, when travel and communication between Korea and the United States was extremely expensive. I watched as my parents built Korean American immigrant community around themselves but could never quite replicate the feeling of "home." I listened to the voices of my family in Korea as they spoke to my parents over the phone and heard the echoes of longing as they dreamed of reuniting. They spoke loudly to one another, emphasizing each word as if to mark the miles and oceans between them. Later, speaking to my grandparents about their family in North Korea, I heard the same longing for family one would never see again and the desperate hope of reunification across borders and time.

Even before transnationalism was sustained and supported through technology,[13] there has always been a spiritual sense of border and boundary crossing and yearning for places one departed. Though for many immigrants, it may be possible to recross particular boundaries and revisit spaces that one has departed, the sense that homelands have transformed and transitioned without them is deep. My mother and father often talk about how Korea has changed beyond their comprehension. The places that they knew are no longer there, the colloquial language used among Koreans in Korea is different from the one they painfully preserved for their children and grandchildren in the United States. When they visit their homeland, they are suddenly "other" and seen as westernized. My grandfather used to tell me that my mother and I "smelled like America" when he tried to describe how we too had changed.

As previously noted, epigenetic scholarship tells us that consecutive generations suffer from the loss and trauma of the experience of forced and sudden geographic movement. Trauma is etched onto our DNA. One generation may undergo displacement directly, but the experience, collective, and individual memory is shared and even multiplied within future generations. This occurs among Black people, Native and Indigenous people, Jewish people, Asian people, Caribbean people, Latinx people, asylum seekers, and others.[14] All this to say, even children born in the United States and North America with parents or grandparents who have experienced necessary immigration due to war or forced displacement bear the consequences of what that journey means upon their psyche, spirits, inherited spiritualities, theologies, their reality of minoritization, and the experience of being religious pilgrims[15] in a hostile land.

Making visible cultural and religious difference in embodiments and practice are ways in which the precious articles of what it means to belong to the *woori-ness* of one's community are passed down, taught, and learned. Though land, place, language, and other tangible things may be lost or forgotten over time, practices of peoplehood, spirituality, and the enculturated ways in which we converse and imagine G_d and ourselves are still very much grounded in those lost places and things. In a way, as we engage in cultural and religious rites and practices together, we revive what was lost before our very eyes.[16] An anticolonial approach to theological education are ways in which language, histories, customs, and entire cultures are preserved. Anticolonial theological education is also where new meanings, both religious and cultural, have the potential to be cocreated and negotiated across cultural, religious, and generational differences. How might teachers embrace what students bring as part of their creative and liminal religious and cultural dissonances to theological education, as part of anticolonial practice and commitment? By centering holistic formation as a part of every classroom, regardless of topic, we can make possible the recognition of the power of liminality in the dissonant experience of self and community among minoritized students in the world.

You might consider student formation which attends to cultural and religious embodiments as an unnecessary part of the work of your particular field, but consider that it is the siloed thinking of a western oriented academy that convinces educators that explicit and implicit formation is not something that occurs or should occur in all classrooms. Formation work is not only for religious educators in theological education. Formation is imbedded in all the ways education operates. Both teachers and students enter classrooms as beings in formation and exist formed in one way or another by what occurred inside. Whether or not formation is explicit in classrooms, it implicitly occurs. We are all formed via the theological educational enterprise, and in many ways, we are malformed by it into patriarchal, white supremacist, and Christian hegemonic modes of being. Formation is multidirectional. Formation is not something teachers *do* to students but *with* them.

The integration of formation as a part of every classroom in theological education is about the recognition of the significance of *interdependence* as a primary mode of being in place of independence. Korean Theologian, Choi Hee An writes about the power of interdependence in the postcolonial self, saying, "The notion of the interdependence and interconnectedness of life values mutuality and justice not only for human beings but also for nonhuman reality. It is about the respect for all life."[17] Choi goes on to describe the insidious reframing of interdependence and interconnectedness that is in reality individualism in sheep's clothing. Interdependence and interconnectedness cultivated for the sake of individual dominance is not truly interdependence or interconnectedness at all. Choi's decolonial understanding of interdependence and interconnectedness as beyond just human life but inclusive of all life is a vision of the disruption of the center and margin binary. This disruption is the very same echo of the experience of dissonance many minoritized teachers and students go through on a daily basis. How might all classrooms in theological education reorient themselves away from the type of individualism that only functions to shut down the possibility of imaginative dissonance in our student's lives and work or worse, sees it as a danger to itself? What kind of holistic environment is possible for teachers and students who are welcome to bring all their truths, even conflicting ones, into classrooms? If theological education were to model decolonial interdependence and interconnectedness, our institutions and subsequent classrooms would think of individual and communal coformation that impacts all of life necessarily a part of all course design. For racially and religiously minoritized students, classrooms that center formation can become places where students are able to witness and perceive the edification of self and community, creative dissonance and all. The formational interconnectedness of *woori* is already a part of many teachers and student's lives. Will our classrooms squash *woori* or nurture it?

It is easy to romanticize *woori* without seeing its underside. To romanticize *woori* is a colonial move that reproduces the erasure of those who have experienced the concept and embodiments of *woori* as painful and traumatizing. As this text strives to engage anticolonial understandings of teaching and learning, I want to also lift up the ways in which *woori* as a concept can do harm when it is wielded through colonial understandings of sameness. The concept of *woori* is challenging to the very justice-oriented interdependence imagined by Choi. The individual self in relation to the communal self is not always the colonial self. Sometimes it is the communal self, the *woori*, that seeks to erase the impact of the individual self on the identity of the whole. Religious and racialized cultural communities are potential places of comfort for those seeking solace from the hostile world that perceives community members as other and foreign, but these same communities can also cultivate confusion and tensions at the intersections of these dissonant liminalities. This ease of comfort and the feeling of belonging in religiocultural spaces can come at a cost to authenticity and even personal values. Culturally, racially, and religiously minoritized people who live intercultural and religiously fluid lives may experience *woori-ed* spaces as insular and unwelcoming of particular identities. Their particular identities and values can be seen as a threat to the common *woori* of the interdependent whole. This is because the interdependent whole is not functioning as interdependent at all. Instead, it reproduces coloniality by setting borders and boundaries around the quality of *woori-ness* and how it is defined. For instance, the queering of Asian American theology as well as the acceptance of LGBTQIA+ people are still difficult and unapproachable topics for many Asian and Asian immigrant communities. Such antiqueer and homophobic positionalities are further theologized by destructive Christian theologies and teachings. I once served a Korean American immigrant church where youth began coming out to the disbelief of the first generation. There was no way for queer identifying youth or their family to be openly queer while remaining a part of the congregation which vehemently theologized a relationship of queerness with sin. Families with adolescents who came out had to practice silence about the queer identities of their teens. Essentially, youth and their families had no support or affirmation for living into their authentic selves within the construct of *woori*. In this congregation, as much as the queer identifying second-generation Korean American's intentionally lived into the dissonant space between two cultures, the culture and theologies of *woori* did not mirror the creative potential of liminal space and instead restricted it. In this particular instance, either they would seek to belong and make themselves fit or they could chose to depart and not belong at all. In this instance, the connectional nature of the Korean and Korean American community which occurs through the auspices of the church ended up winning the day, with the newly "out" youth agreeing to continue to attend the church without openly discussing such a significant part of their personal and even their Christian identity. This uncomfortable and tense truce, which acted as violent erasure, was negotiated because the value of having a community, even with fabricated comfort, was held in higher esteem than the feeling of being adrift and alone without the church and therefore without a religious racial ethnic community. In cases minoritized individuals are seeking to exist as their authentic selves community, the threat of losing the support and comfort of *woori-ness* and becoming an outsider is a real and dangerous compromise. This dangerous erasure through the concept of *woori* is problematic because it assumes that *woori-ness* is a one-sided formation instead of a mutual growth and formation where both the individual and community are pushed to grow and expand their theological frameworks of belonging through shared histories and lived experiences.

There is an insidious side to *woori-ness* as an epistemology that can supersede other identities that people might name and claim outside of a particular community context. Adhering to the communal identity and belief system is seen as the aim even at the cost of someone's individual self-determination. The nail that sticks out gets hammered down. This can leave minoritized people feeling isolated and invisible even within a protective ethnic religious context of *woori*. In these cases where *woori* is detrimental to selfhood and is weaponized against the flourishing of the whole community, classroom formation is necessarily a way in which someone experiencing the negative formation of the collective can visiblize and work out their identities and beliefs among others who can midwife the person who is being called forth.

The concept of *woori* is more than a concrete Korean concept of oneness and community. When expanded to consider the minoritized lives of people in theological education, *woori* is a framework that is transnational, boundary crossing, aware of the creative potential of communal and individual dissonance, and at times, dangerously prioritized over self-determination. *Woori-ness* is part of formation that should be a part of our day-to-day teaching and learning. It is a lens through which minoritized people and dominant culture people might learn to see one another and themselves as grounded in significant places, people, and spiritualities amid feelings of otherness on North American soil. Where does *woori-ness* exist in your spaces of teaching and learning? How might you acknowledge and cultivate *woori-ness* in the lives of your students? Though not a perfect framework or construct, *woori* offers a chance for both teachers and students to thrive as they negotiate what it means to create inhabitable worlds that hold dissonant realities as sacred spaces where people and communities are nurtured and challenged.

Chapter 6

Retelling Histories as Story and Story Formation

ORIGIN STORIES

Everyone has an origin story. Origins stories are particularly important for people with histories of displacement. Origin stories are invisible anchors to people and places. Mine begins with my grandparents. My maternal grandmother and grandfather escaped what is now known as North Korea on one of the last boats traveling south. Together, they packed up whatever they could carry and with one of my young uncles holding my grandfather's hand and my other uncle, a six-month-old infant, strapped to my grandmother's back, they hurried toward the harbor hoping against hope that they would find room on board. My infant uncle died on that journey. He suffocated on my grandmother's back from the hot press of the desperate crowd. My grandmother did not realize he had died until they were on board. The boat was teeming with people and immediately began to sink. My grandmother once described the scene to me saying, "We looked like ants swarming a piece of fruit. You couldn't distinguish one body from another." People were hanging off the boat's exterior and pushing others overboard trying to survive. Others, frantic to keep the boat from sinking, demanded my grandparents throw the body of their infant into the sea, along with others who were sick or injured, so that the boat would stay afloat. My grandmother wrapped my uncle's body in her skirt, clutched him against her, and carried him to their new home in the south. In that way, they remained together, separated by death but not an impassible border. He traveled with them, if only in body. My grandparents left everyone behind, their parents, siblings, aunts, uncles, cousins, and friends. They would never again see their family or home. In the wake of so much loss, they were not about to leave the body of their youngest son behind. For my family, into the next two generations, my infant uncle would become the most significant symbol of what my grandparents had clung to and lost, their biggest sacrifice and the price of war.

Growing up and listening to the story of my grandparent's escape and the many other painful stories in our shared family narrative, I learned about my identity and the power of *woori*. I was not alone. I learned to define myself in relationship to the joy, grief, and pain that emerged from these narratives and within the contextual power of *woori*[1] or the "us" of what it meant to be a Korean person in diaspora. Stories and the tenor of the voices that told these stories grounded me. I began to see myself by extension in the places and people I had never seen or met. I knew who I was and who I wanted to become because of how I was directly connected to the stories shared with me by my family as well as others in my Korean American community. As a second-generation Korean American, born in Los Angeles, these stories connected me directly to the motherland, to the Korean Peninsula and the Korean people. Sitting at the feet of my elders, I felt claimed by a tradition and story larger than my own, a narrative more expansive than what I had been allowed as a nonwhite person in the United States. As a liminal and bicultural person who often experiences life in North America as betwixt and between, these connections, facilitated through story, anchored me in a transnational sense of home, particularly in seasons of my life where I felt invisible or essentialized in an American cultural context that constantly measured me as deficient against the yardstick of whiteness.

This chapter examines the importance of story for teaching and learning among minoritized people, especially immigrants and the second generation as a cornerstone for interculturally and interreligiously intelligent pedagogy and focuses on the magnitude of intergenerational story formation and sharing as a form of resilience, resistance, and survival. Thinking beyond the racialized Black and white North American binary and the dominance of Christian narratives requires we attend to the lives and experiences of diasporic peoples. Anticolonial teachers interested in intercultural and interreligious intelligence must grow curious about the stories of their diasporic students, both immigrants and the second generation. The stories of first-generation immigrants are often the only connections that younger diasporic generations have to motherlands and even mother tongues. Stories shape and form entire generations culturally, communally, and spiritually, carrying with them lessons, warnings, and a thousand hopes. Sometimes the stories that are birthed in immigration and displacement change as they are told and shared, becoming imbued with new meanings for new generations; they are stories and memories that become living coformed histories. Drawing upon oral storytelling traditions and theologies of Asian American peoples and my personal history and family stories, the chapter explores the importance of intergenerational story formation and storytelling for the thriving of coformed interculturally and interreligiously intelligent classrooms.

DECOLONIZING POSSIBILITIES IN STORIES

When we hear the word story, our minds might automatically recall a childhood past time. There might exist assumptions that stories are for children or stories are always positive and make us feel good to tell and hear them. There might exist temptation to relegate the practice of storytelling to one solely about happy endings. Sometimes I hear faith leaders saying that storytelling is something that brings us closer together across differences without considering that stories are also vehicles of separation, erasure, and violence. Stories are not always "feel good." Stories sometimes knock the wind out of us. Stories can tell truths about not only our innermost selves but also our untruths that facilitate confirmation bias, shutting down opportunities for positive transformation. Stories lend both the storyteller and hearer power; the power to mend across difference and the power to rupture relationships and community.

Stories are leveraged and operationalized in classrooms and as part of pedagogy for their power. An anticolonial acknowledgment of story in teaching and learning makes room for the power of story but is constantly aware that power is wielded for both destruction and reconstruction. An anticolonial interculturally and interreligiously intelligent teacher asks about reshaped narratives in storytelling, whether whitewashed histories are corrected, or perpetuated, whether communities and people are humanized or dehumanized, whether telling and hearing stories makes us better versions of ourselves or reduces us to perpetrators of violence. Interculturally and interreligiously, intelligent pedagogues carefully weigh the impact of story in the classroom and beyond, the power of both telling stories and opacity and the complex ways people engage across conflicting narratives.

The first step in the process of understanding of stories requires resisting the urge to soften and romanticize stories, particularly when they are being shared in classrooms by students or by our colleagues. We resist the romanticizing of stories by acknowledging the sacred space we are invited into via the sharing of personal stories. Upon hearing sacred story, the colonial and anticolonial mind operate in starkly different ways. The colonial mind automatically leaps to a place of controlling narrative, seeking places to insert oneself through comparison, rather than approaching what is shared from a place of listening. They might hear a story and think in terms of personal gain, "What a great story! I wonder where I might share this story or retell it somewhere else to make a point?" The anticolonial mind listens in a different way. The anticolonial person begins by acknowledging what has happened, becoming aware of what the systems and structures at play in the stories retelling. The anticolonial mind is awed by the sacred moment and recognizes it has been entrusted with the sacred and resists layering new meaning over what is shared. The anticolonial person resists operationalizing a story which is not theirs. An anticolonial and interculturally and interreligiously intelligent pedagogue pays close attention to what stirs within themselves as the story is revealed and takes time to receive it fully. They do not seek to own what they hear, only to bear witness. The anticolonial pedagogue is fully present to the sacred, naming and suspending assumptions, aware of personal biases, and resists the urge to control what is unfolding.

In order to model for students the power of personal narrative in formation, I often share my own family histories and stories, with permission, as part of my teaching and preaching. Every once in a while, someone will ask me if it is okay for them to share my story as part of their own sermon illustration or teaching. I reply with a firm "No." I am disturbed by the inclination some possess to collect the stories of trauma and pain that are not their own or their family's for the purpose of unfurling them when it serves a personal or professional purpose. I wonder if the fondness for collecting stories that do not belong to us signals our disconnectedness with our own histories and stories and a fear of our own truths? Even more viscerally, perhaps the lure of story collection and curation is the fear that we do not have stories worth telling or hearing. The colonial enterprise of stealing stories or throwing rosy colored glasses over fraught histories has facilitated the erasure of minoritized people all over the world. It is what Ojibwe activist and scholar Winonna LaDuke calls the colonial consumption or the colonial project acting as colon, digesting everything in its path for its own nourishment.[2]

Not all stories and histories are for common consumption. Stories are entrusted to people and communities. Like the origin story, I shared at the beginning of this chapter, many stories that are passed down are about violence, despair, trauma, and the birth of hope. By sharing these stories with permission in this book, I am entrusting you, the reader, with the very core of my personal truth and formation, in hopes that something might also shift and expand in you, not for your voyeuristic consumption. My practice of sharing personal narratives also reconnects me to the bonds of family and community, to religion, faith, and culture and the people that embodied all three for me. By retelling stories of joy, love, hope, pain, and trauma, communities keep alive the legacy of survival and what survival cost. People who cross borders and those who are crossed by borders, carry with them stories and histories that sustain and affirm their human dignity in new and hostile lands even when they can bring little else with them and even when those new lands contribute to their dehumanization. Yet, even in the throes of day-to-day survival, memories, and stories, and the potential for the cocreation of new stories and the intergenerational reinterpretation of stories are invaluable during what can be a new trauma of settling in a new place. For people for whom borders and boundaries marked on their bodies and collective consciousness are a daily reality, these memories and stories contribute to the formation[3] of entire generations of people past the point of immigration and displacement. These memories and stories about violence, survival, and flourishing act as a form of heritage and resistance to the often white, colonist, and western lenses through which the stories of minoritized people are filtered and diminished. To bear witness to the presentation of stories and histories in classrooms is to bear witness to the fierce strength of ancestors embodied in the voices of students. It is an honor and a privilege to bear witness. It is never a right.

For people distanced from memories and stories of immigration and displacement, whether through the passage of time or through internalized narratives of cultural and religious dominance, they need not look deep into the annals of history to witness the living stories that form us. History is always on the table. It is with us now. History repeats itself through human hands with a vengeance. The imposed carceral conditions of today's immigrants and asylum seekers is one public example of stories being written on the bodies of the most minoritized among us. As I write this chapter, an immigration crises is unfolding, again, on the southern border of the United States. Asylum seekers are systematically separated from their families, infants, and toddlers ripped from caregivers and thrown into concentration camps. Children are left to care for other children. Toddlers are given infant formula while infants are stripped of their clothing before being returned to cages. In the state I live in, the state of Georgia, immigrant women in detention camps are undergoing forced hysterectomies. This is and has been a humanitarian crisis. Recently, a photographic image of Oscar Martinez Ramirez and his two-year-old daughter Angie Valeria Martinez was shared on the Internet. They drowned in the Rio Grande seeking asylum.[4] Martinez held his daughter to his body even as they died. I cannot bear to look at this picture and the photographs of many other such deaths.

White supremacy does not just come to collect the lives and bodies of immigrants. George Floyd was murdered by a police officer kneeling on his neck while two others watched. I can still hear the screams of Diamond Reynolds and her four-year-old daughter as they watched Philando Castile shot multiple times at point blank range by yet another police officer who was later acquitted of all charges. Sandra Bland. Breonna Taylor. Ahmaud Arbery. Brayla Stone. There are countless more people we can name and countless more we cannot. All of this death, the ripping asunder of lives, families, histories, and stories eats at my soul. I refuse to normalize the brutality of this murderous and colonial nation against the bodies and lives of Black and brown people. People are dying. People are being incarcerated. People are being tortured. People are being murdered—everyday.

For teachers and students in places of power and privilege, these realities, stories, and memories must shake them to their core that the rosy-hued glasses might never again threaten the erasure of millions. To retell these stories in real time is part of that witness. To utter these stories in spaces where those stories are unwelcome is to keep alive the memory of those the system killed. It throws a mirror in the face of those who look away to preserve their own oblivious comfort. The anticolonial teacher both facilitates an environment where colearners can choose to entrust personal histories to one another and where stories that threaten humanity, shaped in the public sphere today, are made visible and audible.

STORIES IN TRANSMISSION

We share our classrooms with immigrants, documented and undocumented, with Black, Indigenous, and people of color, and the religiously targeted and minoritized. Some of us are also teachers who fit some of all of these descriptions. For those of us whom this describes, stories and storytelling are vehicles for the transmission what is important from one generation to the next. Stories and how communities share, teach, and inform. Stories shape communal and individual identity, pass on familial and cultural traditions and heritage, preserve language, and form faith and spiritual values. Storytelling encompasses folk stories, stories of lived experiences, and created stories. When told intergenerationally, stories impart significant messages from the immigrant generation to those who are growing up in a different time and context. The transmission of stories is more than about stagnant preservation and survival. In the North American context, storytelling is in its essence about the cultivation and deepening of personhood and peoplehood, often over and against a national white supremacist Christian supremacist narrative that seeks to diminish any foreign affiliations, transnational identities, and differentiated religious belonging. Stories facilitate the building up of personhood and peoplehood in an inhospitable land and against all odds. Making space for stories in classroom pedagogy grounds epistemologies of all kinds crucial for intercultural and interreligious intelligence.

However, story transmission in classrooms is not without its tensions and complications. In order to honor and create space for the complexity of stories as part of interculturally and interreligiously intelligent pedagogy, we need to take the time to sit with the actual lives of minoritized people and hear how story is a vehicle for both connection and disconnection. For teachers from privileged dominant contexts, that means reading and elevating the work of minoritized scholars, meditating on their art, and listening to their voices and modeling this practice for students. For minoritized people, sometimes that means telling and retelling your own stories and histories as a way of reconnecting genealogical tissues severed over time or as a way of making sense of your own struggle within white supremacist and Christian centric systems and structures that seek to diminish or essentialize you and your people. In the remainder of this chapter, I tell many of my own family's stories, mostly from my childhood and adolescence, as a way of inviting you, the reader, into my own process of understanding how the story has been transmitted in my own life and how it affects the way I teach and learn. I invite you to listen and consider, to hold space and hopefully expand your heart toward a commitment to deeper intercultural and interreligious intelligence as anticolonial resistance.

MY STORY, OUR STORY

"I'm American!" I blurted to a group of Korean Christian missionaries. I lived with the missionaries for a summer in Thailand when I was eighteen. My statement did not refer to my place of citizenship. I was referring to the self-erasure of my Korean-ness, to the denial of *woori*-ness the women were attempting to cultivate with me. To say that I was American erased the fact that I was Korean, and in my mind's eye, prevented these women from claiming me into a history that was too painful for me to accept.

The second or third generation, or the North American-born generation, may not initially want to hear stories about homeland or the things that they consider gone and past in the midst of what could be considered developmental crises. Hearing stories can hurt and cause crisis. The crisis arises as the chasm between caregivers and children widens. I remember thinking, why am I expected to do the things, other people's parents do? As a child, my nonimmigrant classmates had parents who guided them through the school system. They filled out forms, conferenced with teachers, and socialized with other parents. My parents did none of these things. Not because they did not want to but because they were still learning how. Children and adolescents of immigrant families often find the roles between themselves and their caretakers reversed.[5] Children and adolescents of immigrant families learn language and tacit culture more quickly than their parents because of the education system. Attending school helps them grow wider, multiracial social networks than their caretakers, and they are able to learn English primarily through immersion.[6] In early elementary, my parents asked me to help them read mail and make phone calls. I learned to read in Kindergarten and distinctly remember my frustration at not being able to learn quickly enough. Not only was I impatient to read books on my own, the weight of necessity drove me. I needed to learn to read so that I could translate for my parents, and we could move through life together in the United States as a family unit. I had to grow up quickly and take on roles and responsibilities traditionally reserved for parents and guardians. I visited hospitals with my parents and grandparents as an adolescent translating for them with health-care practitioners. I learned early on that my caretakers were dependent on me to get through many day-to-day activities and realities.

While living in an Asian and Latinx part of Los Angeles, I watched as other children of immigrants also lived into role reversals. Simultaneously, dominant culture people discounted, diminished, and tore down our parents as we helplessly watched. The adults in our lives who had made the greatest sacrifices for the collective good, were dependent on the second generation for survival. The more quickly the second generation acculturated, the more quickly we could assist our parents who depended on us. This diminishment of the first generation in the eyes of the second generation via larger North American culture and society causes deep distress in the psychological development of children and adolescents.[7] Children and adolescents learn that they are unable to count on their caretakers for protection and must instead find ways to protect their parents. I remember being devastated by the emotional tension I felt when helping my parents and grandparents. I was both proud that they could lean on me and I was worried that I would fail them. I lay awake at night grieved and concerned about their safety every time I witnessed them face racism and discrimination. I was also angry at them for letting me see them become so small, therefore, making me feel even smaller. For those of us in the second generation, as acculturation accelerated, the more quickly many of us began to lose touch with our home culture and languages, having now to operate out of two different value systems, two different vocabularies, and two distinct and often oppositional cultures. In cases like these, how does one generation impart storified personhood and peoplehood to a generation that is experiencing the reverberations of immigration in a completely different and disruptive way? How does the immigrant generation retain and regain their authority as elders and storytellers in the eyes of a generation that is losing touch with their home languages and simultaneously learning to negotiate a new culture so that all might survive?

Children and adolescents from minoritized context, who experience role reversals or racialized threats in the form of the diminishment of their caretakers in the public sphere, need to hear and learn the memories of the previous and surviving generations through shared story in order to connect into their kin-group and community. In the midst of the isolating experience of racial and religious minoritization, story transmission helps people course-correct their relationships. Instead of watching their loved ones suffer in inhospitable spaces, transmitted and shared narratives help the younger generation witness their elders as empowered and vibrant. When community elders share personal narratives with those in the younger generation, the story of survival and flourishing against all odds become a collective story of *woori*, or us. Through the sharing of memory through story, racially and religiously minoritized people are able to return to their ancestral homes,[8] their ancestral selves, and in a sense, take their children with them.

For religiously minoritized people and for people of color who are not immigrants, the difference in day-to-day operating frameworks also rings true. Black and brown children and children who wear articles of faith have *the talk* early on with their caregivers. A talk that dominant culture people can opt out of having with their children. "Keep your hands out of your pockets, smile and say hello. Don't you dare run when you see police. When you are pulled over, keep your hands up. Don't walk through neighborhoods where you don't know anyone. If you know you are about to be arrested or attacked, record everything." These are lessons on acculturation, on fitting in and making oneself visible and invisible as it pertains to staying alive. The lessons emerge from the very real grief over the loss of young people—such as Tamir Rice, Trayvon Martin, Deah Shaddy Barakat, Yusor Mohammad Abu-Salha, and Razan Mohammad Abu-Salha.[9] Their stories are remembered, recited, and ritualized as mourning and a spell against the evil of white and Christian supremacy all around.

STORIED LANGUAGE

There are two levels to the use of language in cultural and religious transmission. First, regardless of whether stories are memories or fiction, the ways in which they are shared impart the perspective of the storyteller. Just as when multiple eyewitness accounts are recounted, the stories are different, a memory when recounted reveals the perspective of what is important to the teller. Second, stories are embodied. My maternal grandfather when talking about how he built his own business after he had been internally displaced always glowed with pride. When my mother told me the same stories about how her family started over with nothing, her eyes held the embers of the same lively spark. My mother may have been wearied from working multiple jobs, but when she reminded us of the memories she had of her homeland, her parents, her family, the *Ki*, or the collective familial energy swelled back into her demeanor and voice. The pride and strength she exhibited rebuilt her before my very eyes. She was no longer an immigrant woman who I witnessed berated for not speaking English by a stranger in the grocery store, she was a woman deeply grounded in the words she chose and the culture that formed those words. It was through that demeanor, spark, and form of those words that I felt connected, not only to my mother or the memories she shared but also to an entire culture and an entire collective experience of a people. Her empowerment was contagious. Through her, I began to see myself as powerful too.

Language, culture, and how they are embodied becomes increasingly difficult to transmit in diaspora. I spend copious amounts of time speaking Korean to my third-generation Korean American son. At five years old, he primarily uses English to communicate with his parents and when we respond in Korean, he understands but chooses not to respond in Korean. Interacting with him, I feel the echoes of my own parent's frustration at trying to transmit language to me. For immigrant parents, the transmission of language is more than about another lexicon, it is about the transmission of the stories behind the words, the feeling behind *how* they say *what* they say. The expression of an entire people is embedded in their words, the things, and places important to them, the values they carry, and the experiences they share. For instance, in English we say sometimes that birds sing, in Korean we say, *seh-gah oohn-dah*, or birds cry. As a people who have endured multiple periods of colonization and war, continuing today to be under U.S. military occupation, our words express collective sorrow. The Korean word for this collective pain is called *han*, it is woven into the way we see and describe the world around us.

Jennifer Cho coined the phrase, mel-*han*-choly as the feeling of unfinished mourning behind Korean people's collective grief, often expressed through the Korean language. Cho argues that the mel-*han*-coly of the Korean people and the Korean language is a form of resistance to the oppressive nature of the official global history of the Korean Peninsula.[10] A history that is forever tied to the division of land and people via American intervention and military occupation. Official U.S. history recollects this period as salvific for the Korean people through the strategic implementation of American military aid, while for many Korean and Korean American people it is a period of sadness where the Japanese occupation was traded for an American one. Retaining Korean mel-*han*-choly through language transmission to diasporic generations is a form of resistance to remind ourselves that we are not yet free. We are not done grieving what we have lost.

Teresa Hak Kyung Cha, in her seminal autobiographical work, *Dictee,* writes about diasporic peoples, particularly women, as those with internalized subjugated knowledge.[11] One could understand this as knowledge that subjugates the *woori*-ness of Korean lament to a history filtered through the lens of American exceptionalism, and the knowledge of self, subjugated through the filter of the model minority myth via white supremacist constructs. To resist subjugation in diasporic spaces requires the liveliness of language and all the history and *han* that it carries to continue to flourish. As long as language and lexicon grounded in peoplehood continues to erupt out of generations in diaspora, minoritized people are better able to resist the subjugation and colonization of their minds and tongues by those that desire their erasure. For a Korean American child or adolescent to understand why a bird might cry, rather than sing, signifies an imbedded cultural and historical understanding of mel-*han*-coly and what it means to be part of the Korean culture and narrative.

Despite each generation's best efforts, language can unfortunately be lost over time as generations of immigrants settle into a new land and culture. Sometimes this occurs through coercive force, and at other times, it is from the impact of physical distance. For Indigenous people in North America, the conscription of their children and adolescents into religious boarding schools enforced the loss of language and culture in inhumane ways.[12] For many immigrants, after they depart their homeland, the evolution of language stalls. The home culture no longer affects the way they speak or what they say and how language has formed thus far is fossilized through the process of separation from homeland. For instance, contemporary colloquial Korean is often mixed with words from different languages, abbreviations, and slang diasporic Korean people do not recognize. My cousins are forever telling me that my Korean though fluent, sounds like my grandmother's. Meaning, I inherited the words and perspectives of a bygone era. When my parents visit their homeland now, their friends say the same things about them, their way of speaking is like an artifact from the past, indicating for others that they do not quite belong. The meaning and perspective embedded in languages also become buried over time. The transmission of stories is one way to keep the memories from a particular era, strung together by those very words, alive and whole, even as conversational language changes or disappears. Keeping those memories alive sustains immigrants, keeps them grounded in their culture, and reminds them of their human dignity even as they experience downward mobility and loss of status during immigration.

STORIED RELIGION AND VALUES

Stories share religious and cultural values across generations. To understand the impact of this in early formation, we look to child and adolescent experiences. Why do we need to attend to the lives of racially and religiously minoritized children, adolescents, and their families in theological education? Even though our classrooms are filled with adults, these adults were once adolescents and children. Students from racially and religiously minoritized communities carry with them their earliest formations. Those formations continue to inform their lives, scholarship, and engagement in the classroom.

Some communities understand adolescence as going well into one's twenties and thirties. Some cultures understand childhood and adolescence as an extended period of time beyond what public school systems or legal systems dictate. I am always astounded by how often my students reflect on some of their earliest experiences in community when reflecting on sacred texts, critical social political issues, and other topics in theological education. Those memories and foundational understandings of self and the world in relation to racialization, religion, and spirituality remain palpable well into adulthood. Many of my students earliest formations occurred through stories shared in their communities of nurture. These stories transmitted religious and cultural value to them, and in adulthood, they continue to ponder the meaning of inherited stories, reclaim them, or reject them. What follows is a look into the formation of some of the most vulnerable in our communities, the children and the adolescents of immigrants. As educators of adults, we need to understand how vulnerable communities are formed through story, the impacts of sociopolitical stress on their lives, and the importance of religious and spiritual groundings. In doing so, we are able to reconstruct educational spaces with the intelligence to hold all that our most vulnerable students bring with them.

My first book explored how Korean folktales and biblical stories in Korean immigrant Christian households were ways of transmitting both Christian values and cultural values about identity and gender, particularly with Korean American girls.[13] Research among Canadian Arab immigrant families also reveals how storytelling is a vehicle for the cultivation of both Islamic and cultural values among children and adolescents.[14] Research on the development of children and youth of asylum-seeking communities has shown that the transmission of religiocultural beliefs and values works to bolster their self-esteem and resiliency in the face of experiences of discrimination and erasure.[15] The more children and adolescents of racially and religiously minoritized communities feel grounded in their communities, particularly in communities of faith, the more they are able to internalize a healthy counter-narrative to the damaging messages of North American antiimmigrant, anti-Black, anti-Semitic, and anti-Muslim sentiments.

Storytelling is also an act of profound religiocultural meaning making. Religious stories told in minoritized communities, particularly around rites and rituals, help to make religious and spiritual meaning out of the lived experiences of daily life and experiences. Storytelling brings together the past and the present, bridging the way communities experienced their values and religious commitments of the motherland to the collective reconstruction of those values and religious commitments in the new homeland.[16] Systematic theologians and first-wave Asian American theologians, Sang Hyun Lee and

Joung Young Lee, both discuss the saliency of the biblical exodus narrative for Korean American immigrants. As Korean immigrants and theologians, they embraced the narrative, not as a story of exile but sojourning. They see the Korean American experience as being pilgrims in a foreign land, aliens that are never fully accepted, and a people who are wandering in the wilderness yet with a call upon their lives to bravely venture into new places seeking G_d's presence.[17] Lee and Lee's message and theologically bound story responded to the experience of yellow peril, anti-Asian legislation, and discrimination, as a daily reality for people in their community.

In today's North American political climate, new immigrants are once again bombarded with dehumanizing messages, including the threat of deportation. The impact of dehumanizing messaging, policies and legislation around immigrants affects the entire family system. Studies of children and adolescents of undocumented parents have found slower cognitive development in children beginning at twenty-four months due to the ramifications of social exclusion, economic hardship, lack of social support, and increased parental psychological distress.[18] Undocumented parents often do not seek out necessary social support, legal counsel, or kinship groups for fear of being detained or deported. Children learn secrecy and silence for fear of losing their parents. In the midst of these high-stress lived realities, it is important for religious immigrant communities to believe and internalize a message of divine purpose, guidance, and protection undergirding their experiences of displacement, particularly in the face feelings of isolation, separation from homeland, and the detrimental experiences of bigotry, hostility, and impending loss. Connecting family and community stories to religious ones creates new sacred stories and transmitting them to children and adolescents is a sacral way of weaving the new liminal experiences of the in-between generations into the tapestry of a larger narrative of immigration in the face of fear and trauma.

DISSONANCE BETWEEN STORIES

As discussed in chapter 5, dissonance is part of the human experience. When confronted with one another in the classroom, conflicting narratives create dissonance and as long as all actors are willingly engaged, dissonance can dialogue in ways that unlock new realities across difference. Dissonance is also at play in stories and storytelling. I use dissonance as a way to describe the tension between stories and their telling, not only as a way of marking incongruency. Here, I outline three forms of dissonance between the stories we tell across generations, creative liminal dissonance, the dissonance produced through silence, and the dissonance between what is directly transmitted by the community and the stories produced by colonial and dominant culture perspectives.

The first form of dissonance is the creative liminal. Stories shared between the immigrant and second generations shift and change in their retellings. They are actively renegotiated between generational transmission. The same thing occurs in a classroom when stories are shared. As students or teachers bring their personal stories to the fore in the classroom as a part of anticolonial pedagogy, the stories take on a life of their own, shape-shifting from one retelling to the next. This is how we know stories are incarnational or imbued with sacred life. One could say that the danger of story transmission between one person to another is that alternate meanings might be mapped over the stories as they are cradled by different storytellers, especially across generations. This dissonance and mapping can be a liminally creative space that inculcates a deeper understanding of self and community between generations. This type of generational and familial mapping is different from the mapping of a colonial entity upon those it seeks to colonize. The difference is the direct connection the storyteller in one generation has to the generation who lived the story. When we consider why immigrant communities share stories between generations, it is often to teach not only what has happened but also what they have overcome, and what they will collectively continue to overcome together. The next generation needs to see themselves in these stories. They need to eventually lay claim to the stories they have heard, retelling and reshaping them in their own words, in a new language, and through new religiocultural lenses.

When I share the stories of my grandparents and parents in writing, as I do here in this chapter, I do so in the English language. When students for whom English is a second, third, or fourth language share their stories in classes, they are reaching across linguistic chasms to put new flesh around something familiar to them in order to share its meaning with religiocultural outsiders. There is something about this act of translation that naturally creates creative liminal dissonance. As mentioned previously, there is a cultural and religious essence to how words are shaped, and how they describe our worlds. When retelling stories in a foreign tongue, the story reshapes itself. This shape-shifting adds to the narrative's complexity. For instance, the retelling of the first generation's stories through the eyes of the second generation adds another layer and perspective that creates new meanings for new experiences of displacement. When I reflect on my grandparent's experience of being internally displaced people, their stories hold a different significance for me than they do for them or even for my mother. Their stories and my retelling of them helps me see and connect to a genealogy of resilience and faith. Their strength is my strength, their sorrow, my sorrow. Their stories and the act of retelling their stories connects me to the collective *han* of both my family's personal losses and sacrifices, and the cultural and national lament of an entire people. Weaving my perspective into the stories of my elders reminds me that even with continental difference, language barriers, cultural and contextual misunderstandings, that we in fact do belong to one another across space and time.

A second form of dissonance between stories is created when communities choose silence or modulated disclosure[19] as their narrative. For many immigrants, migrants, and refugees, there are some stories, some experiences and realities that are too painful to verbalize, and too traumatic to share with their children. For many Issei and Nisei Japanese Americans who were interned in concentration camps, the pain of their collective and individual dehumanization was too great to share with the Sansei, Yonsei, and Gosei generations.[20] Though some did not speak of their experiences at all, others used modulated disclosure. For instance, some Sansei report that some in the Nisei generation would choose to refer to chronological time as "before camp and after camp," without reference to what happened in between, thereby creating dissonance.[21] Dissonance occurs when the second and third generations do in fact know what happened, but they hear it through whispers and read about it through textbooks. In the United States, these are textbooks that retell histories from imperial and colonist perspectives if they retell them at all. In the worst case, these stories go untold in both displaced communities and the public narrative. Silence, though understandable and sometimes necessary for survival and sometimes as a choice of resisting cooption, creates a dissonance that results in feelings of disconnection and isolation between generations. Russell Jeung, in his book *Faithful Generations*, retells the story of a Japanese American congregation that though they might not have shared some of their most painful stories found ways to nurture intergenerational connection through an annual bazaar that celebrated their shared culture. As the Nisei generation aged and were unable to continue running the annual bazaar, the Sansei generation took up the tradition, continuing the legacy of embodied narrative sharing. Through shared activities like making traditional meals, they shared the narratives of everyday life.[22] These practices of embodied cultural storytelling, through different from verbally retelling painful histories, knits generations together across even necessary silence and the void it produces to continue to thrive in their lives together.

A third form of dissonance across stories occurs when the children of immigrants hear first-person narratives about homeland and a colonial or imperial one in the public sphere. JoAnn D'Alisera in her study of Sierra Leonian asylum-seeking families discovered that while children and adolescents heard their parents and grandparents describe the land and people of Sierra Leone as vibrant and beautiful, at school and in the media, children and adolescents heard a completely alternative narrative. This alternative described Sierra

Leone and its people as the "heart of darkness," starving, disease-ridden, and without resources. These disparate representations created a dissonance in their understanding of homeland, their understandings of their caretakers, and their own identities.[23] Which narrative should they claim? What was the risk of claiming the edifying narrative over the ugly one? Would claiming the antiimperial narrative isolate them further from communities beyond the American Sierra Leonian community?

When I hear the dehumanizing tropes around North Korea and North Koreans emerging once again from the United States, the caricature of an entire people as brainwashed, uneducated, and disposable, I cringe and remember what it felt like to feel pulled in multiple directions as a child. Then and now, the disparity between what I know about North Korea from the stories my family has told me and what the U.S. government and public opinion says disturbs me. My grandparent's stories, particularly my grandmother's stories about her beloved little brother whom she left behind, the stories about village life, and her descriptions of the beauty of the land, the trees, and the mountains are what hold salience and significance for me. Those are the words and stories embedded in my identity and which mark my soul. Those cords of connection formed in childhood are now so strong that the disparaging narratives emerging from the American public sphere no longer cast a shadow of doubt over my understanding of self and community. It instead affirms in me the profound connection to peoplehood that my grandmother helped cultivate and nurture in me. Because of her and others in my family, the people of North Korea are still my people, they are my family and kin, utterly human, flesh and blood. In cases where a new generation is exposed to injurious and conflicting narratives about homeland, self, and community, the firsthand narratives of the first generation are significant and need to be constantly retold, not only to provide a counter-narrative to the destructive and colonial one, but to edify the personhood of new generations who are quickly identified with the stereotypes that emerge from the distressing narratives of other nations and people produced through the auspices American exceptionalism.

STORYING OUR COMMUNITIES

The memories and stories of the most vulnerable: immigrants, asylum seekers, Black and brown folx, and the religiously targeted are filled with specters that continue to haunt the living. Ghosts of times, places, and people no longer accessible except through the act of sharing and reliving story. Communities are knit together across generations, lands, and time with the resurrecting power of story. The specters never leave but cling to the words and bodies of those that call to them and claim them. Specters bearing stories do not always leave us feeling well, they rightly sicken us out of our narcissistic "health" and cut us to the core. They can force us out of selective amnesia to remember and re-member them and one another across our differences so that new stories for the well-being of all might emerge. Stories remind us of our humanity and the humanity of one other. British Somali poet, Warsan Shire in her piece called *"Home,"* gives words to the plight of the asylum seeker and her own experiences as a displaced person. I end this chapter with lines from Shire's riveting work, a story shared with the world so that we who are both teachers and learners of one another's stories might be transformed and convicted to shatter coloniality in every corner of our lives.

"i want to go home,
but home is the mouth of a shark
home is the barrel of the gun
and no one would leave home
unless home chased you to the shore
unless home told you
leave your clothes behind
crawl through the desert
wade through the oceans
drown
save
be hunger
beg
forget pride
your survival is more important
no one leaves homes until home is a sweaty voice in your ear
Saying—
leave,
run away from me now
i don't know what i've become
but I know that anywhere
is safer than here.[24]

Chapter 7

Reframing Religious and Cultural Borderlands

INQUIRY AND STORIES

For people who daily resist erasure and cooption, stories are ways of reclaiming epistemologies of self and community. Stories are historical, personal, and communal. Stories bear the weight of generations and stretch how we understand time and space. Stories are not neutral, but hold power to deconstruct and reconstruct, to fashion entire events and histories in our image or to reveal truth no matter how painful. As noted in chapter 6, in classroom settings, stories can be operationalized and weaponized against the most vulnerable. Pastoral theologian Gregory Ellison, in his book *Fearless Dialogues*, discusses what he observes as the five most common fears among people in intimate spaces of sharing. One of these fears is plopping, or the act of articulating and revealing your most authentic self for the world, only to have no one acknowledge it.[1] Plopping is violence in classrooms. We've all witnessed it. A student shares something seismic about their life and other students and even teachers don't know how to react to the sudden vulnerability. We stop, frozen in fear, not knowing how to engage the presence of self-revelatory truth. Suddenly, the moment is gone. The opportunity to validate, affirm, and engage has passed. The student is eviscerated. Depending on how we engage stories, they have the power to help us better know one another or the power to erase the pathways of knowledge toward one another. For centuries in North America, our history textbooks have erased the lives of enslaved African Americans, Indigenous peoples, immigrants, women, LGBTQIA+ folx, and incarcerated people. The media continues to narrate a compressed understanding of the world, making invisible the concerns and realities of minoritized people; instead, harnessing white supremacist lenses. How we choose to make space for one another's stories in the classroom determines whether we will facilitate the acts of seeing and hearing or the acts of invisiblizing and silencing.

Stories are universal. All cultures and religions value them. Stories are at the cornerstone of how human beings learn in a vibrant and intersectional world. C. S. Song reflects on the power of story for theological and personal formation in his book, *In the Beginning Were Stories Not Texts: Story Theology*. Song asserts that story-making and storytelling simultaneously deconstructs and constructs the matrix of our theological commitments. It is in childhood that we start this process of inquiry, the deconstruction and construction of our understandings of one another and the world. From the moment, we begin to point at objects, wondering what they are, we enter the process of inquiry, learning how we are influenced by the actions of others, the push and pull of the world, and how our own embodied ways of being might help or harm those around us. As we continue to learn, our stories change, affected by the continued deepening of our experiences of the world and one another. The alteration of our narratives help us learn and hear across human differences, especially lived religious and spiritual commitments, the misunderstanding of which threatens to keep us fearful and separated from one another.

The deep entanglement of ourselves in story, particularly stories about religious, interreligious, and cultural commitments, are what teaches us about others and ourselves. The process of investigating story, creating, sharing, telling, internalizing, and interpreting, helps us wrestle with the deep-seated fears, biases, and assumptions we may harbor against the others with whom we share our world. As we learn more about the ebb and flow of student formation in intercultural and interreligious classrooms, particularly the identity and spiritual formation of Black, Indigenous, students of color in North America, we modify pedagogies to center the power of shifting stories, both our stories and the stories of the collective "we." This chapter begins with a description of the impact of story on the liminal transnational and transspiritual[2] identity formation of students and concludes with how this decolonial lens might impact classrooms and pedagogical approaches of teacher and student learning, particularly within intentionally intercultural and interreligious spaces. I offer a look at how we might simultaneously reconstruct interreligious and intercultural intelligences in classrooms as we continue the work of disrupting and dismantling colonial, white supremacist, and Christian hegemonic and supremacist ways of being in theological education.

STORY AS TRANSNATIONAL AND TRANSSPIRITUAL RECLAMATION

The sharing of stories and narratives is a part of how identities are formed, shaped, and reshaped. My identity and commitments grow increasingly transnational. The stories shared with me by the older Korean immigrant generation reconnects me to the land that my parents left behind. The stories of immigration, war, and refugee experiences of survival and thriving were transmitted and internalized. These same stories continue to connect me to Korea and the Korean people's collective histories and concerns. These stories also connect me to the faith and spiritualities that sustained the Korean people throughout painful periods of history.

Stories that emerge from lived experience make deep epigenetic imprints on our consciousness. Shared narratives across generations and the resulting ways in which we learn to carry those stories in and on our bodies and through our actions, affect us and the stories we tell. They connect us to spaces, places, and often indescribable emotions across oceans and time. Is it possible that trauma both imprints on us and also on the practices that sustain us or cultivate resilience in the face of traumatic experiences? Perhaps spiritual practices and the benefits we receive from them and the religiocultural identities are transmitted through collective experiences and the sharing of stories. If so, how might this alter the way we construct interreligious classrooms and approach interreligious pedagogy to make space for understanding and cultivating transnational and transspiritual identity formations?

Though I was born in Los Angeles, home always felt nebulous, neither here in the United States where I remain a perpetual foreigner,[3] nor in South Korea, where much of my family resides. Home remains both and neither place. Home does not only concern geography or the physical rootedness of my feet but also where I feel the most present in my body, comfortable in my own skin without feeling the need to constantly explain myself or the dynamics of my identity and commitments. This includes how I might or might not cultivate and practice my spiritual and religious beliefs. This transnational and transspiritual identity was facilitated by the way my family has shared story across generations.

Transnational and transspiritual identity formations are dynamic and constantly negotiated. The object of negotiation includes spiritual and religious identities, beliefs, and practices. As negotiation occurs, internal and external third spaces are created. Sociologists Levitt and Waters, in their edited volume on transnationalism among youth and young adults showcase several examples of the formation of transnational identities across newly malleable boundaries. Immigration no longer facilitates the permanent severing of familial or national ties. Many second- and third-generation North Americans identify home as multiple places, and people that are not restricted to national boundaries. While their commitments to these different places, nations, and people can often conflict, they are still held together without the necessity of having to work out the conflictual commitments.[4] For instance, as a child I remember a common question second-generation Korean Americans would ask one another was, "If the United States and Korea ever went to war, which side would you be on?" Though in the United States, our parents, the immigrant generation, worked diligently to carve a path forward for us, many of us still had relatives in Korea with whom visited. Complicating this was the cultural and Confucian value of family loyalty and honoring one's elders and the ever-present racism and discrimination, we still experienced as perpetual foreigners in a white supremacist land.

In the interreligious and intercultural classroom that is intentionally porous and self-revelatory, I increasingly find students choosing to self-identify as transnational and religiously fluid, thereby increasingly negotiating their religion, spirituality, and faith in boundary crossing ways. As students engage and unpack their personal narratives, identities, and inheritances, they discover that their spiritual practices are rooted in more than one community and more than one location. I once had a student in a class on interreligious engagements in diaspora who at first identified as a white Christian man. As the class went on and we focused on what it meant to identify with our personal histories, he revealed to his colleagues that he actually identified as a white Latinx man, raised both as Catholic and Wiccan and now Protestant. He shared that he had initially chosen to identify as a white Christian man because he learned that identifying as a light-skinned and light-eyed Latinx man who practiced Protestant Christianity with Wiccan and Roman Catholic understandings and underpinnings to his faith, was problematic for those he encountered. Identifying with whiteness was a way for him to avoid what he understood as a predetermined Latinx identity that had no room for his particular experiences or spiritual expressions. In response, the student learned to present himself as white, an identity people assumed he claimed, rather than explore who he knew himself to be in his innermost being. The Christian white male identity not only afforded him privilege and social capital but also made a challenging personal and spiritual life shrouded in racial and cultural dissonance.

Transnationalism and its defining characteristics can extend to the landscape of transspiritualism and one's interspiritual and interreligious commitments. Hybrid religious and spiritual practices become embodiments of negotiated transnationalisms. My family are three generations into Christianity. Christianity and its practices took root while my grandparents were still in North Korea. As they embraced Christianity and Presbyterianism in particular, they put away the Confucian-cultural practices that for them could not be assimilated and reinterpreted into their new Christian theologies and beliefs. However, what is consciously buried does not always stay underground. As various historians, theologians, and scholars on Korean American religious practices began to uncover the Indigenous origins of Korean Christian practice ways of transspiritual fluidity also began to emerge.

POROUS BOUNDARIES

One of our family's rejected practices was the practice of *jeh-sah* or ancestor veneration. Counter to what white European and North American missionaries assumed, the practice of *jeh-sah* was not one-dimensional ancestor worship. It was the practice of venerating elders gone before you and the recognition that the boundaries of life and death remained porous. The living set a banquet table for the deceased, placing the dead's picture on the table along their favorite foods, and in contemporary practices, the inclusion of items that held meaning for the individual while they were alive. The living then bow before the table and offer prayers. These prayers are conversational, wishing the spirit well, and asking for guidance and protection for the living. This practice of setting *jeh-sah* table and conversational prayer, articulate the permanence of a relationship between the living and the dead that was not severed with death.

I started practicing *jeh-sah* on the first anniversary of my maternal grandmother's death. Even after her death, I still feel her presence deeply upon my life. At each anniversary, I lay out the banquet table including the handwritten Bible she gave me on the occasion of one of my last visits with her. This practice has helped me feel a profound connection not only with her but with both my Christian understanding of the cloud of witnesses and resurrected body and the Indigenous shamanistic practices of the Korean people for the releasing of *han* or the collective suffering of the people. For me, my transnationalism is also transspiritual and anticolonial practice. I hold both my commitments to the United States and the Korean Peninsula together with my commitments to Christianity and the spiritual practices of my people, now reclaimed from erasure in its encounter with Christian mission and Japanese annexation.

Over the years, other transspiritual practices among transnational immigrant communities have been assimilated and reappropriated for the sake of new religious practices in a new land. The connective tissue of the land, culture, religions, and spiritualties left behind are recultivated for a new place to assure the survival and thriving of the transplanted community. Warner and Wittner in their edited volume, *Gatherings in Diaspora*, describe the hybrid practices of Catholic Haitians in New York who practice elements of Santeria as well as the religious and cultural adaptations made by Jewish Iranians in the Los Angeles area.[5] In the Korean American community, two of these hybrid practices are most prominently reflected in *ttong-song-kido* (fervent prayer) and early morning prayer, both which possibly originated out of very early shamanistic practices of confronting and releasing *han*.[6]

This reinterpretation and transformation of embodied spiritualties and identities does not begin or end with immigration. New converts to and from different religious traditions can also, intentionally and unintentionally, carry with them personally significant religious practices and theological understandings about G–d and self into sacred spaces. Human beings in our fluidity, bring forward our narratives, the histories, theologies, beliefs, and practices of our people into new religious and sacred spaces, particularly in moments of crisis. I was raised in a Presbyterian family and church, but one that practiced reformed traditions in decidedly Pentecostal and charismatic ways. This practice is not uncommon among new immigrant Christian communities in Asian America.[7] To this day, even though I am an ordained Presbyterian minister committed to the theologies behind reformed spiritualties and practices, when in crises, my prayers become decidedly evangelical and charismatic. When I need to expediently communicate with G–d, I do not automatically go a book of prayers or recite creeds. Instead, I will pray spontaneously and unabashedly ask for the things I want and need, including the expectation of divine and miraculous intervention on my behalf. My reformed theology allows for spontaneous prayer but would challenge the logic and ethics of my petitioning of G–d in this manner. However, in crisis, my prayer practices organically overcome these boundaries. What is at the foundation of our spiritual formations cannot always be exorcised from us. I have observed this boundary crossing between religious and spiritual practices occurring in the lives of others as well. Once, at a biennial gathering of Presbyterians, an interreligious guest received stood in line with Christians and received communion at our assembly wide service. An African American Muslim woman, was there as an interreligious dignitary and guest. She had converted to Islam in adulthood and in conversation with me, cited her deep belief in the connectional quality of the Christian sacrament of communion for both people and the divine as her reason for participation. She was embodying her transspiritual and communal commitments in a way that made sense for her religious and spiritual life's journey, the places from whence she came and the new places where her religious identity located her today. For me, as I watched her receive the bread and the wine, the body and blood of Christ, she was crossing back and forth between the same porous boundaries that separated me from my grandmother at the *jeh-sah* table.

Technology

These porous boundaries between national, spiritual, and religious spaces and practices are further facilitated by evolving technology that in turn change the way students engage one another and the world in the interreligious classroom. When my parents immigrated to the United States, it meant they had lost the ability for instantaneous communication with their loved ones. Long-distance calls were too costly to make other than for emergencies and special occasions. Letters had to be handwritten and took weeks to arrive. The feeling of loss and separation was much more permanent than it is now. Today, technology allows transnational peoples to engage their different homelands in a multiplicity of ways and in real time.[8] People are able to experience rootedness and commitments to other places and people via technology. They are even able to observe and participate in worship with communities across the world. Through the power of technology, we are no longer bound to a singular location. With the help of technology interreligious classrooms become interreligious spaces across national and spiritual boundaries through the observation of worship in different places around the world, and the direct engagement with different religious practitioners via video conferencing. Students are no longer bound by texts on paper, but people all over the world become living texts through which students are able to learn. As transnational religious and spiritual people, we are also no longer bound to only the mining and interpretation of our historical stories for the grounding and development of our current theologies and spiritual practices. We are able to make meaning and create new stories with living communities, living practices, and the cultivation of newly formed spiritualties together. We are able to follow different stories and curate our identities and commitments through the encounter of other's identities and commitments as they happen.

Cultivation of Transspiritual and Transnational Identities and Narratives

While technologically transmitted narratives, because they are living texts, sustain the porous quality of interspiritual boundaries in interreligious and intercultural education, they are also susceptible to dangerous romanticizing. The construct of "home" is created and recreated through technologically transmitted narratives that can be romanticized, reimagined communities, and renewed meaning-making around spiritual practices. Confucian practitioners, Korean American Christians, and even members of my own family would most likely profess shock at my practice of *jeh-sah* for my grandmother. Truth be told, perhaps part of my impetus in resurrecting the practice of *jeh-sah* may be a way I have romanticized some of the narratives that have been passed down to me from those in my parent's and grandparent's generation. South Korea and all she possesses is irreplaceable in my mind's eye. She is flawed but not irredeemably so. On the other hand, my cousins who are South Korean citizens are always surprised by how much I long for "home" and how much I dread leaving her when I visit. I always cry upon departure. It is a keening of loss. The loss of the warm feeling of comfort, of a belonging that can only come with hearing your mother tongue all around you and living in a context that does not require you to explain yourself at every turn.

Perhaps it is a loss that is partially my own romanticizing of homeland. I will continually remake my transspiritual practices based on how Korea continues to transform herself in my heart and mind. Unfortunately, this transformation can lead to the erasure of other conflicting but significant narratives.

As with stories, why do we need rose-colored glasses with spiritual practices? Do we need rose-colored glasses for a blanket positivism to cover over the narratives we would rather not see? Cultivated and romantic transnationalism and transspiritualties are dangerous. Rose-colored transnationalities and transspiritualties and the curation of narratives we receive invisiblizes entire narratives and histories including the most painful and unspeakable stories. We risk the danger of the curation of privileged narratives that avoid the sticky and messy stories we hesitate to hear and retell. Romanticizing our transnational and transspiritual identities encourages us to see what we desire and little else. Students and instructors pick and choose what is most meaningful to them, centering their own stories without consideration for the larger narratives where those stories are still grounded. When faced with self-cultivated identities and commitments, how might teachers continue to foster intercultural and interreligious education that encourages students to resist the facilitation of erasures in their practices of culture and spirituality? How do we help students work through the process of holding disparate narratives together for the purpose of a more holistic and communal identity formation? What are our students learning about their constantly curated identities and stories in the classroom? Is what they are learning in the classroom porous enough that they are able to make sense of and room for alternative narratives they will encounter about other places, people, and experiences at home, in worshipping communities and in the media? The interreligious and intercultural classroom necessitates an intentional balancing of transparent narratives, hidden narratives, and the uncovering of the way narratives are destroyed and altered, particularly through the white and colonist gaze and particularly for people in the diaspora who learn about their motherlands through the lacuna of information about them in our textbooks or through the lenses of the conqueror over the conquered and civilized over the savage. The classroom community must equip students to hold these divergent stories in tension, help them sift through them and critically and powerfully examine, deconstruct and reconstruct the stories they encounter as an embodied practice of building intercultural and interreligious intelligence.

As racially and religiously minoritized students receive stories from each previous generation, make new meanings and create fluid spiritual practices, they also hear and internalize an opposing set of narratives from white supremacist culture, from the white gaze on othered histories, religious practices, and peoples. Early in my adolescence during a conversation with my family in Korea, I was astounded to discover that the narrative of American militarism as savior post–Korean War was not the narrative they claimed. Their understanding was of American military occupation on South Korean soil, an occupation that was tolerated because of the nuclear threat of North Korea but not welcome because of the violence from American soldiers, the imbedded American exceptionalism, and the neocolonial white supremacist lens that came with American military presence on Korean soil.

As the studies mentioned earlier in intergenerational trauma reveal, there are continued effects of empire and colonial histories on the transnational identities of BIPOC in the United States including in the ways the white gaze and American exceptionalism have bled into the narratives we have interpreted and internalized about our homelands. This reality and tension leads to a continuous process of unpacking and reimagining of our identities and the spiritual and religious practices embedded within them. Just as I have done with the *jeh-sah* practice, there is a movement by those with colonized histories in North America to reclaim and reimagine the spiritual practices that have been lost or erased through missional histories and other encounters with Christian mission and other forms of imperialism. However, this reclamation can cause individuals to feel simultaneously empowered and isolated in their respective chosen communities, therefore, necessitating a renegotiation not only of religious and spiritual belief and practice but also a renegotiation of the relationship between community and personal identity. My ordained status as a clergy person both empowers me in religious spaces and makes me into a disorienting agent for many in the Korean American community, as a result making me feel isolated in many respects from those in the Korean American community who adhere to more conservative theologies around women's ordination. I embody a negotiation of stories and their meanings remade. My very presence as a woman with spiritual and religious authority is a challenge to the norming of Confucian-Christian practices that identify maleness with holiness. Intentionally dwelling with embodied tension in community creates necessary conflict and conversation toward transformation and creates newly negotiated spaces that disrupt paradigms of power and privilege in Korean American congregational life and theology. Engaging tension deconstructs the overlay of white Christian supremacist narratives that simplify Korean culture as rigid, theologically conservative, and sexist.

RETHINKING PEDAGOGICAL DESIGN TOWARD INTERCULTURAL AND INTERRELIGIOUS INTELLIGENCE

With these complexities in mind, how do we approach interreligious and intercultural classrooms where many of our students nurture transnational and transspiritual identities and realities? First, I define interreligious classrooms and interreligious education as spaces where participants are intentionally learning and negotiating the complexities of interreligious life together with the larger systemic and societal structures of public and religious life. Part of the commitment to intercultural and interreligious teaching and learning is to remain open to one another's particular cultures and traditions for the sake of appreciation without the need for proselytization. How do we encourage students to retain these porous boundaries between one another's narratives and histories in their cultivation of identity through story while retaining a sense of self-esteem and growing their capacity for courageously engaging the tensions and conflicts they encounter? What practices ensure student's identities are not subjected to a secondary erasure by the colonist and white gaze or destructive form of assimilation through the parameters and measures of success and failure set by western forms of theological education?

Conflict in the Intercultural and Interreligious Classroom

In chapter 2, I discussed unbinding conflict and conflict transformation as a part of our pedagogical work toward imaginative liberation. I deepen the conversation on conflict here through transnational and transspiritual understandings. Conflict in the classroom, especially around negotiated identities is not something we need fear. John Shindler in his text, *Transformative Classroom Management*, frames conflict as a way forward, a way to cocreate a culture of listening and respect. Conflict in the classroom, when surfaced and properly engaged can open doors to new ways of hearing one another.[9] Though Shindler is referring mostly to classrooms of adolescents, his theory is applicable in interreligious spaces as well. If adolescence is a heightened time when our identities are tested and selfhood is learned, interreligious and intercultural spaces in theological education are also heightened times of formation for classroom participants, particularly for white Christians who have never before had the primacy of their religious or cultural identities challenged in North American spaces.

Often, our instinct when conflicts arise around contested religious and cultural identities, stories, and perspectives in the classroom, is to quickly and efficiently redirect or diffuse. Yet, when we follow this instinct, what is really challenged and changed in the identities and perspectives of the instructors and students? Only the authority of the instructor is reaffirmed. When properly and carefully midwifed, conflicts can become vehicles toward community and individual transformation for both the instructor and student and by association, other adjacent communities. We cannot avoid or escape conflict in the intercultural and interreligious classroom because bodies of color and how they are adorned naturally disrupt white and Christian norms. A student of color's very presence, as they embody the transnational and transspiritual identities they are constantly renegotiating, transforms and challenges the classroom space. Classmates and instructors learn from these students' perspectives and stories, and from the lenses, they use to interpret and curate their narratives, identities, and spaces which they call home. By lifting up and uncovering what is already occurring in the embodiment of our students, our understandings of identity and spiritual formation become porous together, making learning across difference much more possible and collectively transformative, effectively making extending the classroom toward inward spaces of learning and beyond physical walls.

As potentially transformative as classroom conflict is when encountered strategically, teachers must first attend to the establishment of hospitable classrooms for both the transnational and transspiritual identity formation of students and instructors. Though conflicts are natural in intercultural and interreligious spaces, conflicts arise as an unintended consequence of inhospitable classrooms. Inhospitable classrooms presume rigid identities and expect the performance of caricatured identities[10] instead of remaining open to the negotiation and presentation of fluid identities or identities experiencing transformation and realization.

Students and Presumed Identities

When instructors and students presume identities in the classroom without taking the time to leave borders around identities and identity performance porous and open, key identity markers that are constantly and tenuously negotiated remain invisible. This invisibilization can occur through microaggressions by both students and teachers. Common experiences occur in the presumption of social location and socioeconomic status, the mispronunciation of ethnic names, and the invisibilization of disabilities. Studies have shown the negative effect on students of color when their teachers and others mispronounce their names in public spaces without correction. Entire histories and the meanings are embedded in names become rendered invisible and powerless.[11] Studies of Asian American children and adolescents further reveal that this powerless feeling extends to the formation of the person's self-esteem that can even result in self-harm behaviors.[12] When the instructor's lenses are not self-reflective or examined for bias and racism, presenting identities are privileged in the classroom space over others that are more internal but equally if not more tangible for the person who holds them. In the classroom, this can occur as Christian privilege or the privileging of Christian narratives and persons, clergy privilege, heteronormativity, male privilege, and the centering of the white gaze and white privilege. This can also be true for instructors of color via western institutions and training.[13]

Classrooms environments and our pedagogy, should work to encourage the deepening of self-identification over presumption and the simultaneous self-interpretations of multiple identities including religious, spiritual, national, and others. Good pedagogical practices work to unpack how student, teacher, and community identities are negotiated and understood and lifts meaning out of even the seemingly smallest of identity markers. G. Yamazawa, a Japanese American spoken-word artist describes the power of this father's accent in his poem *The Bridge*. "My father's accent is like climbing a barbed wire fence . . . it means he spent more time cooking for other people in his restaurant, making ends meet for his family than trying to learn English."[14] For Yamazawa, his father's accent was more than a marker of immigration, but of his father's commitments, choices, and even love for his family. What would our classrooms look and feel like if instead of only learning how to pronounce one another's names correctly, we also encouraged the unpacking of our names? How names were born and how we received them, what names meant to the giver and what they mean to us? How names continue to shape us? Sometimes our names are the only link we have left to the mother tongue or our homelands.

My grandfather gave me the Korean name Hong Jin. The Chinese characters Hong means wide, while Jin means small and precious. I received this name from my grandfather. To him, I was a small and precious person across the wide expanse of the ocean whom he was waiting to meet. I cannot think about my given Korean name without thinking of this story, the origin of my name, the person who gave it to me, and the deep longing and sorrow he must have felt at not being able to meet his first grandchild until much later. Just as names have deep rootedness in how our identities are shaped and how our transnational ties are carried and sustained, spiritualties and spiritual practices are also inheritances and legacies that connect us to our many "homes" within the classroom space.

Hospitable Intercultural and Interreligious Classrooms

The idea of hospitable intercultural and interreligious classrooms is grounded in the posture of humble modesty as a commitment of intelligence. The hospitality we offer facilitates the coformation of identities and spiritualties and complexify the relationship between them. Students, teachers, and educational institutions are shaped and reshaped in their encounters with one another—in joy, grief, conflict, and creation. For the intercultural and interreligious educator, the goal of any rigor within the classroom is transformation of the participant, institution, and society. This mutual transformation occurs with the perpetual asking of the question, "Who are we?" and the close examination of how we draw lines around the "we." For instance, whose interests are served in the boundaries we draw around "we"? Who is permitted to draw the lines? Who is excluded? Who benefits from the established "we" and who is minoritized?

Christian theologian Amos Yong explores the function of expanding the notion of we in Christian theology to include those of other religious traditions. Yong is a Pentecostal theologian who specializes in pneumatology toward interreligious engagement and life identifies radical interreligious hospitality as a function of the Spirit of G–d. Yong postulates that the Christian understanding of conversion includes attitudinal conversion and reconversion to one's own doctrines of neighborliness and hospitality. For Yong, both are required for deep engagement and commitment to Christian life.[15] If we follow Yong's understanding of we-ness, intercultural and interreligious education is a way in which by deeply embodying radical hospitality toward one another by opening ourselves up and deepening our appreciation of difference, we become truer adherents of the religious traditions and cultures we claim.

The porous classroom, like our porous identities and spiritualties, requires an understanding that the learning and formation of religious and spiritual identities continue outside of the classroom and deeply dynamizes the classroom experience. The classroom is porous and borderless in the sense that intercultural and interreligious dialogue and life is not only shaped through words but also through the art, music, silence, taste, communal memories that occur outside of the classroom context. The experience of these different mediums only enhances how we embody ourselves as we navigate our interactions with each other in the classroom. Outside the classroom, the news cycle vacillates between the continual domestic terrorism of white men murdering Black people, the hate crimes against Black churches, mosques, and synagogues, constant xenophobia, and stories of minoritized communities constantly pitted against one another in the fight for visibility and resources. These stories and experiences enter the classroom too. The very same dynamics and tensions, the mechanisms of white supremacy, reproduce themselves in classroom interactions and in the vulnerabilities of students.

Pedagogy for the porous classroom, or a classroom that fosters hospitable spaces for the shifting identity and spiritual formation of students and teachers, constantly lifts up and tracks the varied dimensions of power and privilege in the classroom and tracks how they change or are changed through encounters.[16] Some of the markers of difference within structures of power and privilege include religion, gender, nationality, language, age, sexuality, among others. As facilitators of these spaces, we try and to this with care, through the understanding and working with the vulnerable experiences of tracking identity formation through self-reflexivity in marginal spaces. We do this by eviscerating the false notion of safe spaces and moving into the emboldened and democratic spaces bell hooks names for us.[17] There are some people who are never fully safe regardless of where they are in society. Some people are always on the defense because of safety concerns, having to explain themselves or intentionally invisibilize parts of their identities in order to survive. To call a space "safe" in North American society privileges heteronormativity, men, nondisabled bodies, Christianity, and whiteness. Individual and communal identities, religious, and otherwise, can hold power in one space, but remain liminal in others. For example, as previously described, my clergy woman status is empowering within my ecclesial family, the Presbyterian Church (USA) is currently 92 percent white, but my clergy status and denominational leadership gives me access to transformative avenues of conversation. In my Korean American context, I am a paradox. A woman with spiritual and religious authority is perceived with suspicion for subverting normative Confucian and patriarchal structures and systems.

Dismantling Binaries and Assumptions about Students

We further the aim of hospitable intercultural and interreligious classrooms by integrating antiracist and antisupremacist approaches and critiques into our pedagogy and posture. The negative impacts of white supremacy and Christian supremacy through hegemony were discussed as part one of this book. As we work to lift up the creative liminal dissonance between narratives and make visible stories, realities, and histories that have been buried through the centering of colonial narratives, we must also work to deconstruct dangerous binaries named in chapter 2. The two most common binaries that work against the cultivation of holistic identities are the racial binary of Black and white as well as the religious binary of Christian and other. The Black/white binary works to suppress the complex narratives of different people of color communities while the Christian and other binary centers the Christian agenda and story over and against the rich diversity of religious and spiritual narratives in our world. We cannot hope to maintain the porous boundaries between transnational and transspiritual identities and practices within binary constructs that work to keep the complexities of identities and commitments hidden and ultimately pits vulnerable communities against one another.

Other constructed assumptions that do not foster the complexities of identity and story coformation in the classroom are generational and vocational assumptions. Particularly, in theological education, we can no longer assume that our students hail from a monolithic millennial generation with all the pigeonholed stereotypes this label carries with it. Generational theories having to do with generational assignments and patterns are based on data that norms the lives and experiences of white North Americans. The experiences across generations are not generalizable when we are considering wealth disparities, educational disparities, and different access points to citizenship and immigration. Assumptions about generational belonging and identities do damage to the porous identities and borders of intercultural and interreligious education. The experience of immigrant adolescents in gen Z dealing with the impact of role reversals are not the equivalent to the experiences of white gen Z adolescents. Generational assumptions work against potential intergenerational cooperation between traditions, cultures, and peoples. We do not even possess the same understanding of the transition between adolescence and adulthood across our different communities and cultures. In some cultures and communities, adolescence stretches out until one is married and moves out of one's parent's home. In others, you are a youth until you are an elder. Still in others, you are an adult once you turn eighteen. Today, it is common in theological education to have students from generation z, millennial, generation x, and the boomer generation sharing space and learning together.

Another intersection where assumptions live are around professional differences. In theological education, second and third career students are learning alongside students with multivocational and professional realities. Many community religious institutions such as churches and synagogues can no longer sustain full-time staff and leadership. This shortage of traditional religious leadership roles has forced students to harness their creativity, patching together different leadership roles simultaneously along their career paths. The bringing together of second and third career students with students who will eventually need to experiment to insure income security brings to light socioeconomic disparities that in turn affect the different narratives in the classroom. In addition, the growth of nontraditional masters programs reveals students are entering theological education for professions other than religious leadership. As instructors, how are we allowing for the different reasons for students who are seeking theological education coexist in the classroom layered with the different textures of their transnational and transspiritual commitments and formations and their socioeconomic and potential career realities?

Students bring their different lived experiences, histories, perspectives, generational and intergenerational gaps and realities, community and group resources, points of access, and communication styles into one collective space. This range of deep diversity may seem daunting at first because of the potential for conflict and misunderstanding. However, the gathering of these dissonant narratives becomes less resistant to transformation when they are in coformation together. By being in the presence of profound differences, student and instructor assumptions wear down and the boundaries between self and other become porous in the same way as our transnational and transspiritual identities and practices. It is possible that because of the growing generational and social location differences in our theological education classrooms, we are poised, more than ever before, to cultivate increasing capacity for conversation about and through difference that in turn supports the formation of students with transnational and transspiritual identities and commitments.

The stories we hear, learn, and share shape us and those around us. Our stories are constantly shifting as they encounter different generational religious and cultural realities. They speak of our deepest commitments, transnational and transspiritual, even those commitments that we are still learning to understand and unpack. They flesh our religious beliefs and practices both personal and communal. Our identities are threaded through with narratives that are simultaneously fragile and resilient, narratives that work against one another and exist in tension within the confines of our bodies and minds. Our identities both transnational and transspiritual are coformed in our encounter with one another, in particular in the intentionally vulnerable spaces of theological education.

Transformative pedagogy as embodied intercultural and interreligious intelligence builds bridges between diverse and dissonant stories, our histories, social locations, and understandings of religion and practices without requiring students to assemble rigid and permanent definitions of self. Transformative pedagogy is anticolonial in that it fosters classrooms that are hospitable and individuals who hold their identities, commitments, and practices in porous ways, as to allow for the continual formation of selfhood that comes with the encounter of others. The way we nurture hospitable classrooms can encourage the breakdown of dangerous binaries and assumptions that promote hostility and fear among our students while encouraging mutual transformation toward one another. We practice mutual thriving and then we hold narratives, commitments, and embodiments in ways that lean into creative liminal dissonance, both within ourselves as teachers and for our students.

Chapter 8

Restoring Genealogies of the Intangible

GENEALOGIES

There are many kinds of genealogies. Genealogies locate where we come from and how we arrived to this particular place and time. There are familial genealogies that detail family histories, and there are genealogies that address scholarly affiliations like those between a doctoral student and a *Doktor Vater*. There are genealogies of thought and art where creators attribute the inspiration of their work to the work of those who have come before. For systems and structures of colonialism, white and Christian supremacy, genealogies are weapons wielded to control and destroy. The enslavement of African peoples destroyed entire communities and their genealogies. The same occurred for Native and Indigenous people all over the world as colonization stole land, erased histories, and produced genocide. The processes of enslavement and colonization dehumanizes, making it impossible for people to possess the familial and historical records upon which Empire is based, wealth accumulated, and nations built. Throughout world history, monarchies rise and fall due to the mapping and remapping of genealogies, and what they say about who is included and who is not. In the anticolonial classroom committed to intercultural and interreligious intelligence, genealogies are always active, intentionally subverting histories written by the victors. Genealogies are intangible ways of being and knowing that are real, valuable, and traceable.

In the Korean tradition, there is a genealogical chart called the *ho-juk*. A family's *ho-juk* details the names of each generation and the common *dol-im*, a shared character for each name in that generation. Traditionally, only men's names are recorded in a family's *ho-juk*. Even though my name is not written in my family's official genealogical chart, I can still trace the places and persons from whence I came in other, perhaps more meaningful ways.

When I cook Korean food, I can taste the *ho-juk*, a *ho-juk* that includes me, my mother, my grandmother, and all the mothers before her. In the Korean language, we have a phrase called *sonmat*, or the flavor of one's hand. There are no recipes, only an intuition of taste that comes from the intimate knowing of how something should taste, smell, and feel. Religious Educator Boyung Lee writes about *sonmat* in her essay on Asian/Asian North American feminist pedagogy. Lee speaks of *sonmat* pedagogy as the recreation of communal connections that teach across geography, space, and time.[1]

I internalized *sonmat* by enjoying my mother's food and the food of my grandmothers. Through their *sonmat*, I taste the food of my ancestors, the soil that grew their food, the labor of the harvest, the earthy goodness of vegetables grown in fields and on the sides of craggy mountains, the sweetness of fruit ripened by the hot sun of the motherland, and the salt dried and collected from wild kelp in the Korean sea. I have never been to the villages and the places where my grandmothers were born. The Korean War separated them and us from those places. Like so many people whom war has displaced, I do not possess access to the lands now part of North Korea. I may never be allowed to set foot upon those fields and mountains. My name may not reside in an official family registry with the South Korean government, but I know my name, and I know from whom and from whence I came. In our classrooms, numerous genealogies of the intangible, are present. They may not be written down, but they are worth naming, remembering, and honoring as part of our commitment to intercultural and interreligious intelligence and anticoloniality.

WHAT HAS BEEN LOST?

Genealogies of the intangible *are* epistemologies. We will never fully comprehend the many epistemologies and ways of being, stolen and lost due to colonization's rampant destruction and reordering of the world. Colonial representations of knowledge and knowledge production emphasized text-based forms of education, mapping over the histories and current realities of the colonized, enslaved, and murdered. Calculating our losses is something we do as people striving for the dream of decolonization. For some of us, coming face to face with what we lost or the things that have never had a chance to flourish is excruciatingly painful. For instance, Korean American Christians struggle with our understanding of what makes Korean American worship unique. Many Korean American churches and communities possess a tendency to emulate, sometimes without critical intention, a white evangelical form of worship. Worship is based heavily on the personality of the male preacher whose persona is cool and relatable. The direct opposite of the austere holiness which is usually the status quo in many mainline immigrant Korean American churches. Around this pastoral persona, the rest of worship is oriented around contemporary worship music and prayer out of primarily white evangelical traditions and mega churches. The emphasis is on one's personal relationship with God, repentance, forgiveness, and the Christian identity as moral guide. There is nothing that makes Korean American worship Korean American except for the bodies in the room. Though, I do think this should be enough to constitute it being Korean American worship, I always hope for more in terms of a distinctively Korean American practices and theologies that distinguish worship from its white evangelical counterparts.

This particular style of worship emerges not as a set of practices on its own but in relation to a white evangelical theology that does not always affirm racial, cultural, or religious difference as part of Christian ways of being and knowing in the world. The theology undergirding this tenet touts identity in Christ over identities or labels "the world" might put on someone. I once saw a YouTube clip from an evangelical megachurch in which a sprinkling of people of color including Black, Asian, and Latinx people, among mostly white evangelicals looked into the camera saying, "I'm a Christian first." This clip expressed a unifying vision from a self-described evangelical church but epitomized for me the danger of theologies that constitute erasure of meaningful identities and rootedness for the sake of unity. Unity is not sameness. Neither is unity a tolerance of differences. Ethnocultural and Interreligious differences are not markers to overcome or reorder to serve an overarching agenda of getting along. Instead, we work together and coexist with our racialized, ethnocultural, and religious differences in tact.

Christianity came to most Asian nations and people through the auspices of the colonial enterprise, which made quick work of assessing and doing away with Indigenous spiritual practices and religions, is an important entryway into understanding why some in the AIPDA Christian community experience such a lacuna when it comes to theology and worship that incorporates significant ethnocultural markers. Much of western colonial Christianity did not open itself up for incorporation into the religious life and landscape of Asian peoples but worked to eradicate and subjugate what existed before Christianity's arrival. Though some APIDA Christian communities have begun to include understandings and representations of religious and spiritual fluidity including practices that reach back to Indigenous roots, APIDA Christians may never grasp the fullness of what we lost due to Christianity's arrival among Asian peoples and their Indigenous religions and spiritualities.

Intercultural and interreligious classrooms naturally attempts to keep track of the things people have lost. Through assignments and discussions that incorporate the self-reflexive study of self in community, colearners, integrate narratives of survival and thriving with communal and personal stories that contest the accounts of colonial and missional histories, students actively engage in the naming and reclaiming of what was lost. In acknowledging what we have lost, we can also look toward what we might gain and prophetically claim new narratives of mending as we engage the process of decolonization through anticolonial teaching and learning together.

THE SIGNIFICANCE OF LANGUAGE: KEPT, LOST, AND FOUND

Language is a significant marker and tool of preserving culture, religion, and peoplehood. In North American classrooms, we teach in the English language and those teachers for whom English is their first or only language may not grasp how difficult it is to learn in a second, third, or fourth language. Teachers who teach and communicate primarily in English may not understand how cumbersome it is to read and write in a foreign language and to wrestle with words twisted on your tongue. Denice Frohman, a queer and Latinx spoken word artist performs a poem called, "Accents."[2] As a second-generation Latinx person, Frohman's poem talks about how her mother's tongue and lips undergo a type of gymnastics to usher forth English and how certain pronunciations are still elusive to her. Frohman is not in any way being pejorative when she speaks of her mother's pronunciation of English. She speaks of her mother's accent and way of speaking as the homing beacon from which she finds herself and her own Spanish. Her mother's struggle to speak in English, and the ways her words are beautifully reshaped and recreated as they float across her tongue and lips is a way Frohman reinterprets the meeting point between her family's heritage and colonialism.

In theological education and in institutions of higher education, we talk about the study of everything, including language, in terms of mastery. We assume that language, like culture and religion, is something we can dominant and tame to our own purposes. In seminaries and doctoral programs, we emphasize and even require the study of European languages as well as Hebrew and Greek. Academe still ignores the ways Black, Indigenous, and people of color embrace and reshape the English language as resistance and to reclaim power. When immigrants speak English by bridging multiple languages and understandings, people call it broken. During an event for a doctoral mentoring institution, I was invited to colead a group of first-year doctoral students. My coleader and I requested each student map on a large piece of butcher paper their academic path for the next four years. Our mentees were from various institutions, all which had different ways of marking a doctoral student's progression through the rigors of PhD life. Despite institutional differences, I noticed that each of these students, Black, Latinx,

Asian, and multiracial students, were listing language exams and calculating the years they needed to spend studying for exams that emphasized not only biblical languages, but European languages like German and French. As an educator who spends her time thinking about ways to decolonize the classroom, the appearance of these language requirements across many beloved institutions as a way to mark whether or not a scholar of color was ready to join the academy was jarring and infuriating. Sure we can argue that for some academic fields it is important for new scholars to learn European languages. Yet have we considered how these languages are doing anything but preparing Black, Indigenous, and other scholars of color to make themselves more palatable and acceptable to white-dominant academic spaces? How will these European and colonial languages assist scholars of color in their work toward accountability to the communities who named, raised, and nurtured them? I recall speaking with my mother after my first book was published. I gave her a copy and when she was halfway through I asked her what she thought. I can still see in my mind's eye, the steady gaze of my mother's eyes as she looked at me and said, "I know this is a book about Korean and Korean American women, and I am a Korean and Korean American woman, so I don't understand why you made it so hard for me to understand what you are saying about us." It was one of those moments where I once again realized that it was not my mother's English that was broken, but my own. I had recreated her world and my world in a framework, theory, and concepts no longer tethered to *woori* or us.

Language is more than just a system of words that communicate and describe. Language ties people to one another, to land, to place, to communal and personal memory, to histories, and to belief. The same descriptor words in different languages do not bear the same meaning. There are stories and histories behind how people have come to use certain words and how a word's meaning is expanded and deepened to hold more than the description of one thing. In the documentary, *A Seat At The Drum*, filmmaker and journalist Mark Anthony Rolo, a member of the Bad River Band of Lake Superior Chippawa Nation, names the difficulty of language and displacement. The film shows Pricilla, a Dine´(Navajo) mother and her daughters walking along the beach while she teaches them the different Dine´ words for what they see as they walk, the ocean, the sun, and the sand. Rolo says,

> Here's the problem, Navajo is a desert language. A language of red rock canyons, pinion pines, willows on the edges of small streams, it's a language of flash floods and scorching summer heat. It's a language of place, and the sadness of losing it is that we lose real knowledge about the desert Southwest that is thousands of years old, but it goes deeper than that. These lessons are all that Pricilla has to link her daughters to Navajo culture.[3]

In classrooms, we have both students who are learning English as a second language as immigrants and international students and students who have never had the opportunity to learn the languages tied to their heritage, place, and land. Students whose mother tongues were stolen from them. In particular, students of African American heritage who have violent histories of enslavement and trafficking and students of Indigenous heritage whose ancestors had their languages stripped from them along with their names, relationships, and religions. Just because someone is a native English speaker and also a person of color does not mean there is not deep pain associated with the loss of language and the relationships represented through that lost language. Educators with intercultural and interreligious intelligence do not attempt to draw false equivalencies between the two groups of students, but hold them together while distinctly honoring their diverging experiences. We can speak English both as a way of celebrating what we access through it and at the same time mourn that we have to speak it at all.

In North American classrooms, too few of us know how to model equity among languages as a form of intercultural and interreligious life together. Lingual equity at its most visionary means a classroom in which multiple languages are used at all times and where each language that is used bears unique significance to both the person speaking and those who hear. Though multilingual classrooms are indeed the way of the future, many of our North American institutions still prioritize the English language as the primary mode of teaching and learning mostly because institutions of theological education in North America were not built to sustain and support more than one primary language. Theological education was built to control the use of non-English languages, destroy them, or to subjugate it to the colonizer's tongue. We are still far from the reality of a multilingual environment for teaching and learning in theological education, but we can still practice models of language appreciation in our classrooms that acknowledges and visibilizes the meaningful nature of how language works among people through ethnicity, culture, and religions. How do we learn and teach the deep appreciation for how language functions across ethnicities, cultures, and religions? For some, language is what ties individuals to our religious traditions and communities. I am always struck by how Arabic functions among Muslim Americans who hail from all over the world. A language that edifies personhood and communalism in the Islamic tradition, educates in religious tradition, and has the potential to bridge across racial and ethnic differences. Arabic is also a language that provides access to scared text for some and not others in the Muslim American community.

In North American classrooms, we are taught from a young age that only the English language matters. It is assumed that only the English language can communicate across cultures and different people. It is our common lingual ground. All other languages are periphery and considered only for their commodifiable value. Some foreign languages are worth learning because they are advantageous to us in our professional lives. In my Seattle suburban high school, when we had to choose which foreign languages we wanted to learn as part of the core curriculum, our choices were French, German, Spanish, and Japanese. French and German were seen as important Romance languages while Spanish was seen as a progressive language to learn ahead of a more global future. Learning Japanese was seen as a potentially savvy direction for secondary languages because of our geographic proximity to Japan and the Japanese business interests held by many of the school's families. Not much has changed from my adolescence to my children's experience. When my son was in nursery school, the principal pulled me aside and said that she noticed I spoke to him mostly in Korean. She suggested I speak to my child in English from now on since Korean was not a commonly used language and would put him behind the other children in his class. My high school and my son's daycare principal were of the same mind when it came to languages. Languages exist to serve the purpose of preparing someone to enter into dominant culture society, governed by a set of rules and hierarchies that perpetuate racialized stereotypes that are also mapped onto languages. When considering the power of language from that worldview, the significance of language is reduced to the transactional. The ability it gives someone to subjugate another and to give the bearer of the language abilities to assimilate and attain economic wealth.

These mother tongues were carried across oceans and over lands that also bore the wetness of tears from experiences of departures and forced separations. For many of our ancestors, upon arrival, language and all that it tied together in the form of relationships to people, community, land, history, and memory was systematically silenced. The vehicle for such erasures included Christian education.[4] Our classrooms cannot continue to act as extensions of this atrocious educational history. The insistence in our classrooms and in theological education of adopting reverence for languages that were once forced upon some of our ancestors perpetuates a violent act. It might be the only way forward to scholarly validation and equipping for academe, but it is a violent and jarring process of undoing the profundity of generations. Such emphasis in higher education on first learning and validating mastery of scholarship beyond what has already been passed down and nurtured in racially and religiously minoritized scholars is a colonial endeavor. The concept of lingual mastery intentionally works to separate scholars of color and religiously minoritized scholars from the places, people, and languages that are inscribed on their flesh and bone. Roy I. Sano, a United Methodist Bishop wrote about the impact of white theological institutions on the lives of immigrants by saying, seminaries in the United States worked like bleaching vats for the cream of the crop of immigrant churches, taking the youth of immigrant communities seeking theological education and reshaping them in their own image.

As educators, we know languages spoken and unspoken are more than a colonizer's cudgel. Some languages are painstakingly preserved, created, recreated, lost, and found. We bear these words and experiences in our names. For some of us, our names tie us to colonial histories. I think back to my students of Filipino heritage who possess Spanish surnames, reminders of a colonial legacy and of pain. Names that today create divisive understandings of racial identity and miscognition in self and others. Many teachers and students come to classrooms with the weight of mother tongues heavy in their bodies, minds, and hearts. We might be unable to form or say the words, we might have a different relationship with them, we may have lost and forgotten language over generations but they still matter to us and are part of us. My younger brother and I grew up in a household where Korean was the primary spoken language. Though we had the same opportunities with language, my brother did not retain much Korean while I became fluent. Some of this has to do with gendered language preservation. In immigrant families, girls are often expected to carry on culture and language. However, most of this was because my brother never had much interest in learning Korean. English felt much more accessible and useful to him in daily life. The only Korean words he uses are *Umma* and *Appa*, the words for mother and father as well as words for some of his favorite Korean foods like, *kimbap* and *jjigae*. Foods that my mother still lovingly makes from scratch for her beloved son when she visits him. It is not an accident that relational words are the ones my brother retained. He retained the connectional words. The nourishing and nurturing words. Though some of us never learned our native languages or the meanings behind them, they are still buried in our bones along with the blood of our ancestors. When we discover them again what a joyous reunion it is! How do we honor both the presence and absence of language and the depth of what they signify and carry for each of us and for all people?

TECHNOLOGY AND LANGUAGE

Technology is a powerful tool for recognizing the genealogical power of language in the classroom. Many of us who teach online or in hybrid course formats have access to online discussion boards. Some of us have tech assessable classrooms that allow students to be online while attending class. We are kidding ourselves when we think students can and will disconnect when they are in our classes. The potential for technology to enhance multilingual learning is exciting for intercultural and interreligious commitments. Some of the ways, I have experimented with a multilingual classroom untethered from multilingual fluency is by asking students to chat online with one another as they are engaged in class. For international students who speak the same primary language, create a chat group hosted by either a third-party platform like Google or by the institution's online course platform. Encourage them to have side conversations in their own language about what they observe and hear in class. For international students that come from cultures, where speaking in class and asking questions is not an acceptable form of engagement, this allows for them to engage one another as a community within the larger classroom community in live time, instead of saving the conversation for the break or after class is dismissed for the day. I also use a Google doc shared to the entire class where we collectively generate lists of new English words and U.S. concepts in live time. I do my best to visually project this document in the classroom. As the class goes on, one student might type in a word or concept they do not understand, and another student will chime in with the definition. Students can work in the document in any language they see fit. It is amazing at the end of a class session to see how many languages, different ideas, and definitions there are around the room, around even a single word or concept.

GRIEVING AND NAMING

Among the cultural and religious markers that we lose across time and space, there are also markers that are stolen, markers that are intentionally let go, and markers that are never fully possessed but remembered ancestrally. Naming what we have lost and how we have lost them is a valuable and sacred practice across cultures and religions that we can practice in our teaching and learning. Naming helps us grieve and mourn so that we might have room for the creation of the new and possess joy. As a second-generation Korean American, a part of me will always mourn that my third-generation children will have even less knowledge of the Korean language than I do. I also grieve that their connection to significant pieces of family history like the Korean War and the Japanese Occupation of Korea will feel more distant to them than it does to me. Their connection to those formative and traumatic events is further distanced from them as my grandparents pass away and as my parents age. Those memories, stories of loss, survival, and strength, will fade unless we choose to retell them and embed them into our collective consciousness. As a second-generation person, there are things I will never understand about the Korean culture, things that will always feel a bit distant and things that will never align with my bicultural experience. This experience of distance will be exacerbated for my children and their children.

Immigration patterns rupture communities, connections, and transmissions. Yet, amid the loss and grief, there exists the hope that the creation of new markers offers us.

My mother has a different sort of grief. For her, it was her Christianity that she hoped would take root in all our lives. In some ways, it has. I became a Presbyterian minister and teach in theological education. However, my lived Christianity looks radically different from hers, and it is difficult for her to recognize her Christianity in my embodiment of the same faith. The Christianity of my children, should they choose it, will look radically different from mine. Hopefully, for the better. With the progression of time and the creation of homes in new lands, we also knowingly and unknowingly give up articles of our cultures and religions that once grounded us and called to us. These articles do not die, only transform. We honor the old ways through faithful critique and fierce love, a crucible which allows the rebirth of the old for new generations.

The shared practice of naming loss, grief, creation, and joy facilitates anticolonial practice in classrooms and other environments of teaching and learning. Anticolonial practice in classrooms makes possible the recognition of histories that our textbooks would otherwise malign or leave out. It makes possible for even those with conflicted histories to speak from places of personal truth and still participate in mutual recognition and respect in the face of differences. One way of facilitating an intentional naming is to start each course by giving students the opportunity to not only name themselves but to also name the communities they come from and the intersectional identities and solidarities they possess. Religious educator Sheryl Kujawa-Holbrook has a wonderful exercise that invites students to share their names and how their names connect them to histories and communities. Students are invited to share their full name, the story of how they received their names and what their names mean. Students are invited to write their names on the board in the language of their preference. This exercise is deceptively simple. Unpacking one's name also unpacks the histories and legacies given to you. Names are personal and connectional. They are given to us by those who love us and have big dreams for us. Many people's names have both familial and religious significance.[5] Names are uttered and remembered by communities that nurture us and hold us accountable. I know that when my mother or father call me by my Korean name, Jin, that they are about to say something either loving or hard, often it is both. When our names are uttered, we call up the ancestors. Our names remind us of who we are and who we are becoming. Exercises like unpacking names invite students and teachers into vulnerability and invoke personal and collectives histories of families that are intrinsically linked to peoplehood, spirituality, and religion. Naming works to diminish stereotypes and bias, creating space where students and teachers can truly begin to see one another through the lens of decolonial futuring. We are becoming, together. Exercises like these help both teachers and students firmly resist and shed the masks coloniality insists we must don for one another.

Grieving and naming what is lost gives way to new energies to restore and revision what we have lost both culturally and religiously. Creating space for grieving and naming does not mean we forget and move on. It is an imperial notion that we can simply bury knowledge or rename it as something new. Anticolonial teaching and learning are about undoing and resisting colonialism's continual press upon our souls and lives through reclamation and creativity. Colonialism desires to disconnect us from the genealogies of the intangible: religious and cultural. In response, we collectively work to restore and redefine the categories of knowledge and knowledge production for ourselves and for one another. We do so by redefining and constituting what we mean when we talk about the text, sacred or otherwise, by working as guardians of alternate histories and memories, keepers and transformers of culture and religion, and by seeing one another as co-conspirators in our work against white and Christian supremacy.

SACRED TEXTS

Access to sacred texts is controversial across religious communities and in the halls of theological education. In some religious traditions, the text is only accessible to those of a particular gender or group. One of the Korean immigrant churches I grew up in only allowed men to pray and read scripture in front of the congregation. Sometimes the sacred text is written in a language that only some can access, like the *Qu'ran* in its Arabic form. What exactly the sacred is and how we define sacral nature are up for contestation. In some religious traditions like among the Abrahamic traditions and in some Dharmic traditions like Tibetan Buddhism, people are embodiments of the sacred alongside the written form of the text. The divine incarnates or reincarnates into flesh and is for many, the text. The gospel of John begins with the phrase, "The Word is made flesh and dwelt among us."[6] For many traditions that have been relegated to folk religions or spirituality, there is not a primary written text. For some people and traditions, there have been bodies and people who have been deemed sacrilegious, or outside the realm of the holy. Christianity has done this to Black, Indigenous, people of color, to its religious neighbors and spiritual traditions, and to queer folx over the centuries. The reality is, what is determined sacred and who possesses access to the sacred has changed across history. Knowing this helps us to expand our understanding of what the term "sacred" means and how we might liberate it.

Like genealogies of the intangible, texts are more than the written word. An anticolonial approach to sacred texts remembers that the sacred is not always textually bound. The sacred is often ephemeral and embodied, sometimes simultaneously. The texts in our written canons sometimes contradict the epistemologies we carry in our lives and on our bodies. One way this is real for me is the way some Christian biblical texts are exclusive, privileging male, cisgendered, hetero bodies, and narratives. What I know from my own experience of G-d's love and the love between people contradicts what Christians have called sacred text. As many others have, I accept that our embodied knowledge of G-d and humankind is also a powerful form of knowledge that can and will challenge what religious communities have understood as truth over the ages. For me, as a Presbyterian, this is permissible and even necessary, as our reformed theology requires us to ever reform our thinking and being. For teachers of anticolonial classrooms, what would change if we saw ourselves and our students as the sacred text? As part of a canon that is no longer closed but open to various possibilities? What if we were the living texts that existed beyond space and time, the histories we carry, the stories, the memories, both collective and individual, all of it sacred and complex, bearing just as much if not more knowledge as a written canon? What marvelous knowledge might we witness newly created and with fresh eyes?

SHOWING UP FOR MEMORY

The notion of "showing up" is rooted in activism. Showing up means to put our whole selves forward for those who are most vulnerable. In some religious and cultural traditions, this is known as witness. A student of mine in a Christian worship course once challenged her peers about their understanding of Christian witness. Her colleague argued that witness was a weak form of activism, that in today's technological world, witness was reduced to voyeurism. Her rebuttal named the act of seeing as only the surface of Christian witness. To witness meant seeing injustice, but seeing injustice meant also challenging it, and preparing for possible backlash. My student's definition of Christian witness has bearing on showing up. Activists show up not only for causes but for actual people, calling them by name and amplifying their voices. Voiceless-ness does not exist. Showing up for our students means we bear witness to who they are, how they choose to represent themselves, their cultures, their religions, their spiritualities, and the way they desire to engage one another and the world. We witness them in the fullness of who they are and exclaim, "I see you! You are seen!" Showing up in the classroom for our students, especially racially and religiously minoritized students, means we grieve with them, celebrate with them, and advocate for them in white and Christian serving institutions.

As teachers, we also show up for ourselves and the people we carry into the classroom. One of the most contested issues I've seen and heard of at various institutions is the issue of titles. We argue about whether or not a professor should go by their first name or their earned title. Women of color mostly choose to go by their earned titles, Rev. Dr., Dr., or professor. The issue of titles or first names is a gendered and racialized issue if there ever was one! I was once asked by a white male colleague why I wanted to be addressed as Rev. Dr., Dr., or Professor Hong versus Christine. After some thought I told my colleague that it was not that long ago people who looked like me could not earn PhDs or become ordained as clergy in my denomination. I told him that there were still many Korean Christians who did not believe in my ordination or my teaching in theological institution. I named for him the many Asian American feminist theologians who had gone before me who fought long and hard so I could be here. I told him that when my students called me by my title, Dr. Hong or Professor Hong, they were also calling out to my ancestors, to my mentors, to the many who had paved the way for me and others. I carry these people and communities with me into classrooms as they have also carried me into the future they created. It is also my practice to call students by the titles and names they prefer to use. At the end of the day, showing up for one another is a foundational aspect of anticolonial teaching and learning. Showing up is about human dignity and its acknowledgment and preservation in spaces of education. One way we do this is by showing up for religious and cultural representation by honoring memories, practices, and the people who keep memory alive, including Indigenous and Native peoples.

Lifting up Indigenized pedagogy as part of our accountability to First Nations people, is a significant way we begin to repair the erasure of colonial education on Native bodies and memories. Indigenized pedagogy embraces the knowledge of Indigenous people as part of how we understand teaching and learning. Not as periphery knowledge, or for a week in the syllabus, but holistically as a part of how we understand the birth and transformation of knowledge. Tuck and Yang speak of decolonial classrooms as first naming how our fields, guilds, and practices have done violence to Native peoples.[7] Teaching students the histories of our fields is our responsibility as educators. Teaching the honest history of our fields, even if those histories put into question our very existence and practices is an anticolonial commitment and action that embraces the possibility of a collective decolonial future. A significant way theological educators can do this is through the naming and acknowledgment of collective, communal, and individual memories as the knowledge itself. Knowledge does not have to come from a text, or be written down in order to be real. These memories as knowledge are not always written down and agreed upon as the collective history, but they are passed down through story, through collective feeling, and sometimes as part of a larger fabric of cultural memory, which can also exist as many faceted. Hyeran Kim-Cragg used the word Orature, or Oral literature, a term that originated from Indigenous and African historians to counteract the denial of orality as a lexicon of memory and knowledge.[8] The spoken word artists mentioned at the Preface of this book, William Nu'u'tupu and Travis T, describe the impact of colonization on the oral histories and lives of their people in their poem *Oral Traditions*. They state, "When a person dies, it's like a library burning down."[9] Memory as embodied by those in communities both religious and ethnic are alive. They are our most primary texts. The way we organize and catalog knowledge and even art in academic libraries and museums is itself a colonial enterprise. This European modality of curating and disseminating knowledge originates from a philosophical attempt to hoard knowledge and give access to a select few. Sometimes our most revered classroom texts are written by outsiders to communities or by insiders who have to preform knowledge for the academy in order to have their qualifications validated and accepted. When we begin to notice and accept the ways the academy has treated and understood the creation of knowledge does not always include all sources of knowledge, we are able to imagine a different type of classroom, course, and teaching and learning inclusive of religious, spiritual, and cultural forms of creating, bearing, and preserving what people know and hold dear.

The memory keepers for many communities of color and Indigenous communities around the world are their elders. Eldership is not something you age into. Eldership is a status bestowed upon someone who is not only advanced in years but also has given something profound to the community. We become elders through the passage of time and also through the blood, sweat, and tears of what we give back to the people and places from whence we came. I sometimes say to my students that in some of our cultures, we don't become adults until we become ancestors. Religious and communal elders do not always write down their stories, and they do not always acquiesce to have their stories told and retold. Elders decide what and how knowledge is shared, withheld, and how space is created for the burgeoning of the new in communal and familial history. As I write this book, my two living grandparents, my paternal grandmother and my maternal grandfather have entered their final days. We have been told by our relatives to prepare. Their impending loss weighs heavy on my heart and even brings my shoulders down with the gravity of what it means that an entire generation of our family is about to enter their transition. All four of my grandparents were both born in what is now known as North Korea. All four were born into and survived Japanese occupation and the following U.S. military occupation which continues to this day. They survived the Korean War, a war which never ended, but entered a cease fire. Two of them lived to see the real possibility of unification in 2018, the leaders of a divided people shaking hands across the DMZ. My paternal grandmother lived through two marriages, immigration to the United States, the founding and closing of multiple businesses, and the rebuilding of a new life from nothing. My maternal grandfather, a centurion, celebrated his 100 years in 2019, surrounded by his children, grandchildren, and great grandchildren. He grieved the death of two of his eldest children and one grandchild. Both of my surviving grandparents passed down their tremendous faith to their children and grandchildren. Their Korean Christianity survived the attempted erasure of Japanese rule and the crossing of multiple borders, a theology of survival, life, and death. When they pass, much will pass with them. So much of what they know, they have chosen to keep for themselves, desiring not to pass down to us the most painful stories so that we might begin anew, a gift and a burden. Some memories are intentionally not passed on at the will of memory keepers and so knowledge is let go. This is quite different from memories becoming historically erased or lost through colonization. Through colonization when a memory is erased, that empty space is taken up and devoured. When memory keepers withhold memories and stories, the empty space is not filled, but suspended and held. The emptiness itself teaches and speaks into our lives. The intention behind silence is not the erasure of people and peoplehood but for survival and flourishing only possible through the hope of expanding, holding space for the old, and making room for the new.

SHOWING UP FOR CULTURE

In teaching and learning, we cannot take for granted the depth of how culture is represented and how it shows up. As stated in chapter 1, culture is not only ethnicity but also nationality. It cannot be reduced to food or clothing, though these are important aspects of culture.[10] Culture is much more intricate in the way it shows up in our everyday lives. Culture in the classroom is present even if the demographics appear homogenous. In my classroom in Louisville, my students were predominantly white, Black, and African American; however, the cultures represented across traditions, geographies, and spiritualities were abundant and required careful navigation. Diversity though appearing only racially binary in nature was remarkably varied and complex. Appalachian Christianities, cultures, traditions, and dialects, intersected with East and West Coast slang, evangelicalisms, progressive Christianities, and religious fluidity. Among my African American students, the ways they identified as either Black or African American varied contextually, politically, generationally, and by community. Ghanaian students identified differently than my Black and African American students due to histories shared and unshared. White students named traditions in their families that carried over from immigrant generations a hundred years ago. In classrooms that are dynamic toward visible and tangible representation across religion, race, culture, and ethnicity, difference is an embarrassment of riches. Difference and complexity is the teacher and the guide for all we attempt to do together. The assumptions we make about what culture is and how it is represented are held at bay if we keep in mind that culture is first and foremost either high or low context. Culture always shows up. It is up to teachers to show up for culture in its various forms as embodied by us and by our students, and the ways culture transforms spaces of mutuality through continuous unpacking, repacking, and engagement.

Among our students, there are those who come from traditions of culture keepers. These students are preparing themselves to take on the role of culture keepers, maybe living into these roles, or interacting with others who hold these roles in both religious and ethnic communities. Culture keepers, like memory keepers are those in our families, our cultural communities, and religious communities that preserve culture in all its forms. Not all aspects of culture necessitate explanation in classrooms. There is some aspect of opacity that is necessary for the well-being of people who are constantly targeted as a part of the xenophobic North American political environment. Culture is also one of those tangible and intangible things. However, this does not mean that all aspects of culture, shared and unshared, knowable and unknowable, are not always in play in our classrooms. Rather than demand that students share with teachers the tools of how to navigate their cultural codes, the anticolonial approach to teaching and learning creates space where those codes and perspectives are invited to reveal themselves and participate through our students should they so choose. This lives into bell hook's value of teaching democratically so that *how* one participates is always a choice, particularly for those who are vulnerable.[11]

In our classes, we do the work of teaching and learning one another's cultural values, codes, and languages, but there are things we can only know by being insiders to a community. In my own culture, I still study all the ways Korean people speak without actually speaking. Though I am an insider for all intents and purposes, there are still aspects of communication and living together that are intangible and tacit. Intangibility is also cultural. For Korean people, intangible cultural knowledge is *noon-chi*, or the measure of the eye. This term is so ethnoculturally embedded that there is not an equivalent linguistic word in a different language. The meaning of *noon-chi* is closest to the English word, tact. To possess *noon-chi* is to be able to read between the lines, to read context as the primary source of information. This means being able to hear a "no" when someone is saying "yes." It also means to anticipate other's needs before they are spoken. *Noon-chi* is often gendered. It is something Korean women are implicitly taught and utilize as a part of maintaining relationships. For instance, it is not always wise to state an opinion or desire directly in relationships. Sometimes it is more polite to say no first or to object to an overture of kindness or care. I might ask my mother-in-law what she would like for her birthday. She might reply, "Nothing," but she certainly does not mean nothing! There is a polite dance back and forth of my asking and her saying, "Nothing" and reading the context of what she says. During one such exchange, she might say something in passing to me about a certain scarf's nice material. If I use *noon-chi*, I would hear her hinting that she would appreciate the scarf as a gift. *Noon-chi* does not always translate across cultures. A story about the cultural importance of *noon-chi* always stuck with me from my mother's experiences as a high school exchange student in Flemington, New Jersey. My mother loves fresh squeezed orange juice. Orange juice was an extravagance in Korea during the 1960s and 1970s. For this reason, it was customary for guests to bring orange juice as a gift to someone's home as a gesture of gratitude. When my mother first sat down to breakfast at her host family's home as a Korean exchange student, she was offered a glass of orange juice. Her eyes lit up and she thought, isn't it amazing! American families have orange juice at breakfast every day and not only on special occasions. Eager for a glass of the precious orange juice, she used deferential *noon-chi* and said, "No, thank you." She thought her host mother would continue to offer it to her as a Korean host might do. She was dismayed to find that the host mother did not continue to offer her the orange juice, assuming my mother did not enjoy it. My mother eventually discovered that in low-context American culture one simply asks for the things they want, rather than waiting for someone else to anticipate what she wanted or needed.

Michelle LeBaron, in her text *Conflict Across Cultures*, discusses high- and low-context cultures. High-context cultures emphasize nonverbal and indirect communication paired with more reserved reactions. Low-context cultures emphasize verbal and direct communications with overt reactions. In our teaching and learning, it is important for us to provide space for students from both high and low contexts to engage.[12] We need to become knowledgeable and possess acumen in both types of cultural communication as part of our intercultural intelligence and anticolonial teaching. How might we shape assignments or assessments for students in our classrooms who come from high-context cultures, where direct and autonomous engagement is not the preferred mode of communication? For instance, in my current classroom context, I have several international students per course. Not all of them come from cultures that engage teachers or peers by speaking up when one has a thought or question to contribute. Most often, the students who raise their hands to speak, or who speak without raising their hands for that matter are domestic students. To create space that is amenable to high-context students, I pose the questions I plan on asking prior to class. When it is time to discuss I give students a minute or two to review the questions and perhaps make notes for themselves. It is amazing what can occur when there is time given for processing new information and for thoughtful input, rather than quickly jumping into discussions where only some students might feel prepared or comfortable thinking out loud. I then open up a discussion period where I invite responses from high-context students by calling on them by name while understanding that my low-context students will jump in when they feel ready. In this way, participants get an opportunity to hear from all their peers instead of only peers who are acculturated to speaking on the fly and autonomously without invitation. Students who feel uncomfortable with answering can pass or defer to one another. As part of the transparency integral to the anticolonial classroom, I let my students in on the strategy behind how I frame class discussions.

TEACHING PRACTICES, HEALTHY DIALOGUE, AND SYLLABUS EXORCISM

"How do we decolonize our teaching? What are the best practices?" I am asked these common questions when I teach workshops on antiracist teaching or present at conferences. These questions assume that there are quick start ways to decolonize how we have been trained to think of ourselves, our students, and our collective work. These questions assume that the patterns of teaching and learning we internalized as educators were not formed in the crucible of colonialism over centuries, now crystalized in our syllabi and assignments, and even perhaps in the need for their existence in the first place. There is not a prescriptive way to decolonize teaching and learning. There is not a listicle of ten things you must do. Believing there is a simple solution, a ten-step process, is in itself a colonial way of looking at the world, at the grief and terror that colonialism has inflicted on us, on our ancestors, and the world. If there is a first step at all, it would be to let go of the notion that we can decolonize our classrooms in one fell swoop and that we can do it alone. As Tuck and Yang write, decolonization is not a metaphor for social justice, it is the very real return of land, culture, and peoplehood back to those it was stolen from.[13] Decolonization means that settler-colonizers leave and leave no trace. It means we give the land back. We are not there yet. Until we are, we take part in the decolonial futuring of theological education through anticolonial practice and commitments. We are creating the future together, now. The futuring of decolonization will take all of us. It will take all that we possess, all our intellect, our passion, and our resources. It is the posture, work, and the goal of a lifetime.

Meanwhile, because not all of us can wait a lifetime, there are tools for anticolonial practice that we try, tweak, and try again so that we might thrive, teachers and students, together. One of the most effective ways to concretely commit to anticolonial practice in the classroom is to perform a syllabus exorcism, that is, to exorcise the syllabus of the demon of whiteness. Not white people, whiteness. Whiteness as a gaze, lens, and demand. You might see this as an excessive move, and it might be, depending on the topic or the goal of the course at hand, but I have come to realize that no matter how many of my syllabi I exorcise, I will still have colleagues who refuse to decenter white voices, white thought, and whiteness in general. Most of us work in white serving institutions, after all. Unfortunately, my students will still have their fill of white theologies, white histories, and colonial methods of teaching and learning, even with all my efforts. Until the day comes where everyone is on board, I will continue the practice of exorcising my syllabi. In addition, focusing one's syllabi on minoritized voices and communities makes incredible impacts on student's lives. I am always amazed how racially and religiously minoritized students comment on feeling seen and heard for the first time in a class when I take the time to decenter white thought and white voices in my courses, whether through eliminating racially and religiously unconscious white scholarship from my readings or by undoing and unbinding some of the dominant forms of written assignments and assessments. Critical intercultural and interreligious engagement in theological education is no longer a sidelined exercise, it is central to the anticolonial academic pursuit of truth and health.

CO-CONSPIRATORS

Dismantling and disrupting the colonial enterprise and the Christian, white supremacist, patriarchy requires that we cooperate with one another and that we become co-conspirators with each other toward those ends. For some, conspiring has negative connotations. Images of plotting behind people's backs comes to mind. Some conspiracy is bad, but others, particularly by those who are minoritized, is necessary in the work of solidarity and justice. However, when we are faced with powers that do not even acknowledge that we exist or when there are such great power differentials that it is no longer a fair fight, co-conspiring is what we must do to survive and to hope for flourishing. Genealogically speaking, our ancestors, families, ethnic and racialized communities, religious communities, have all invested in our survival and flourishing so that we might join in the overt and covert work toward unbinding the fruit of liberation and justice. Co-conspiring toward antiracism and interreligious understanding with everyone in the classroom is part of the process of decolonization and honoring the people, communities, and places we call home.

Co-conspiring requires us to divest ourselves from the notion of enemies. In fact, dissenters are seen as stakeholders and are invited into the room. Even among friends and people who have nourished us, we sometimes disagree. We must let go of the fantasy that solidarity and the common work toward justice does not take effort across differences. We must cease to become surprised and dismayed when we realize all of us, regardless of racialized and religious minortizations have internalized supremacist understandings of race, religion, gender, human sexuality, and ability and perpetuate them in so called safe spaces. I am well aware that even though I claim Korean American Christians as my people that many of them will not claim me since I am an ordained clergywoman and "liberal" in my political and communal leanings. This does not mean I will abandon them. Though I have indeed considered this in my lowest moments! It means I double down and do the work of co-conspiring, which means we struggle together and breathe together. Breathing in the good and breathing out that which no longer edifies our lives together.

Co-conspiring, breathing together and working together, requires that we commit to the long game of justice rather than short-term rewards. That we keep our eyes on permanent change which might not occur in our lifetime, rather than temporary satisfaction. Co-conspiring with students means we see them as full participants in the unbinding of our mutual liberation in teaching and learning. It means we view them as individuals, tied to ethnic and cultural communities, to religious and spiritual practices and beliefs, that have stories to share with us as teachers and also as learners. Being co-conspirators in the classroom means, we work together toward being antiracist, interculturally and interreligiously intelligent in our awareness of one another and in the world.

ACCOUNTABILITY

Accountability is an essential part of co-conspiring toward hoping for and creating justice. Accountability is not a moment, an instance, but a long-term commitment. Accountability is both being held accountable and holding others accountable. There are rhythms to a life of being accountable and being held accountable. Though it is ideal that both forms of accountability occur together, sometimes it is a one-way street. Some accountabilities are minimally such because they are between structures and people with great power differentials. True accountability requires risk on all sides and efforts toward equity between the actors in relationship with one another.

As educators, we are accountable to our institutions, to do the work they hired us to do in their midst and to help, not harm the institutions and those inside of it. This type of institutional accountability, though well-intentioned, is tested when educators challenge embedded structures and systems that continue to disenfranchise and work against minoritized people. The type of accountability I wish to discuss here are those that are helpful for anticolonial teaching and learning toward intercultural and interreligious intelligence.

There are different types of accountabilities that are meaningful in anticolonial spaces and work toward the advancement of intercultural and interreligious intelligence. I will discuss two here. We are accountable to the communities that nurtured and raised us, and we are accountable to the work we commit to together in classrooms. These two types of accountabilities will crisscross in the classroom; they work to inform each other. For example, my accountability to women of color communities informs the way I present myself as an educator, structure syllabi, and engage students. My institutionally "outside" commitments are internalized and become concrete in the way I think and live my teaching. Since we are in the room not only with likeminded people, but in the midst of dynamic diversities that are meaningful not ornamental, we hold one another accountable as we teach and learn and are also held accountable by invisible threads to the people, communities, and places from whence we came.

We are accountable to the communities that nurtured us and raised us, to the stories we were told, and made to remember. These are a mix of racialized and ethnic communities and religious and spiritual communities. There might be very little distinction between these two types of communities. They may be deeply entwined. Religion becomes enculturated in its most embodied form, after all. As a scholar and a practical theologian who identifies as a woman of color, and a Korean American, I am accountable to the communities and places that root me to those identities. I am accountable as a woman of color in solidarity with other women of color, particularly Black and Indigenous women, and their communities. Accountability is messy and chaotic and the communities we see ourselves accountable to might view us with suspicion because of particular histories and the white supremacist gaze that infiltrates all of our interactions in North America. For instance, though solidarity between Asian people and Black people has a rich history in the United States, particularly on the west coast, it has also been rife with anti-Black and anti-Asian sentiment. These sentiments are facilitated by the white supremacist gaze through which we see and identify one another. We witness these dynamics play out in our classrooms between students and between students and ourselves, and we have to constantly commit to working together to see one another beyond the frameworks white supremacy has given us.

For me, accountability to the women of color community means I work on my biases and work on checking them in community. In particular, I work to call out the anti-Black racism within the larger Asian American community that work against a commitment to solidarity and accountability. As a Korean American, I am accountable to the larger Korean American community, to work on the issues that harm us in North American society, honoring our elders both living and passed, remembering our shared histories, and passing them on to my children. Through the Korean American identity, I am also held accountable to the land. The motherland of the Korean peninsula, a place I have journeyed back and forth from, a land that is still divided, in the midst of a ceasefire, and militarily occupied. I am accountable to her mountains and to her fields, her oceans, and streams. Through her, I am accountable to my ancestors, who ground me to a place where I was not born, yet constantly yearn for. As a Korean Christian and a Presbyterian, I am accountable to my shared faith and my denomination, and I work to hold them accountable as well in our pursuit of the beloved kin–dom that is both intercultural and interreligious. I am accountable to other Korean American Christians, and I hold them accountable in the pursuit of equity in our shared world and in light of a more conservative Korean American Christianity, and along with others, I push for the visibility and affirmation of queer folx, and a deeper commitment to interracial, intercultural, and interreligious solidarity.

In our classrooms, we are accountable to the work set before us. Just as our syllabus sets out our expectations for our students in terms of their work and what they will learn, an anticolonial classroom also sets out expectations for the environment of teaching and learning. I like to begin each class with negotiated and shared guidelines, or the values and commitments, for our collective work. This is the concretized work of co-conspiring toward decolonial futuring. I ask students to call out or write down guidelines that they would like their peers or myself to abide by. Students will name guidelines for what not to do as well as guidelines for different postures of openness in learning. This exercise takes time, but I find the values and commitments process helpful for constructively naming the fears students might share of what it might feel like to take risks in the classroom. Unlike rules, guidelines are less permanent. Students may alter guidelines, create new ones, or strike them as the class progresses. I leave the guidelines posted in the class or present them to students at the beginning of each class and ask for suggested revisions. Some days there are no revisions or suggestions, other days there are radical shifts. This is essential in the anticolonial paradigm of teaching and learning because we expect to transform and change our perspectives as we undo internalizations and work through some of the fears and biases we possess. It also helps me as the teacher see how different topics, discussions, and interactions are affecting the classroom environment. At the beginning of a course, most students might have met before but may not feel ready to make themselves vulnerable nor accept the vulnerability of their peers. As the course progresses and students build trust as guidelines are upheld, and start to advocate for making them more precise. At the end of the course, we have a strong set of guidelines for life together that has been coshaped, a model for how accountability functions in community, and a living example of how we negotiate and transform our values from fear-based and untrusting to affirming and trusting. Find ways to co-conspire with students toward decoloniality through the process of naming fear, discomfort, and risk in classrooms and point toward the transitions that occur as they work collectively toward the dismantling and disruption of cultural and religious assumptions and biases.

Conclusion
Begin Again

LET'S START OVER

Here at the end of this book, I invite you to make a commitment to the decolonial futuring of theological education through tangible anticolonial work. Your commitment, *our* commitment, is a beginning. The decolonial futuring of theological education is an embodied dream. It is not a figment of our imaginations, but the very real commitment to the daily pursuit and practice of liberation unbound, and freedom as necessity. In teaching and learning, anticolonial practice honors intercultural and interreligious encounter, not in seeking to master it but out of love for it. A commitment to anticolonial teaching is a commitment to holistic intercultural and interreligious intelligence. Intelligence as curiosity and the anticipation for the expansion of understandings across difference and self-revelation. In theological education, we dream the decolonial futuring together, in community with teachers and students by recreating a genealogy of shared experiences and authenticity. We story ourselves into one another's lives as a way to tell truths about ourselves and our communities of accountability. It is the loving work of resistance against a coloniality that seeks to overcome, erase, and diminish personhood and peoplehood.

The decolonial futuring requires all of us to dream it into being. How do you dream decolonial futuring where you are? In your institution? In the building of your courses, readings lists, and syllabi? In the greeting of your students by their names, in the greeting of the communities your students carry on their shoulders and in their hearts? How do you live into intercultural and interreligious intelligence as you facilitate spaces of hearing, speaking, feeling, and showing that are beyond verbal expression? How are your assignments constructed to reward curiosity and creativity, to redirect the energy of regurgitation and memorization to the creation of something new and powerful? How are you noticing the use of power where you are, in your school, your classroom, between yourself and your students? How are you noticing your relationship with conflict in the classroom? How is your pedagogy related to the transformation of people and their attached communities toward the pursuit of liberative imagination and flourishing?

It is my fervent hope that anticolonial teaching and learning will transform theological education, but it is going to take all of us together to catalyze that change. The transformation we usher in together will be stunning. It will be beautiful to behold. Living, breathing poetry. Literary prophet, Audre Lorde wrote about poetry as necessity. She writes, "Poetry is not a luxury. It is a vital necessity of our existence. It forms the quality of the light within which we predicate our hopes and dreams toward survival and change, first made into language, then into idea, then into more tangible action . . . the farthest horizons of our hopes and fears are cobbled by our poems, carved from the rock experiences of our daily lives."[1] Likewise, anticolonial teaching and learning toward a decolonial futuring is necessity for all of us, it is a moment and an instrument for now. It is not something we save for later when there is a better time. We lay the foundation of our collective futures today. We do not save this work for tomorrow. In our anticolonial teaching and learning, if our institutions try and shut us down, as they are built to do, we know it is because what we are creating together, the poetry of decolonial futuring is the wild wind of disruption, shaking institutions to their foundations. There is new life when coloniality is finally thrown into disarray.

WHAT IS YOUR ROLE?

As we commit to enter to the work of decolonial teaching and learning together, I invite you to think about your role. What is the particular intercultural and interreligious intelligence that you bring to your classroom and to the greater work of seeking a collectively decolonial theological education in our lifetime? Activist and educator Deepa Iyer writes about the different social responsibilities of activism as the social change eco-system.[2] Iyer warns activists and organizers of trying to do and be everything to everyone in the pursuit of justice and liberation. Knowing our role, what only we can do, and what others might do, helps us with our decolonial vision. Iyer's warning helps us avoid the savior model that falls into the colonial model of education. There is not one person or one entity that can save us from the structural and systemic mess of racism, religious bigotry, and empire. Instead, how might we think more collectively and expansively about time, space, gifts, and roles for the common struggle today. Iyer's eco-system model includes healers, builders, visionaries, disrupters, caregivers, frontline responders, bridge-builders, storytellers, and artists. All of these identifiable people in our communities work together toward a future built on equity, inclusion, liberation, justice, solidarity, resiliency, and interdependency. Which of these roles is yours for today? Which of these roles can you identify as the shared work of the people and communities around you? Iyer's social change ecosystem model can also inspire the way we build classrooms together with our students. If we are creating courses that ultimately seek to contribute to the decolonial vision of equity, inclusion, and liberation, what are the roles different students and teachers take on as co-conspirators? Together, we recognize the long game of anti-oppression work and the varied intercultural and interreligious intelligences it requires to survive the journey.

TO HOPE AND TO FLOURISH

Part of our role as theological educators is to continue to hope and to hope desperately. We hope that what we teach and what we learn makes a difference in the world we share. What is it that you hope your students will leave the classroom with? What is it that you hope you will gain in your teaching? Theological Education that embraces anti-colonial teaching and learning is about the power of hope as an anti-oppression tool within systems and structures of oppression. We teach and learn out of a hope inspired by one another's gifts of intercultural and interreligious intelligence. At the start of each semester and at the end of each academic year, it is my deepest hope that something has shifted both in my students and in myself. I hope that the shifts are essentially movements toward one another, closing the gap across difference through bridges of understanding, hospitality, empathy, and compassion. It is my hope that both my students and I have learned and internalized strategic and subversive ways of flourishing in an institution and a world that was seemingly only built for the thriving of some and not all. Toni Morrison, in a 1975 keynote at Portland State University famously said,

> The function, the very serious function of racism is distraction. It keeps you from doing your work. It keeps you explaining, over and over again, your reason for being. Somebody says you have no language and you spend twenty years proving that you do. Somebody says your head isn't shaped properly so you have scientists working on the fact that it is. Somebody says you have no art, so you dredge that up. Somebody says you have no kingdoms, so you dredge that up. None of this is necessary. There will always be one more thing.[3]

Morrison was speaking of the way systems and structures of oppression steal the flourishing of Black folx by drawing their energy toward proving their existence and worthiness to the colonial enterprise. For Morrison, flourishing is not for the purpose of explaining oneself so that the oppressor might finally recognize you as an equal. It is easy to believe that anticolonial teaching and learning is the work of proving ourselves and our students worthy within systems and structures that have historically sought to erase difference. In times of desperation, we might indeed resort to this mode of survival, but survival is not flourishing. Flourishing is the intentional attention to the creation and process of freedom, in spite of systems and structures of oppression, not because of them. The anticolonial commitment to teaching and learning through intercultural and interreligious intelligence is a celebration of tenacious mutual flourishing, to freedom on our own terms. First, it is the taking back of power and energy by racially and religiously minoritized people from the colonial undertaking. Second, it is the sharing of power and energies by white and Christian people with Black, Indigenous, other people of color and religiously minoritized people for the sake of mutual liberation and freedom.

In order to flourish, we resist using our energies and the energies of our people to reproduce ourselves for the colonial gaze. One person's flourishing need not come at the expense of another's life. Our commitment to anticolonial teaching and learning and decolonial futuring is anchored in the mutuality of this flourishing life together. Lives full of joy and grief. Lives full of love and conflict. Lives that are curious, storied, and connectional, always. We must flourish on our own terms, for the sake of ourselves, for the love of ourselves, in a time such as this. I deserve to flourish. You deserve to flourish. Our students deserve to flourish. We all deserve to dream. May it be so.

Notes

PREFACE

1. William Nu'utupu Giles and T. Travis, "Oral Traditions," *WNG*, 2015, https://www.willgilespoetry.com/poetry.

INTRODUCTION

1. Eve Tuck and K. Wayne Yang, "Decolonization is Not a Metaphor," *Decolonization: Indigeneity, Education, and Society* 1, no. 1 (September 8, 2012): 1–40, https://americanarchive.org/catalog/cpb-aacip_508-cc0tq5s173.

2. Frank B. Wilderson III's work on Afro-Pessimism refers to nonwhite men as junior partners to whiteness. He writes that junior partners include non-Black people and "LGBT people who are not Black and Indigenous communities." For Wilderson, non-Black people "suffer at the hands of contingent violence rather than the gratuitous or naked violence of social death"—146. According to Wilderson, non-Black people of color will never be white but the lure of whiteness makes them into instruments of whiteness through their anti-Black violence. He writes, "White people and their junior partners need Anti-Black violence to know that they are alive"—94.

3. Frank B. Wilderson III, *Afropessimism* (New York, NY: Liveright Publishing Corporation, 2020), 146.

4. Clive Staples Lewis, *The Voyage of the Dawn Treader* (New York, NY: HarperCollins, 2019).

5. A helpful model for thinking about anti-racist institutional life is the Continuum on Becoming an Antiracist, Multicultural Institution by Crossroads Ministry. A copy can be found in Stephanie Speller's book, Radical Welcome. Pg. 70–71.

6. Brenda J. Allen, "Introduction," in *Presumed Incompetent: the Intersections of Race and Class for Women in Academia*, ed. Muhs Gabriella Gutiérrez y (Boulder, CO: Univ. Press, 2012), 17–20.

7. Grace Chang, "The Promise and Perils of Teaching Women of Color Studies," in *Presumed Incompetent: The Intersections of Race and Class for Women in Academia*, ed. Muhs Gabriella Gutiérrez y (Boulder, CO: Univ. Press, 2012), 200–1.

8. W. E. B. Du Bois (William Edward Burghardt), 1868–1963, *The Souls of Black Folk: Essays and Sketches* (Chicago, IL: A. G. McClurg, 1903; New York, NY: Johnson Reprint Corp., 1968), 2–3.

9. *Wiconi International*, "Richard Twiss: A Theology of Manifest Destiny," May 7, 2008, https://www.youtube.com/watch?v=4mEkMy1KNW0.

10. Roy I. Sano, *From Every Nation without Number: Racial and Ethnic Diversity in United Methodism* (Nashville, TN: Abingdon, 1982), 83.

CHAPTER 1

1. Ania Loomba, *Colonialism/Postcolonialism* (Abingdon, Oxon: Routledge, 2007), 4.

2. Loomba, *Colonialism-Postcolonialism*, 12.

3. Loomba, *Colonialism-Postcolonialism*, 12.

4. Kate Ford, *Competency-Based Education: Histories, Opportunities, and Challenges* (UMUC Center for Innovation in Learning and Student Success, 2014), 1–3.

5. Margaret Kovach, *Indigenous Methodologies: Characteristics, Conversations, and Contexts* (Toronto, ON: University of Toronto Press, 2009), 77.

6. Kovach, *Indigenous Methodologies*, 76.

7. Kovach, *Indigenous Methodologies*, 79.

8. Stephen R. Prothero, *Religious Literacy: What Every American Needs to Know—And Doesn't* (New York, NY: Harper One, an imprint of Harper Collins Publishers, 2008), 11–12.

9. Prothero, *Religious Literacy*, 12.

10. Stephen Prothero defines religious literacy as ". . .the ability to understand and use in one's day-to-day life the basic building blocks of religious traditions—their key terms, symbols, doctrines, practices, sayings, characters, metaphors, and narratives"—in Stephen Prothero, Religious Literacy: What every American needs to know—and doesn't, pg. 11–12.

11. Prothero, *Religious Literacy*, 14.

12. Tacit culture is the part of a culture that one can learn via observation though nothing explicitly instructional might exist. We learn tacit culture through interaction and immersion in particular communities. In our home, part of our tacit culture is to remove our shoes before entering. I do not explicitly ask the people invited to our house to take off their shoes, but a careful observer will notice all of our shoes lined up outside the door and also take their shoes off. This tacit cultural learning by some visitors to our home occurs through observation, not verbal instruction.

13. I use the terms "outsiders" and "insiders" here to refer to people who belong to particular cultures and religious traditions. I find that outsider and insider dichotomies better describes the dynamics of people who create and sustain tacit culture in racial, ethnic, and religious communities, and those who desire to understand it from outside communities.

14. Expansive Definitions: Definitions, creating them, stating them, and recreating them, are a cornerstone for the academy. As academics, we love to pin down a definition concretely and permanently for future use. We like to make up words to describe new ideas and do the good work of attributing their use to one another. For this book, definitions, like my definitions for intercultural and interreligious intelligence, are held expansively to affirm human understanding and knowledge as always transforming and in flux. I also acknowledge that my definition and other's definitions of the same word are not always the same, nor should they be. By seeking the concretization of definitions, particularly definitions connected to religion and culture, we run the danger of the reification of the systems and structures that have historically erased or reduced entire peoples and entire traditions from the colonial map. Instead, this book works to hold definitions expansively as a posture of openness to what is possible and as an act of honoring the liminality necessary for decolonial teaching and learning. The terms defined in this book are starting places for mutual conversation, not an end to them.

15. Gardner's eight criteria for qualifying as an intelligence included: potential for brain isolation, a place in evolutionary history, the presence of core operations, susceptibility to encoding, distinct developmental progression, savants, support from psychology, and support from psychometric findings.

16. Gardner initially proposed seven intelligences, including musical-rhythmic, visual-spatial, verbal-linguistic, logical-mathematical, bodily-kinesthetic, interpersonal, and intrapersonal.

17. Howard Gardner, *Intelligence Reframed: Multiple Intelligences for the 21st Century* (New York, NY: Basic Books, 1999), 33–34.

18. The word "intelligence" has been used to belittle and diminish many people over centuries. Indigenous and Native scholars Margaret Kovach, Graham Smith, and Linda Tuhiwai Smith have noted the use of intelligence as measurement against whiteness and assimilation to whiteness. Here, I attempt to reclaim intelligence as more than the way people are assessed for knowledge and measured against one another. Intelligence in the anticolonial frame is both concrete and intangible. It requires curiosity for both cultural and religious literacy, but it does not end there. Cultural and religious literacy and well as authentic relationships with those of cultural and religious difference, open the door to other forms of intelligence. Some of those intelligences encompass grasp of language, insider and outsider knowledge of communities, religious and cultural codes, self-reflection, and transformation.

19. Gardner, *Intelligence Reframed*, 34.

20. Jeannine Hill Fletcher, *The Sin of White Supremacy: Christianity, Racism, and Religious Diversity in America* (Maryknoll, NY: Orbis Books, 2017), 9.

21. Gaile Sloan Cannella and Radhika Viruru, *Childhood and Postcolonization: Power, Education, and Contemporary Practice* (New York, NY: Routledge Falmer, 2004), 30.

22. As part of my work, I have been invited to serve on planning committees for antiracism workshops and conferences. Post event there are telling signs that the burden of antiracist and anti-oppression education has fallen on the most affected by those very oppressions. I almost always leave workshops or conferences on antiracism physically and emotionally depleted. I fall ill soon after the event concludes. White identified co-conspirators might also leave feeling spent, having participated in holding their community members accountable through the teaching of anti-oppression solidarity and contending with their own power and privilege. However, those who attend only to learn from the labor of others often leave feeling restored, refreshed, and energized.

23. Formal relationships are often transactional until *jeong*; the feeling of affection and affinity is established. Even after establishing *jeong*, the custom of giving gifts may remain as a sign of recognition, care, and gratitude.

24. Code-switching describes the way people can modulate between different languages, cultures, and ways of being, depending on their current space. Code-switching is more than multilingualism. It is the intentional changing of one's perspective, vernacular, behavior and the way one interacts with others depending on the space and community. Code-switching is a learned skill common among many culturally and religiously border fluid people.

25. Jonathan Franzen, *The New Yorker*, Conde´ Nast, September 8, 2019, https://www.newyorker.com/culture/cultural-comment/what-if-we-stopped-pretending.

26. Hansi Lo Wang, "Code Switch, Chinese-American Descendants Uncover Forged Family Histories," *NPR*, December 17, 2013. The creation of Paper Sons was the direct result of the Chinese Exclusion Act of 1882, which banned Chinese laborers from entering the United States. The term "Paper Sons" refers to Chinese immigrant men who attempted to enter the United States with forged papers that claimed they were children of Chinese American citizens. Chinese Americans would return to China, marry, and create paperwork for their "children." Paper sons would then apply for immigration, which during the Chinese Exclusion Act, allowed for blood relatives of Chinese Americans, among others, to immigrate. Today, many Chinese Americans are still recovering family surnames due to their family history of immigration through the creation of Paper Sons.

27. Judith A. Berling, *Understanding Other Religious Worlds a Guide for Interreligious Education* (Maryknoll, NY: Orbis Books, 2004), 13.

28. This type of categorical "demotion" also assumes that folk traditions, home religions and spiritualities personal spiritualities are less significant than traditions that are deemed world religions. As we will see, this is a colonial hierarchical system of evaluation that those of us who teach must work at dismantling and disrupting.

29. Vine Deloria, *God Is Red* (New York, NY: Dell Publ., 1979), 259.

30. Mircea Eliade, "The Quest for the 'Origins' of Religion," *History of Religions* 4, no. 1 (1964): 154–169, Accessed September 27, 2020, http://www.jstor.org/stable/1061877.

31. *Indigenous Reflections on Christianity*, "Sacred Land Project," 2015, https://www.youtube.com/watch?v=OoxNyNWFvZw.

32. Michelle LeBaron and Venashri Pillay, *Conflict Across Cultures: A Unique Experience of Bridging Differences* (Vancouver, BC: Access and Diversity, Crane Library, University of British Columbia, 2016), 27.

33. LeBaron and Pillay, *Conflict Across Cultures*, 26.

34. Phil Wilnon and Alexa Diaz, "California Becomes First State to Ban Discrimination Based on One's Natural Hair," *Los Angeles Times*, July 3, 2019, https://www.latimes.com/local/lanow/la-pol-ca-natural-hair-discrimination-bill-20190703-story.html.

35. Merrit Kennedy, "George Washington Professor Who Reportedly Faked Being Black Resigns," *National Public Radio*, September 10, 2020, https://www.npr.org/sections/live-updates-protests-for-racial-justice/2020/09/10/911391817/george-washington-professor-resigns-after-scandal-over-fake-racial-identity.

CHAPTER 2

1. Linda Tuhiwai Smith, *Decolonizing Methodologies: Research and Indigenous Peoples* (New York, NY: Zed Books, 1999), 99.

2. Khyati Y. Joshi, *White Christian Privilege: The Illusion of Religious Equality in America* (New York, NY: New York University Press, 2020), 82.

3. When I worked for the national PC(USA) offices in 2014, a policy that was deemed to discriminate based on religion was set to come before Congress. Those of us who advocated in the realm of politics and religion quickly found the information of the self-identified Presbyterian congresspeople to make phone calls and write letters to significant effect. It is astounding how much influence mainline Christian denominations have with elected officials in the U.S. government, both local and national, in sheer numbers. That a mainline Christian denomination can make an impact advocating for this or that by calling on their congressional membership is a remarkable feat and privilege. Access to such swift actionable advocacy is not something religiously minoritized people in the United States possess.

4. Elliot Eisner's theory of curriculum as delivered through explicit, implicit, and null mediums are standard ways for educators to think about where and how teaching and learning takes place.

5. Even as I write this book, I recognize I am working within a construct of a particular form of epistemological commitments that centers monographs as colonial academic norms!

6. bell hooks, *Teaching to Transgress: Education as the Practice of Freedom* (New Delhi: Dev Publishers & Distributors, 2017), 50.

7. hooks, *Teaching to Transgress*, 39.

8. Showing Up for Racial Justice or SURJ has written helpful definitions for white supremacy culture and other racialized and supremacist concepts. Their webpage states, "White supremacy culture is the idea(ideology) that white people and the ideas, thoughts, beliefs, and actions of white people are superior to people of color,

their ideas, thoughts, beliefs, and actions. White Supremacy culture is an artificial, historically constructed culture which expresses, justifies and binds together the United States white supremacy system." https://www.showingupforracialjustice.org/white-supremacy-culture.html.

9. American exceptionalism is a particular perspective of chosen-ness embedded into the way the nation-state functions and interacts with the world. It can also personify as an internalized perspective carried by people identifying as American. For political discourse, American exceptionalism is the narrative of a free and democratic nation seeking to spread freedom and democracy across the globe. The meaning of American exceptionalism is far more insidious than that. According to Kelly Brown Douglas, the belief of American exceptionalism considers the United States of America as divinely sanctioned to dominate and protect with force all of its possessions, including land, property, and at one time, enslaved people. It is in many ways self-aggrandizement of the American colonial enterprise and subsequent way of life. A prime example of American exceptionalism is the world news. When traveling to other countries, I am always struck by how world news in other nations have a much broader and connectional understanding of what is considered essential to know as part of the daily news cycle. Stories from across the globe abound regardless of whether or not they are stories about modern military might and conquest. In the United States, the world news cycle is fixated on the political and military power of the United States on the global stage, only interested in connection if it either confirms or threatens U.S. sovereignty.

10. Kelly Brown Douglas, *Stand Your Ground: Black Bodies and the Justice of God* (Maryknoll, NY: Orbis Books, 2015), 15.

11. Douglas, *Stand Your Ground*, 16–17.

12. Gloria Anzaldúa, *Borderlands: The New Mestiza* (San Francisco, CA: Aunt Lute Books, 2007), 1.

13. hooks, *Teaching to Transgress*, 131.

14. I use the word "immigrant" throughout the book to include documented and undocumented peoples as a way of resisting the narrative that only documented people can be immigrants. However, I do not wish to conflate the radically different experiences of documented and undocumented immigrants.

15. The language of stakeholders is rooted in community organizing, but I have used it in theological education settings as well. Students find the term helpful to think about divisive communal issues and the stakes each member of a community has in the success or failure of a change initiative. The term "stakeholder" emphasizes the value of each community member impacted by a movement or a systemic change and helps organizers think beyond the binaries of them and us, for and against, friend and enemy.

16. Eboo Patel, "Commencement Address," *CST Commencement*, Presented at the CST Commencement, May 2013.

17. hooks, *Teaching to Transgress*, 42.

18. Marcia Y. Riggs, "A 21st Century Paradigm For Transforming Religiously Motivated Conflict And Violence," *Religious Ethical Mediation*, Accessed September 28, 2020, https://www.marciayriggs.com/.

More on Religious Ethical Mediation and Marcia Y. Riggs can be found here.

19. Frank B. Wilderson III, *Afropessimism* (New York, NY: Liveright Publishing Corporation, 2020), 163.

20. Along with Marcia Riggs' Religious Ethical Mediation, John Paul Lederach's Conflict Transformation method is helpful to us here. Lederach's pedagogy assumes that conflict is unavoidable and potentially present in every space where people gather. Lederach also works from a mindset that harnesses different lenses that work to complexify conflict in order to resist the flattening of narratives. Conflict transformation works to unleash creative engagement of conflict rather than avoid it altogether. Lederach's method engages relationships between people, systems, structures, and works to help actors join together in an effort and commitment to transform and liberate.

21. In my personal and academic life, I have to work to resist utilizing *only* the lens of unforgiving critique. Critique is necessary but should emerge from appreciation, not disdain. The academy has ingrained in me the falsehood that it is only through the critical engagement of other's work, finding holes and poking at those holes, that we can discover something wondrous. Critique is essential, but so is generous listening. The colonial impulse to destroy what it cannot possess and to appreciate only what it can commodify should not be the central way we teach students to engage their world. The mimicry of this colonial impulse through reading and writing is not what we should be looking for when assessing our students.

22. Gaile Sloan Cannella and Radhika Viruru, *Childhood and Postcolonization: Power, Education, and Contemporary Practice* (New York, NY: Routledge Falmer, 2004), 30.

23. Jonathan Freund is the vice president of the Board of Rabbis of Southern California at the Jewish Federation of Greater Los Angeles. I have heard him teach this point many times as a way of articulating how different communities understand pain, atrocities, and time differently.

24. Michael Langford, "Youth Ministry and Disability," Audio blog, *The Distillery* (blog), Princeton Theological Seminary, https://thethread.ptsem.edu/distillery/youth-ministry-and-disability, n.d., https://thethread.ptsem.edu/distillery/youth-ministry-and-disability.

Michael Langford's scholarship on youth ministry and disability discusses the difference between inclusivity and belonging. According to Langford, inclusivity makes room for disabled people but does not transform the community. The community is unchanged whether disabled people show up or not. Belonging takes community beyond inclusion. When disabled people are not present and involved, the community is not whole. I find this understanding helpful in the ways institutions have expressed their understandings of inclusion without putting forth effort to ensure belonging takes place.

CHAPTER 3

1. Jessica Vazquez Torres, Decatur, Ga. March 2019.

2. Whiteness is the lens through which we even engage publishing and antiracism work. A popular social media post in late 2018 by an anonymous person in publishing showed a photo of two stacks of books on antiracism. The first stack was noticeably more substantial. The larger pile of books were authored by white scholars writing on antiracism, the second much smaller pile belonged to people of color. The photograph's point was that even though publishing houses actively seek to publish books on antiracism, ultimately, it is economics and sales that drives whose scholarship is more marketable and profitable.

3. David Lanham and Amy Liu, "Not Just a Typographical Change: Why Brookings Is Capitalizing Black," *Brookings*, September 23, 2019, https://www.brookings.edu/research/brookingscapitalizesblack/.

The politics of capitalization is one way we code our words and language. Which words receive capitalization and which do not? In this book, I choose to capitalize the words Black, Indigenous, and Native along with other nouns for minoritized people like Asian and Latinx. These nouns are more than colors and geographic locations. The capitalization of these names honors and makes visible the tenacious personhood and peoplehood sustained against all odds. A web of communal identity that connects people across all the lands, memories, and human dignity which systems and structures of colonialism and white supremacy have decimated throughout histories. W. E. B. Dubois led the movement for the recognition of personhood through capitalization as resistance. The scholarship of Nikole Hannah-Jones and The 1619 Project, reenergized conversation about the politics of naming. In her work, Hannah-Jones rejects the word "slave" for "enslaved people." In response to The 1619 Project, The Brookings Institute also changed its standards, convicted that, "Without Black might, there would be no white wealth. Yet for over three centuries since the first colonists landed on American soil, Black people were considered less than equal under the law."

George M. Johnson, "Yes, 'Black' Is Capitalized When We're Talking about Race," *MIC*, October 10, 2019, https://www.mic.com/p/yes-black-is-capitalized-when-were-talking-about-race-19208252.

Reflecting on Hannah-Jones choice and the capitalization of Black, Journalist George M. Johnson writes, "Hannah-Jones's work got me thinking about the capitalizing of the 'b' in the word "Black" as a racial identifier. It's not always done, and that capitalization is important because the word is not just describing the color of skin, or of a car or a desk for that matter. It describes a race—one whose existence has historically been plagued by erasure. Formatting the name of a race accurately, in books, on Twitter, in the media, is a glaring demand for our humanity."

4. Brittney C. Cooper, *Eloquent Rage: A Black Feminist Discovers Her Superpower* (New York, NY: Picador, 2019), 4.

5. Maggie Astor, "Dove Drops and Ad Accused of Racism," *The New York Times*, October 8, 2017, https://www.nytimes.com/2017/10/08/business/dove-ad-racist.html. Soap advertisements depicting the transformation of Black people to white continue today. Dove released television ad in 2017 that showed a Black woman who uses Dove soap. She takes off her shirt to reveal a white woman underneath.

6. The term third-world originated as cold-war terminology, but colloquially became economic hierarchical categorizations of different nations. In some cases, the

phrase is used to portray African, Asian, and Latinx nations and people as uncivilized and barbaric, familiar tropes of the colonial imagination. Fanon, Loomba, and others have written extensively on this topic.

7. R. Seema, "Https://Medium.com/@Artlust/Coded-Language-Community-Diversity-and-Other-Racist-Words-a0a19f3b3a5bS," Web log, *Medium* (blog), August 29, 2018, https://medium.com/@artlust/coded-language-community-diversity-and-other-racist-words-a0a19f3b3a5b.

8. Robin DiAngelo, *White Fragility: Why It's So Hard for White People to Talk about Racism* (London, UK: Allen Lane, an imprint of Penguin Books, 2019).

9. The term "Asian American" is a race-conscious term that promotes solidarity between disparate Asian communities and people. It was born out of the Asian American Movement in San Francisco, in response and solidarity with the Black Liberation and Native Liberation movements.

10. Django Paris and Maisha T. Winn, *Humanizing Research: Decolonizing Qualitative Inquiry with Youth and Communities* (Thousand Oaks, CA: SAGE, 2014), 30.

11. Even though the term dialogic spiral indicates the privileging of dialogue as the primary form of communication and knowledge transfer, the modality of the dialogic spiral also informs and teaches about the productivity and strategic use of silence, nonverbal forms of communication, time for intentional processing, and the production and use of empathy in difficult communication.

12. Paris and Winn, *Humanizing Research*, 30.

13. It is vital in the process of giving and receiving feedback that there is every intention of incorporating said feedback into the process for a different set of dialogical spirals. Every classroom comes with a different set of vulnerabilities, potential conflicts, and necessary conditions, and intimacies. With each contextual environment at play, there is not a one-size-fits-all model that will work. Instead, teachers and facilitators are encouraged to include debriefing and take the critical experiential feedback to heart for any future processes of dialogue.

CHAPTER 4

1. "History," *The High Line*, November 11, 2019, https://www.thehighline.org/history/.

2. Assessment itself can become an extension of the colonial enterprise. We may begin by defining assessment as evaluation or measurements of learning but can we ever truly assess the value of how and what someone has gained in their time with us? We can assess only what we have set out to measure, but what if what we had intended to measure is not helpful at all? What if what we set out to measure and assess is about measuring the adaptation to the colonial enterprise of teaching and learning, rather than the value it has taken on and embodied in a person's mind, heart, and life? bell hooks discusses the power of her student's experience with learning extended beyond the life of classroom and as teachers learning to acknowledge our need for immediate professional gratification via assessment limited to a course. We

must ask these questions, even if we have no answers at the moment in order to move toward decolonial space and place in our teaching and learning.

3. John Gast, "American Progress," a woman leads pioneers west toward manifest destiny. Native Americans and wildlife flee in their wake, *Library of Congress*, 1872, Gene Autry Western Heritage Museum, https://www.loc.gov/pictures/item/97507547/.

4. Genocide includes the stealing of children, or the separation of children from their families. These types of child separations prevent the perpetuation of peoplehood, the connectionality of families, and in the most practical sense, the discontinuation of cultures, languages, religions and spiritualities. It is the very real destruction of identity and the end of a people in one fell swoop.

5. Cumberland County Historical Society. Carlisle Indian School Students, "Photograph," *The Sentinal*, https://cumberlink.com/news/local/indian-school-new-research-puts-carlisle-indian-school-enrollment-closer-to-8-000-students/article_82f8fbdc-db62-5191-bc92-5fc37d9d661e.html.

6. Jacqueline Fear-Segal and Susan D. Rose, eds., "Introduction," in *Carlisle Indian Industrial School: Indigenous Histories, Memories, and Reclamations* (Lincoln, NE: University of Nebraska Press, 2016), 1–2.

7. Fear-Segal and Rose, "Introduction," 1.

8. Jacqueline Fear-Segal and N. Scott Momaday, "The Stones at Carlisle," in *Carlisle Indian Industrial School: Indigenous Histories, Memories, and Reclamations*, ed. Susan D. Rose (Lincoln, NE: University of Nebraska Press, 2016), 43.

9. Homi K. Bhabha, *The Location of Culture* (London, UK: Routledge, 2004), 142.

10. I use Christian right instead of religious right. I notice that the phrase religious right is used in place of Christian right. The assumption being that Christianity is the apex religion. I use right and left here to emphasize the binary ways we have learned to think and speak about political opinion.

11. I use the phrase "Trump era" to point to the lasting impact of the Trump administration beyond the presidential term itself.

12. The narrative of mental illness as the cause for white supremacist violence feeds into the ableism that harms communities and individuals struggling with mental illness.

13. "China Suppression of Uighur Minorities Meets U.N. Definition of Genocide, Report Says, Episode," *Weekend Edition Saturday*, July 4, 2020, https://www.npr.org/2020/07/04/887239225/china-suppression-of-uighur-minorities-meets-u-n-definition-of-genocide-report-s.

14. Asian Pacific Islander Desi American.

15. Smith, *Decolonizing Methodologies*, 139.

16. I use both the signifiers people of color and BIPOC (Black, Indigenous, and people of color) throughout this book. My hope is that my use of these phrases do not negate the Black and Native experience but names racial solidarities and collective histories within systems and structures of white supremacy, while also naming Black and Native experiences in ways that mark differences of experience and impact.

17. Nadra Widatalla, "Op-Ed: The Term 'People of Color' Erases Black People. Let's Retire It," *Los Angeles Times*, April 28, 2019, https://www.latimes.com/opinion/op-ed/la-oe-widatalla-poc-intersectionality-race-20190428-story.html?fbclid=IwAR1EhWsO22MILZ5ujwy7176UZt_5cxUkboBkssEg5Y_upNadhfwl8o9nAig.

18. Muslim Americans are widely considered a racialized group post 9/11 after experiencing an increase in racial profiling and hate crimes.

19. Nancy Lynne Westfield, "Personal Practice Aimed @ Austere Reality," *Wabash Center for Teaching and Learning Theology and Religion* (blog), Wabash College, July 17, 2017, https://www.wabashcenter.wabash.edu/2017/06/personal-practice-aimed-austere-reality/.

CHAPTER 5

1. On July 15, 2019, President Donald Trump tweeted that four sitting congresswomen of color should "go back to their own country." Trump's racist tweet is not a far cry from the question, "Where are you from?" The insinuation that nonwhite people are not "American" or citizens of the United States is one that has historical roots of erasure of Indigenous people, Anti-immigrant policy, Yellow Peril, and anti-Black racism in the United States.

2. Nayyirah Waheed, "Lands," in *Salt* (San Bernardino, CA: Nayyirah Waheed, 2019).

3. Defining people in the negative, as what they are not, centers what is dominant in society thereby putting minoritized individuals in contestation with dominant cultures.

4. There is a danger to this unidirectional theological and individual formation that will be addressed later in this chapter.

5. Rita Nakashima Brock, *Off the Menu: Asian and Asian North American Women's Religion and Theology* (Louisville, KY: Westminster John Knox Press, 2007), 298.

Religious educator, Boyung Lee discusses *Uri* positionality as We-ness juxtaposed with I-ness. For her, the "I's are melted into one we."

Hee An Choi, *A Postcolonial Self: Korean Immigrant Theology and Church* (Albany, NY: SUNY Press, State University of New York, 2015), 33.

Choi Hee An has also explored the concept of *woori* as the Korean ethnic self, versus the western concept of self. – 33. A Postcolonial self: Korean Immigrant theology and church.

6. LeBaron, *Conflict Across Cultures*, 27.

7. Gilbert C. Park's concept of the preconstruction of American identity as model-minorities taken on by Korean immigrant students can be extended to the experience of adopting preconstructed identities in Korean immigrant congregational spaces. For instance, preconstructed gender roles and identities and obligations of filial piety which are theologically and spiritually grounded in the practice of Korean immigrant Christianity.

8. Gilbert C. Park, "Becoming a 'Model Minority': Acquisition, Construction and Enactment of American Identity for Korean Immigrant Students," *Urban Review* 43 (2011): 622.

9. Findings from studies (Grace J. Yoo and Barbara W. Kim, "Remembering Sacrifices: Attitude and Beliefs Among Second-generation Korean Americans Regarding Family Support," *Journal of Cross Cultural Gerontol* 25 (2010): 168.) of second-generation Korean Americans who are now in adulthood reveal that the choices they made in adulthood to remain connected with their parents to the point of becoming their caretakers, providing for them financially, and cohabitating with them, were linked to their experiences in childhood and adolescence of the cultural and religious practice communalism as well as their witnessing of their parent's struggles and sacrifices as immigrants.

10. Leah Anderson, "You Ask Me What I Am So You May Know How To Fear Me," *Button Poetry*, May 14, 2019, https://buttonpoetry.com/leah-anderson-you-ask-me-what-i-am-so-you-may-know-how-to-fear-me/.

11. Bhabha, *The Location of Culture*, 139.

12. Wonhee Anne Joh, *Heart of the Cross: A Postcolonial Christology* (Louisville, KY: Westminster John Knox Press, 2006).

Theologian, Wonhee Anne Joh in her book *Heart of the Cross* writes about interstitial space in the Korean American experience as being an in-between space that cultivates resilience and resistance. Likewise, the children and adolescents of Korean immigrants, travel an in-between space that cultivates abilities like code-switching that ease the transition between cultures and expectations, though they may not always be able to reconcile the tensions between two distinct sets of cultural codes and expectations.

13. Philip Kasinitz, John Mollenkopf, Mary C. Waters, and Merih Anih, "Transnationalism and the Children of Immigrants in Contemporary New York," in *The Changing Face of Home: The Transnational Lives of the Second Generation*, ed. Mary C. Waters and Peggy Levitt (New York, NY: Russell Sage Foundation Press, 2002), 97–99.

14. Mary Annette Pember, "Trauma May Be Woven Into DNA of Native Americans," Web log, *Indian Country Today* (blog), October 3, 2017, https://indiancountrytoday.com/archive/trauma-may-be-woven-into-dna-of-native-americans-CbiAxpzar0WkMALhjrcGVQ.

15. Sang Hyun Lee, *From a Liminal Place: An Asian American Theology* (Minneapolis, MN: Fortress Press, 2010).

Sang Hyun Lee wrote extensively about the Korean American immigrant experience through the theological lenses of both perpetual foreigners and pilgrims.

16. Su Yon Pak, et al., *Singing the Lords Song in a New Land: Korean American Practices of Faith* (Louisville, KY: Westminster John Knox Press, 2005).

Singing the Lord's Song in a New Land, describes distinct Korean American practices of faith using auto-ethnography and historical research. The authors share how particular forms of Korean American spiritualities like *ttong-song-kido* or fervent prayer are both inherited and sustained across generations.

17. Choi, *A Postcolonial Self*, 118.

CHAPTER 6

1. As discussed in chapter 5, *woori* is a Korean word that is used to describe a collective we. It is used in both the personal and familial realm and the political sphere. Korean people will commonly refer to the Republic of Korea as *woori nahrah*, or "our Nation" rather than as South Korea. The possessive term emerges out of the collective mindset of the Korean people which is opposed to individualism, particularly when it is counter to the good of the whole. *Woori* also carries with it, a feeling of collective responsibility for what is being claimed.

2. Winnona LaDuke, *Indigenous Reflections on Christianity*, Sacred Land Project, 2015, https://www.youtube.com/watch?v=OoxNyNWFvZw.

3. I use the term "formation" as both a positive and negative reality.

4. Natalie Gallón, "A Woman Watched Her Husband and Daughter Drown at the Mexican Border, Report Says," *CNN*, June 26, 2019, https://www.cnn.com/2019/06/26/politics/mexico-father-daughter-dead-rio-grande-wednesday/index.html.

5. Alvin Alvarez, Barbara W. K. Yee, Jenny Su, Su Yeong Kim, and Loriena Yancura, "Asian American Pacific Islander Families, Essay," in *Asian American Psychology: Current Perspectives*, ed. Nita Tewari (New York, NY: Psychology Press, 2009), 302–3.

6. Hirokazu Yoshikawa and Niobe Way, "From Peers to Policy: How Broader Social Contexts Influence the Adaptation of Children and Youth in Immigrant Families," in *Beyond the Family: Contexts of Immigrant Children's Development* (San Francisco, CA: Jossey-Bass, 2008), 3–4.

7. Alvarez et al., "Asian American Pacific Islander Families," 302–3.

8. Jane Iwamura, "Ancestral Returns, Essay," in *Off the Menu: Asian and Asian North American Women's Religion and Theology*, ed. Rita Nakashima Brock, Jung Ha Kim, Pui Lan Kwok, and Seung Ai Yang (Louisville, KY: Westminster John Knox Press, 2007), 112.

9. On February 26, 2012, Trayvon Martin was shot and murdered by George Zimmerman in Sanford, Florida. Martin was a seventeen-year-old Black child and Zimmerman was a twenty-eight-year–old multiracial man. Trayvon was unarmed, carrying only a bag of skittles in the pocket of his hoodie. Zimmerman claimed self-defense. Ultimately, Zimmerman was acquitted. On November 22, 2014, Tamir Rice, a twelve-year-old Black child, was killed in Ohio by police officer Timothy Loehmann, a twenty-six-year–old white man. Like Trayvon, Tamir was unarmed. The murder of Trayvon Martin and Tamir Rice are two of many instances where unarmed Black folx, including children, are shot and murdered by law enforcement. On February 10, 2015, college students Deah Shaddy Barakat, Yusor Mohammad Abu-Salha, and Razan Mohammad Abu-Salha were murdered by their neighbor in their home in Chapel Hill, North Carolina, in a racial and religious hate crime.

10. Jennifer Cho, "Mel-Han-Cholia as Political Practice in Theresa Hak Kyung Cha's Dictée," *Meridians* 11, no. 1 (2011): 36–61, doi:10.2979/meridians.11.1.36.

11. Teresa Hak Kyung Cha, *Dictee* (Berkeley, CA: University of California Press, 2001).

12. "The Residential School System," *Indigenous Foundations*, Accessed September 28, 2020, http://indigenousfoundations.arts.ubc.ca/the_residential_school_system/.

13. Christine J. Hong, *Identity, Youth, and Gender in the Korean American Church* (New York, NY: Palgrave MacMillan, 2015).

14. Lynda M. Ashbourne and Mohammed Baobaid, "Parent-Adolescent Storytelling in Canadian-Arabic Immigrant Families (Part 2): A Narrative Analysis of Adolescents' Stories Told to Parents," *The Qualitative Report 19* 60 (2014): 1–18.

15. Ashbourne and Baobaid, "Parent-Adolescent Storytelling," 3.

16. Iwamura, "Ancestral Returns," 1–8.

17. Sang Hyun Lee and John V. Moore, eds., "Asian American Theology in Immigrant Perspective: Called to Be Pilgrims, Essay," in *Korean American Ministry: A Resourcebook* (Louisville, KY: Consulting Committee on Korean American Ministry, the Program Agency, Presbyterian Church (USA), 1987), 52.

18. M. Brinton Lykes, Kalina M. Brabeck, and Cristina J. Hunter, "Exploring Parent–Child Communication in the Context of Threat: Immigrant Families Facing Detention and Deportation in Post-9/11 USA," *Community, Work & Family* 16, no. 2 (2013): 123–46, doi:10.1080/13668803.2012.752997.

19. Modulated disclosure refers to the sharing of traumatic narratives with children and adolescents in disconnected snippets rather than as a whole.

20. Nobu Miyoshi, "Identity Crisis of the Sansei and the American Concentration Camp," *Pacific Citizen*, December 19, 1980: 41–55.

21. Donna K. Nagata, *Legacy of Injustice Exploring the Cross-Generational Impact of the Japanese American Internment* (Plenum, NY: Springer, 1993), 26–35.

22. Russell Jeung, *Faithful Generations: Race and New Asian American Churches* (New Brunswick: Rutgers University, 2005), 139.

23. JoAnn D'Alisera, "Images of a Wounded Homeland: Sierra Leonean Children and the New Heart of Darkness, Essay," in *Across Generations: Immigrant Families in America*, ed. Nancy Foner (New York, NY: New York University Press, 2009), 114–30.

24. Warsan Shire, "'Home' by Warsan Shire," *Facing History and Ourselves*, Accessed September 28, 2020, https://www.facinghistory.org/standing-up-hatred-intolerance/warsan-shire-home.

CHAPTER 7

1. Gregory C. Ellison, *Fearless Dialogues: A New Movement for Justice* (Louisville, KY: Westminster John Knox Press, 2017).

2. I am using the term "transspiritual" to describe religious and spiritual commitments, beliefs, and practices that originate from different experiences, places, histories, and religious and spiritual traditions but are embodied and held together in one individual. Like transnationalism and its commitments, transspirituality does not merge, synthesis, or syncretize distinct commitments, but these commitments, practices, and beliefs exist, present, and transform in tension and conversation with one

another. Transspirituality is not a cherry-picking of religious beliefs and practices but rootedness in them through communal, familial, and personal histories, experiences, and commitments. Transspiritual practices, for persons and groups with colonized histories and experiences, can be practices that were once Indigenous and have been reinterpreted, and reindigenized.

3. A perpetual foreigner refers to Asians and Asian Americans who because of the stereotypes and prejudices associated with their appearance cannot assimilate to the context of North American life. They are assumed to always be foreign, visiting, or traveling through, never at home.

4. Peggy Levitt and Mary C. Waters, *The Changing Face of Home: the Transnational Lives of the Second Generation* (New York, NY: Russell Sage Foundation, 2002).

5. R. Stephen Warner, *Gatherings in Diaspora: Religious Communities and the New Immigration* (Philadelphia, PA: Temple Univ. Press, 1998).

6. *Han* is the Indigenous Korean terminology for collective sorrow, grief, and pain. *Han* can be personal, connectional, and national. Practices of prayer like ttong-song-kido can be in effect a cry of lament and releasing of *han*.

7. Charismatic practices among Korean American Mainline Protestant Christians echo the Indigenous shamanistic roots of Korean spiritualities.

8. Waters and Levitt, *The Changing Face of Home*.

9. John Shindler, *Transformative Classroom Management: Positive Strategies to Engage All Students and Promote a Psychology of Success* (San Francisco, CA: Jossey-Bass, 2010).

10. Judith Butler notes that gender is performed and essentially fluid outside of societally constructed perfomativity. I am asserting that national, racial, ethnic, religious, and spiritual identities are also fluid but that students and instructors learn to perform out of more rigid societal expectations of identity out of necessity and survival in inhospitable environs.

11. Hari Sreenivasan, "A Teacher Mispronouncing a Student's Name Can Have a Lasting Impact, Episode," *PBS Newshour*, May 16, 2016, https://www.pbs.org/newshour/education/a-teacher-mispronouncing-a-students-name-can-have-a-lasting-impact.

12. Nita Tewari and Alvin Alvarez, *Asian American Psychology: Current Perspectives* (New York, NY: Psychology Press, 2008).

13. Indigenous scholars like Linda Tuhiwai Smith and Andrea Smith reflect on the decolonizing of the Indigenous scholar's mind from Western epistemologies and research processes.

14. G. Yamazawa, "G Yamazawa—The Bridge," *Genius*, Accessed July 18, 2019, https://genius.com/G-yamazawa-the-bridge-annotated.

15. Amos Yong, *The Missiological Spirit: Christian Mission Theology in the Third Millennium Global Context* (Cambridge, United Kingdom: James Clarke & Co., 2015), 55–63.

16. Sheryl A. Kujawa-Holbrook, *God beyond Borders: Interreligious Learning among Faith Communities* (Eugene, OR: Pickwick Publ., 2014).

17. hooks, bell. *Teaching Community: A Pedagogy of Hope* (New York: Routledge, 2003).

CHAPTER 8

1. Boyung Lee, "Re-Creating Our Mother's Dishes: Asian and Asian North American Women's Pedagogy, Essay," in *Off the Menu: Asian and Asian North American Women's Religion and Theology*, ed. Rita Nakashima Brock, Pui Lan Kwok, Jung Ha Kim, and Seung Ai Yang (Louisville, KY: Westminster John Knox Press, 2007), 294–95, 293–308.
2. Denise Frohman, "Accents," *Denice Frohman*, Accessed September 28, 2020, https://www.denicefrohman.com/watch.
3. "Indian Country Diaries: A Seat at the Drum," *American Archive of Public Broadcasting*, 2006, https://americanarchive.org/catalog/cpb-aacip_508-cc0tq5s173.
4. Christian education continues to be a place where the perspectives and language become colonizing agents. This happens anywhere where Christianity arrives via the auspices of non-Native peoples into any Indigenous community. I spent some months teaching the English language in Bangkok, Thailand, as part of a private Christian school run by South Korean missionaries. The Korean missionaries also held Sunday services. Thai teachers were required by contract to become members of the church and attend Sunday services even though the majority of them were Buddhist by practice. Each Sunday, the content of the worship including the songs and the sermon were laboriously translated from Korean to Thai. Each worship service lasted for four hours to accommodate for the translation. The worship consisted of no involvement from Thai Christians, only Korean missionaries and their families had any leadership roles. Thai members participated by listening and singing the translated Korean Christian hymns and contemporary songs in Thai. In this instance, the Thai language was retained but was coopted into use by Korean missionaries for the sole purpose of forcing Christianity onto the lives of Thai employees.
5. A 2005 documentary called Grace Park explores the lives of Asian women with the shared name of Grace Park. In the documentary, we discover that there are common stereotypes associated not only with the name but also with Asian women in general. We learn about the inner and public lives of various Grace Lees as well as the meaningful stories behind their names.
6. John 1:1 NRSV translation.
7. Eve Tuck and K. Wayne Yang, "Decolonization Is Not a Metaphor," *Decolonization, Indigeneity, Education, and Society* 1, no. 1 (September 8, 2012): 1–40, https://americanarchive.org/catalog/cpb-aacip_508-cc0tq5s173.
8. HyeRan Kim-Cragg, *Interdependence: A Postcolonial Feminist Practical Theology* (Eugene, OR: Pickwick Publications, 2018).
9. Giles and Travis, "Oral Traditions," Accessed September 28, 2020.
10. I remember an exchange in one courses where upon hearing that I was Korean American a well-intentioned student asked when I would make *bulgogi* for them. I was quite taken aback by this question as it assumed so many things about who I was, what culture meant to me, and leaned into gendered biases and stereotypes about Asian women in general. In a later conversation with the student, they commented that their question was intended to "honor" my heritage and engage with

me on what they understood as an important part of my identity. Their comment was indeed engaging with my heritage and a part of my identity, but it presumed too much. Presumptions about how different people engage with their cultures and how they choose to represent or not represent parts of their cultures are dangerous. It reduces people's identities to cultural markers and denies the conscious choices people make about representation.

11. hooks, *Teaching to Transgress*, 39.
12. LeBaron, *Conflict Across Cultures*, 35–36.
13. Tuck and Yang, "Decolonization is Not a Metaphor," 1–40.

CONCLUSION

1. Audre Lorde, *Sister Outsider* (New York, NY: Penguin Books, 2020), 37.
2. Deepa Iyer, "My Role in a Social Change Ecosystem: A Mid-Year Check-In," *Medium*, May 13, 2019, https://medium.com/@dviyer/my-role-in-a-social-change-ecosystem-a-mid-year-check-in-1d852589cdb1.
3. Toni Morrison, "Black Studies Center Public Dialogue. Pt. 2," *Public Dialogue on the American Dream Theme*, Address presented at the Public Dialogue on the American Dream Theme, March 20, 2020, http://archives.pdx.edu/ds/psu/11309.

Bibliography

Allen, Brenda J. "Introduction. Essay." In *Presumed Incompetent: The Intersections of Race and Class for Women in Academia*, edited by Muhs Gabriella Gutiérrez y, 17–20. Boulder, CO: Univ. Press, 2012.

Alvarez, Alvin, and Nita Tewari. *Asian American Psychology: Current Perspectives*. New York, NY: Psychology Press, 2009.

Alvarez, Alvin, Barbara W. K. Yee, Jenny Su, Su Yeong Kim, and Loriena Yancura. "Asian American Pacific Islander Families. Essay." In *Asian American Psychology: Current Perspectives*, edited by Nita Tewari, 302–303. New York, NY: Psychology Press, 2009.

Anderson, Leah. "You Ask Me What I Am So You May Know How To Fear Me." *Button Poetry*, May 14, 2019. https://buttonpoetry.com/leah-anderson-you-ask-me-what-i-am-so-you-may-know-how-to-fear-me/.

Anzaldúa, Gloria. *Borderlands: The New Mestiza*. San Francisco, CA: Aunt Lute Books, 2007.

Ashbourne, Lynda M., and Mohammed Baobaid. "Parent-Adolescent Storytelling in Canadian-Arabic Immigrant Families (Part 2): A Narrative Analysis of Adolescents' Stories Told to Parents." *The Qualitative Report 19* 60 (2014): 1–18.

Astor, Maggie. "Dove Drops and Ad Accused of Racism." *The New York Times*, October 8, 2017. https://www.nytimes.com/2017/10/08/business/dove-ad-racist.html. Soap advertisements depicting the transformation of Black people to white continue today. Dove released television ad in 2017 that showed a Black woman who uses Dove soap. She takes off her shirt to reveal a white woman underneath.

Berling, Judith A. *Understanding Other Religious Worlds a Guide for Interreligious Education*. Maryknoll, NY: Orbis Books, 2004.

Bhabha, Homi K. *The Location of Culture*. London, UK: Routledge, 2004.

Brock, Rita Nakashima. *Off the Menu: Asian and Asian North American Women's Religion and Theology*. Louisville, KY: Westminster John Knox Press, 2007.

Cannella, Gaile Sloan, and Radhika Viruru. *Childhood and Postcolonization: Power, Education, and Contemporary Practice*. New York, NY: RoutledgeFalmer, 2004.

Carlisle Indian School Students. "0AD. Photograph." *Children and Youth in History*. http://chnm.gmu.edu/cyh/primary-sources/291.

"China Suppression Of Uighur Minorities Meets U.N. Definition Of Genocide, Report Says. Episode." *Weekend Edition Saturday*, July 4, 2020. https://www.npr.org/2020/07/04/887239225/china-suppression-of-uighur-minorities-meets-u-n-definition-of-genocide-report-s.

Cho, Jennifer. "Mel-Han-Cholia as Political Practice in Theresa Hak Kyung Cha's Dictée." *Meridians* 11, no. 1 (2011): 36–61. doi:10.2979/meridians.11.1.36.

Choi, Hee An. *A Postcolonial Self: Korean Immigrant Theology and Church*. Albany, NY: SUNY Press, State University of New York, 2015.

Cooper, Brittney C. *Eloquent Rage: A Black Feminist Discovers Her Superpower*. New York, NY: Picador, 2019.

Deloria, Vine. *God Is Red*. New York, NY: Dell Publ., 1979.

DiAngelo, Robin. *White Fragility: Why It's So Hard for White People to Talk about Racism*. London, UK: Allen Lane, an imprint of Penguin Books, 2019.

Douglas, Kelly Brown. *Stand Your Ground: Black Bodies and the Justice of God*. Maryknoll, NY: Orbis Books, 2015.

D'Alisera, JoAnn. "Images of a Wounded Homeland: Sierra Leonean Children and the New Heart of Darkness. Essay." In *Across Generations: Immigrant Families in America*, edited by Nancy Foner. New York, NY: New York University Press, 2009.

Du Bois, W. E. B. *The Souls of Black Folk: Essays and Sketches*. Amherst, MA: UMass Amherst Libraries, 2018.

Ellison, Gregory C. *Fearless Dialogues: A New Movement for Justice*. Louisville, KY: Westminster John Knox Press, 2017.

Fear-Segal, Jacqueline, and N. Scott Momaday. "The Stones at Carlisle. Essay." In *Carlisle Indian Industrial School: Indigenous Histories, Memories, and Reclamations*, edited by Susan D. Rose. Lincoln, NE: University of Nebraska Press, 2016.

Fear-Segal, Jacqueline, and Susan D. Rose. "Introduction." In *Carlisle Indian Industrial School: Indigenous Histories, Memories, and Reclamations*, 1–2. Lincoln, NE: University of Nebraska Press, 2016.

Fletcher, Jeannine Hill. *The Sin of White Supremacy: Christianity, Racism, and Religious Diversity in America*. Maryknoll, NY: Orbis Books, 2017.

Franzen, Jonathan. *The New Yorker*. Condé Nast, September 8, 2019. https://www.newyorker.com/culture/cultural-comment/what-if-we-stopped-pretending.

Frohman, Denise. "Accents." *Denice Frohman*. Accessed September 28, 2020. https://www.denicefrohman.com/watch.

Gallón, Natalie. "A Woman Watched Her Husband and Daughter Drown at the Mexican Border, Report Says." *CNN*, June 26, 2019. https://www.cnn.com/2019/06/26/politics/mexico-father-daughter-dead-rio-grande-wednesday/index.html.

Gardner, Howard. *Intelligence Reframed: Multiple Intelligences for the 21st Century*. New York, NY: Basic Books, 1999.

Gast, John. "American Progress." Print shows an allegorical female figure of America leading pioneers westward, as they travel on foot, in a stagecoach, conestoga wagon, and by railroads, where they encounter Native Americans and herds of bison. *Library of Congress*, 1872. Gene Autry Western Heritage Museum. https://www.loc.gov/pictures/item/97507547/.

Giles, William Nu'u'tupu, and T. Travis. "Oral Traditions." *WNG*. Accessed September 28, 2020. https://www.willgilespoetry.com/poetry.

"History." *The High Line*, November 11, 2019. https://www.thehighline.org/history/.

hooks, bell. *Teaching to Transgress*. New Delhi: Dev Publishers & Distributors, 2017.

hooks, bell. *Teaching Community: A Pedagogy of Hope*. New York: Routledge, 2003.

"Indian Country Diaries: A Seat at the Drum." *American Archive of Public Broadcasting*, 2006. https://americanarchive.org/catalog/cpb-aacip_508-cc0tq5s173.

Indigenous Reflections on Christianity. "Sacred Land Project." 2015. https://www.youtube.com/watch?v=OoxNyNWFvZw.

Iwamura, Jane. "Ancestral Returns. Essay." In *Off the Menu: Asian and Asian North American Women's Religion and Theology*, edited by Rita Nakashima Brock, Jung Ha Kim, Pui Lan Kwok, and Seung Ai Yang, 112. Louisville, KY: Westminster John Knox Press, 2007.

Iyer, Deepa. "My Role in a Social Change Ecosystem: A Mid-Year Check-In." *Medium*, May 13, 2019. https://medium.com/@dviyer/my-role-in-a-social-change-ecosystem-a-mid-year-check-in-1d852589cdb1.

Jeung, Russell, and Robert Neelly Bellah. *Faithful Generations: Race and New Asian American Churches*. New Brunswick: Rutgers University Press, 2005.

Joh, Wonhee Anne. *Heart of the Cross: A Postcolonial Christology*. Louisville, KY: Westminster John Knox Press, 2006.

Johnson, George M. "Yes, 'Black' Is Capitalized When We're Talking about Race." *MIC*, October 10, 2019. https://www.mic.com/p/yes-black-is-capitalized-when-were-talking-about-race-19208252.

Joshi, Khyati Y. *White Christian Privilege: The Illusion of Religious Equality in America*. New York, NY: New York University Press, 2020.

Kasinitz, Philip, John Mollenkopf, Mary C. Waters, and Merih Anih. "Transnationalism and the Children of Immigrants in Contemporary New York. Essay." In *The Changing Face of Home: The Transnational Lives of the Second Generation*, edited by Peggy Levitt and Mary C. Waters, 97–99. New York, NY: Russell Sage Foundation, 2002.

Kennedy, Merrit. "George Washington Professor Who Reportedly Faked Being Black Resigns." *National Public Radio*, September 10, 2020. https://www.npr.org/sections/live-updates-protests-for-racial-justice/2020/09/10/911391817/george-washington-professor-resigns-after-scandal-over-fake-racial-identity.

Kim-Cragg, HyeRan. *Interdependence: A Postcolonial Feminist Practical Theology*. Eugene, OR: Pickwick Publications, 2018.

Kovach, Margaret. *Indigenous Methodologies: Characteristics, Conversations, and Contexts*. Toronto, ON: University of Toronto Press, 2009.

Kujawa-Holbrook, Sheryl A. *God beyond Borders: Interreligious Learning among Faith Communities*. Eugene, OR: Pickwick Publ., 2014.

Langford, Michael. "Youth Ministry and Disability." Audio blog. *The Distillery* (blog). Princeton Theological Seminary. https://thethread.ptsem.edu/distillery/youth-ministry-and-disability, n.d. https://thethread.ptsem.edu/distillery/youth-ministry-and-disability.

Lanham, David, and Amy Liu. "Not Just a Typographical Change: Why Brookings Is Capitalizing Black." *Brookings*, September 23, 2019. https://www.brookings.edu/research/brookingscapitalizesblack/.

LeBaron, Michelle, and Venashri Pillay. *Conflict across Cultures: A Unique Experience of Bridging Differences*. Vancouver, BC: Access and Diversity, Crane Library, University of British Columbia, 2016.

Lee, Boyung. "Re-Creating Our Mother's Dishes: Asian and Asian North American Women's Pedagogy. Essay." In *Off the Menu: Asian and Asian North American Women's Religion and Theology*, edited by Rita Nakashima Brock, Pui Lan Kwok, Jung Ha Kim, and Seung Ai Yang, 293–308. Louisville, KY: Westminster John Knox Press, 2007.

Lee, Sang Hyun, and John V. Moore, eds. "Asian American Theology in Immigrant Perspective: Called to Be Pilgrims. Essay." In *Korean American Ministry: A Resource book*, 52. Place of publication not identified, KY: Consulting Committee on Korean American Ministry, the Program Agency, Presbyterian Church (U.S.A.), 1987.

Lee, Sang Hyun. *From a Liminal Place: An Asian American Theology*. Minneapolis, MN: Fortress Press, 2010.

Levitt, Peggy, and Mary C. Waters. *The Changing Face of Home: The Transnational Lives of the Second Generation*. New York, NY: Russell Sage Foundation, 2002.

Lewis, Clive Staples. *The Voyage of the Dawn Treader*. New York, NY: HarperCollins, 2019.

Lorde, Audre. *Sister Outsider*. New York, NY: Penguin Books, 2020.

Lykes, M. Brinton, Kalina M. Brabeck, and Cristina J. Hunter. "Exploring Parent–Child Communication in the Context of Threat: Immigrant Families Facing Detention and Deportation in Post-9/11 USA." *Community, Work & Family* 16, no. 2 (2013): 123–146. doi:10.1080/13668803.2012.752997.

Miyoshi, Nobu. "Identity Crisis of the Sansei and the American Concentration Camp." *Pacific Citizen*, December 19, 1980: 41–55.

Morrison, Toni. "Black Studies Center Public Dialogue. Pt. 2." *Public Dialogue on the American Dream Theme*. Address presented at the Public Dialogue on the American Dream Theme, March 20, 2020. https://pdxscholar.library.pdx.edu/orspeakers/90/.

Nagata, Donna K. *Legacy of Injustice Exploring the Cross-Generational Impact of the Japanese American Internment*. Plenum, NY: Springer, 1993.

Pak, Su Yon, Myung Ji Choi, Unzu Lee, and Jung Ha Kim. *Singing the Lord's Song in a New Land: Korean American Practices of Faith*. Louisville, KY: Westminster John Knox Press, 2005.

Paris, Django, and Maisha T. Winn. *Humanizing Research: Decolonizing Qualitative Inquiry with Youth and Communities*. Thousand Oaks, CA: SAGE, 2014.

Patel, Eboo. "Commencement Address." *CST Commencement*. Presented at the CST Commencement, May 2013.

Pember, Mary Annette. "Trauma May Be Woven Into DNA of Native Americans." Web log. *Indian Country Today* (blog), October 3, 2017. https://indiancountrytoda y.com/archive/trauma-may-be-woven-into-dna-of-native-americans-CbiAxpz ar0WkMALhjrcGVQ.

Prothero, Stephen R. *Religious Literacy: What Every American Needs to Know--and Doesn't.* New York, NY: HarperOne, an imprint of Harper Collins Publishers, 2008.

"The Residential School System." *Indigenous Foundations*. Accessed September 28, 2020. http://indigenousfoundations.arts.ubc.ca/the_residential_school_system/.

Riggs, Marcia Y. "A 21st Century Paradigm for Transforming Religiously Motivated Conflict and Violence." *Religious Ethical Mediation.* Accessed September 28, 2020. https://www.marciayriggs.com/.

Sano, Roy I. "Essay." In *From Every Nation without Number: Racial and Ethnic Diversity in United Methodism*, 83. Nashville, TN: Abingdon, 1982.

Seema, R. "Https://Medium.com/@Artlust/Coded-Language-Community-Diversity -and-Other-Racist-Words-a0a19f3b3a5bS." Web log. *Medium* (blog), August 29, 2018. https://medium.com/@artlust/coded-language-community-diversity-and-oth er-racist-words-a0a19f3b3a5b.

Shindler, John. *Transformative Classroom Management: Positive Strategies to Engage All Students and Promote a Psychology of Success*. San Francisco, CA: Jossey-Bass, 2010.

Shire, Warsan. "'Home' by Warsan Shire." *Facing History and Ourselves*. Accessed September 28, 2020. https://www.facinghistory.org/standing-up-hatred-intolerance /warsan-shire-home.

Smith, Linda Tuhiwai. *Decolonizing Methodologies: Research and Indigenous Peoples*. New York, NY: Zed Books, 1999.

Sreenivasan, Hari. "A Teacher Mispronouncing a Student's Name Can Have a Lasting Impact." Episode. *PBS Newshour*, May 16, 2016. https://www.pbs.org/newshour/ education/a-teacher-mispronouncing-a-students-name-can-have-a-lasting-impact.

Tuck, Eve, and K. Wayne Yang. "Decolonization Is Not a Metaphor." *Decolonization, Idigeneity, Education, and Society* 1, no. 1 (September 8, 2012): 1–40. https://am ericanarchive.org/catalog/cpb-aacip_508-cc0tq5s173.

Waheed, Nayyirah. *Salt*. San Bernardino, CA: Nayyirah Waheed, 2019.

Wang, Hansi Lo. "Morning Edition. Episode. Code Switch: Chinese-American Descendants Uncover Forged Family Histories." *NPR*, December 17, 2013.

Warner, R. Stephen. *Gatherings in Diaspora: Religious Communities and the New Immigration*. Philadelphia, PA: Temple Univ. Press, 1998.

Westfield, Nancy Lynne. "Personal Practice Aimed @ Austere Reality." *Wabash Center for Teaching and Learning Theology and Religion* (blog). Wabash College, July 17, 2017. https://www.wabashcenter.wabash.edu/2017/06/personal-practice -aimed-austere-reality/.

Wiconi International. "Richard Twiss: A Theology of Manifest Destiny." May 7, 2008. https://www.youtube.com/watch?v=4mEkMy1KNW0.

Widatalla, Nadra. "Op-Ed: The Term 'People of Color' Erases Black People. Let's Retire It." *Los Angeles Times*, April 28, 2019. https://www.latimes.com/opinion

/op-ed/la-oe-widatalla-poc-intersectionality-race-20190428-story.html?fbclid=IwAR1EhWsO22MILZ5ujwy7176UZt_5cxUkboBkssEg5Y_upNadhfwl8o9nAig.

Wilderson, Frank B. III "Essay." In *Afropessimism*, 146. New York, NY: Liveright Publishing Corporation, 2020.

Wilnon, Phil, and Alexa Diaz. "California Becomes First State to Ban Discrimination Based on One's Natural Hair." *Los Angeles Times*, July 3, 2019. https://www.latimes.com/local/lanow/la-pol-ca-natural-hair-discrimination-bill-20190703-story.html.

Yamazawa, G. "G Yamazawa—The Bridge." *Genius*. Accessed September 28, 2020. https://genius.com/G-yamazawa-the-bridge-annotated.

Yong, Amos. *The Missiological Spirit: Christian Mission Theology in the Third Millennium Global Context*. Cambridge, United Kingdom: James Clarke & Co., 2015.

Yoshikawa, Hirokazu, and Niobe Way. "From Peers to Policy: How Broader Social Contexts Influence the Adaptation of Children and Youth in Immigrant Families. Essay." In *Beyond the Family: Contexts of Immigrant Children's Development*, 3–4. San Francisco, CA: Jossey-Bass, 2008.

Index

Note: Page locators in italics refer to figures.

ableism, 21
abortion, 42
"Accents" (Frohman), 148
accessible technology, 47
accountability, 69–70, 164–67; in classrooms, 166–67; in communities, 165–66; institutional, 165; relational, 30
acculturation, 118, 119
activism, 156, 170
activities, shared, 125
adjacency, white, 2
advertisements, soap, 66, 180n6
affection and affinity (*jeong*), 176n23
Afro-Pessimism, 53, 173n2
Afropessimism (Wilderson), 53
Alger, Horatio, 103
allegiance, pledge of, 41
ally-ship anxiety, performative, 77
American exceptionalism, 178n9; binding, 46–49; imbedded, 137
American Muslims, 48, 183n17
American Progress, *81*, 81–82
Americans: Asian Americans, 10, 71, 166; Japanese Americans, 125; Korean American girls, 122
ancestor veneration (*jeh-sah*), 133, 135

Anderson, Leah, 104
anger, 65
anti-Blackness, 2, 36, 58, 66, 90
anticolonialism, x, 15–16; in classrooms, 154; spaces, 37, 39–40; strategies, 95; in theological education, 107, 169–70
anti-oppression, 40
antiracism, 11, 163–64, 179n2; in institutions, 61, 173n5; workshops, 63, 176n22
anxiety, ally-ship, 77
Anzaldúa, Gloria, 46
APIDA. *See* Asian, Pacific Islander, and Desi American people
appropriation, cultural, 35, 36
art, 80–82
Asian, Pacific Islander, and Desi American people (APIDA), 61, 64, 91, 147
Asian American community, 10, 71, 166
Asian American term, 181n10
assessment, 54–55, 181n2
assignments, research, 22–23
assumptions, 68–69, 86, 142–44, 188n10

197

audacity, of civilization, 79–84
audience, xi–xii

behavior, 70
belonging and unbelonging: educational binaries, 44–46; politics, 92
Berling, Judith, 34
between worlds, 104–5
Bhahba, Homi, 84, 104
biases, 2, 6, 62–69, 86
binaries, 25, 55, 84–85; belonging and unbelonging, 44–46; dark and light, 66–67; about students, 142–44; unbinding, 44–46
binding, 39–40; American exceptionalism, 46–49; purity narratives, 55–59; white and Christian supremacy, 40–43. *See also* unbinding
Black, Indigenous, and people of color (BIPOC), 4, 5, 8, 62, 94; experiences, 182n15; intersectional power dynamics, 91
Black hairstyles, 35–36
blooms, 77–78
boat, 111
body language, 72, 73
body scan, 73–74
border crossings, 46–47, 101
borderlands, 46–47, 100–1
borders, for teaching and learning, 99–100, 102–5
boundaries: porous, 133–37; for teaching and learning, 99–100, 102–5
"The Bridge" (Yamazawa), 140
Butler, Judith, 187n10

call-out culture, 31
Canadian Arab immigrants, 122
Cannella, Gaile Sloan, 25, 54–55
capitalization, politics, 180n3
card exercise, 89–90
caretakers, 118–19, 183n9

Carlisle Industrial Boarding School, 82–83, *83*
case studies, 25–27
categorization, 34, 93, 94
CBE. *See* competency-based education models
Chang, Grace, 5
children, of immigrants, 106, 118
China, 91
Chinese Exclusion Act, 176n26
Cho, Jennifer, 120
Choi Hee An, 107–8, 183n5
Christian dominance, 32–33
Christian hegemony, 1–3, 7, 40–41, 82
Christian institutions, 3, 61–62
Christianity, 76, 188n4; APIDA, 147; conversion in, 141; religions and, 32–34
Christian mastery, 33–34
Christian right, 84–85, 182n9
Christian supremacy, 24; binding, 40–43; navigating, 4–6
churches: Korean immigrant, 26; PC(USA), 177n3
civility: classroom conversations on, 85–86; violence of, 84–86
civilization: audacity of, 79–84; domination of, 79–80
classrooms, 37, 75, 165; accountability in, 166–67; anticolonialism in, 154; civility conversation in, 85–86; conflict in intercultural and interreligious, 138–39; framing, 82; hospitable intercultural, 140–42; North American, 150–51; porous, 141; power dynamics in, 94–96; trauma and pain in, 70. *See also* interreligious classrooms
climate crisis, 28
clothing, cultural, 56
co-conspirators, 163–64, 167
code-switching, 5–6, 26–27, 176n24, 184n12

code words, 62–69; of EDI, 67–68; high and low context culture, 65–66; minority as, 68; Mr. Seymour using, 63; racist, 67
coding, of whiteness, 64–65
cognitive development, 21
collective familial energy (*Ki*), 119
collective pain (*han*), 120–21, 125, 187n6
Collins, Patricia Hill, xi
colonial consumption, 114
colonial education, uncivilizing, 86–87
colonialism, 1–2, 15, 16, 86–87
Colonialism/Postcolonialism (Loomba), 15
colonization: of China, 91; three Ms, 6
commitments, xi, 7–9, 28–30, 131, 169
communication, cultural, 161–62
communities, 30, 171; accountability in, 165–66; Asian American, 10, 71, 166; Indigenous, 18–19; insiders and outsiders in, 20, 175n13; storying, 126–27; terminologies about, 92–93
competency, 8, 17, 95; in theological education, 18; undoing, 33
competency-based education models (CBE), 17–18
complexities: of conflict, 51–52, 179n20; of power dynamics, 88–89; unbinding, 55–59
comprehension, perfecting, 17
Conflict Across Cultures (LeBaron), 161
conflicts, 50, 57; complexifying, 51–52, 179n20; disproportionate risk in, 52–53; in interreligious classrooms, 138–39; unbinding, 51–53
consciousness, double, 5, 103
consequences, of failure, 28–29
consumption, colonial, 114
contexts, global, 47–48
Continuum on Becoming an Antiracist, Multicultural Institution, 173n5
conversations, hard, Dialogic Spiral for, 72–74

conversion, in Christianity, 141
Cooper, Brittney, 65
courses, Western Civilizations, 80
COVID-19 pandemic, xi
creative liminal, 123–24
crisis: climate, 28; immigration, 115
critiques, 54, 179n21
Crofutt, George, 81
crossings, border, 46–47, 101
Crossroads Antiracism Organizing and Training, 63
cultivation, of transspiritual and transnational identities, 135–37
cultural appropriation, 35, 36
cultural clothing, 56
cultural communication, 161–62
cultural fluency, 35
cultural literacy, in theological education, 19
culture, 34–36; call-out, 31; high context, 65, 161; keepers, 160; low context, 65–66, 161; religion entwined with, 36–37; showing up for, 159–62; tacit, 19, 20, 117, 174n12; transformation of, 58

D'Alisera, JoAnn, 125–26
dark and light, binary of, 66–67
DeAngelo, Robin, 68
death, 116–17
decolonial studies, ix
decolonization, 16, 113–16, 162
deconstruction, ix–x, 7
definitions, expansive, 175n14
Deloria, Vine, Jr., 34
dementia, 21–22
demography, 41
demotions, 176n28
devastation, of mastery, 15–20
development: cognitive, 21; psychological, 118
Dialogic Spiral, 72–74, 181n12, 181n14
dialogue: healthy, 162–63; tables, 47–49
Dictee (Hak Kyung Cha), 120

differences, vocational, 143
dignity, 63
Dine´(Navajo), 149
disclosure, modulated, 125, 186n19
disparaging narratives, 126, 136–37
displacement, histories of, 111–12
dissenters, 164
dissonance: formational, 105–10; of identities, 104; between stories, 123–26; teaching, 102–5
diversity: deep, 143; religious, 34
doctoral programs, 45
dominance: Christian, 32–33; civilization and, 79–80
double consciousness, 5, 103
Douglas, Kelly Brown, 46, 178n9
dreams, 6–7, 169, 172
drought, 78
DuBois, W.E.B., 5, 103, 180n3
dynamics, power. *See* power dynamics

eco-systems, social change, 170–71
EDI. *See* equity, diversity, and inclusion
education: belonging/unbelonging binaries in, 44–46; CBE, 17–18; colonial, 86–87; theory, 7. *See also* theological education
educators, 17, 22, 24, 29, 45
Eisner, Elliot, 177n4
eldership, 158–59
elected officials, 43, 177n3
Ellison, Gregory, 129
Eloquent Rage (Cooper), 65
emotions, xiii, 65, 95, 118, 131, 176
empowerment, 120
enculturation, of religions, 165
enemies, 164
energies, 172
English, 148, 150–51
epigenetic imprints, 131
epistemologies, 80, 109–10, 146–48, 177n5
equity, diversity, and inclusion (EDI), 67–68
equity, lingual, 150

erasures, 109, 151
ethics, ix, x, xi, 134
ethnicity, 35, 159
ethnic minority Muslims, 91
euphemisms, 62
exceptionalism, American, 178n9; binding, 46–49; imbedded, 137
exercises: card, 89–90; on naming, 154–55; privilege walk, 88–89
exorcising whiteness, 163
expansive definitions, 175n14
expectations, 5, 45–46
experiences, ix, 8; BIPOC, 182n15; lived, 18, 131; of religion, 34–37
eye-measure (*noon-chi*), 8, 160–61

failure: consequences of, 28–29; inequity of, 27–32
Faithful Generations (Jeung), 125
Fanon, Franz, 77
Fearless Dialogues (Ellison), 129
fears, 4, 104, 129
feedback, 181n14
feminist theologians, 157
fervent prayer (*ttong-song-kido*), 133
flattened narratives, 51–52, 55
flavor of one's hand (*sonmat*), 146
Fletcher, Jeannine Hill, 24
flourishing, 57–58, 171–72
fluency, cultural, 35
fluidity, 10, 134, 136
food, 146
foreigner, perpetual, 131, 187n3
foreign languages, 151
formations, 122, 185n3; dissonance in, 105–10; holistic, 107, 108, 136
fragility, 25, 68, 96
frameworks, 61, 119
framing: classrooms, 82; Dialogic Spiral questions, 73
Franzen, Jonathan, 28
freedom, 172
Freire, Paulo, 45
Freund, Jonathan, 57, 179n23
Frohman, Denice, 148

Gardner, Howard, 20–21, 175nn15–16
Gast, John, 80–82, *81*
Gatherings in Diaspora (Warner and Wittner), 133
gazes, 75
genealogical chart (*ho-juk*), 145–46
genealogies, 10–11, 145–46
generational theories, 142–43
generational trauma, 70–71, 106–7, 137
generations, 143
genocide, 182n4
Georgia, 42
girls, Korean American, 122
glasses, rose-colored, 136
Glissant, Édouard, 25
global contexts, 47–48
Google, 153
Grace Park, 188n5
grading, unbinding, 54–55
grieving, naming and, 153–55
guidelines, 166–67
guilt, upsetting, 74–75

habits, 70–71
hairstyles, Black, 35–36
Hak Kyung Cha, Teresa, 120
han (collective pain), 120–21, 125, 187n6
hard conversations, Dialogic Spiral for, 72–74
healthy dialogue, 162–63
Heart of the Cross (Wonhee), 184n12
hegemony, Christian, 1–3, 7, 40–41, 82
high context cultures, 65, 161
Highline (park), 79
hijab, 77
histories, 1, 57, 80, 145; of displacement, 111–12; repeating, 115
ho-juk (genealogical chart), 145–46
holistic formations, 107, 108, 136
Hollywood movies, 64
home, 131, 135
"Home" (Shire), 127
hooks, bell, 45, 52, 160
hope, 171–72

hospitality, 26
humble modesty, x, 11, 23–24, 30–31
humility, 23, 31–32
hunger, 61–62
hybrid religious practices, 132–34

identities, 68–69, 102, 144, 187n10, 188n10; dissonance of, 104; students and presumed, 139–40; theology of, 147; as threat to interdependence, 108–9; transspiritual and transnational, 130, 138–39
illness, mental, 85, 182n11
imagination: loosening, 76–78; wild, 79
imbedded American exceptionalism, 137
immigrants, 28–29, 42, 178n14; Canadian Arab, 122; children of, 106, 118
immigration crisis, 115
imperialism, 15, 35, 57
imposter syndrome, 4
imprints, epigenetic, 131
inclusion, 33, 179n24
independence, 103
"Indian Problem," 82–83
indigeneity, 2
Indigenized pedagogy, 157–58
Indigenous communities, 18–19
Indigenous Methodologies (Kovach), 18–19
inequity, of failure, 27–32
inquiry, stories and, 129–30
insiders, community, 20, 175n13
institutions, 1–2, 43, 56–57; accountability in, 165; antiracism in, 61, 173n5; Christian, 3, 61–62; flourishing, 57–58; inclusion in, 33
intelligences, x, 4; measuring, 22–24, 175n18; multiple, 20–21, 175nn15–16; posture of, 8–9, 16; reframing, 9–11; reimagining, 21. *See also* intercultural and interreligious intelligence
interactions, student, 5

interconnectedness, 107–8
intercultural and interreligious intelligence, 8, 20–22, 169–70; case study, 25–27; commitment to, 28, 29–30; pedagogy of, 113, 116, 137–44; teaching and learning, 30
intercultural classrooms, hospitable, 140–42
interdependence, 107–9
interracial solidarity, 91–93, 166
interreligious classrooms: conflict in, 138–39; hospitable, 140–42
interrogation, 99
In the Beginning Were Stories Not Texts (Song), 130
inventory, 17
invisibilization, 139
ivy, 40–41
Iyer, Deepa, 170–71

Japanese Americans, 125
jeh-sah (ancestor veneration), 133, 135
jeong (affection and affinity), 176n23
Jeung, Russell, 125
Johnson, George M., 180n3
Joshi, Khyati Y., 41
joy, 3
juice, orange, 161
justice, 164

keepers, culture, 160
Ki (collective familial energy), 119
Kim, Jung Ha, 184n16
Kim-Cragg, Hye-ran, 158
kindness, 63
knowledge, 146; memories as, 157–58; subjugated, 120; theft of, 54–55
Korean American girls, 122
Korean American Mainline Protestant Christians, 187n7
Korean immigrant church, 26, 101
Korean language, 20
Korean Peninsula, 106, 120, 126, 166
Koreans, 92

Kovach, Margaret, 18–19
Krug, Jessica A., 36
Kujawa-Holbrook, Sheryl, 154

labors, of learning, 105
LaDuke, Winona, 34, 114
Langford, Michael, 179n24
language, 20, 188n4; body, 72, 73; English, 148, 150–51; foreign, 151; Korean, 20; loss of, 121, 150; requirements, 148–49; significance of, 148–52; stories and, 119–21; technology and, 152–53; transmission of, 120
Latinx, 69, 132
layl (night/dark), 67
learning, 54; borders and boundaries for, 99–100, 102–5; intercultural and interreligious intelligence, 30–31; labors of, 105; mediums for, 80–81; multilingual, 152–53; questions for, 6–7; spaces for, 9–11
LeBaron, Michelle, 35, 161
Lederach, John Paul, 179n20
Lee, Boyung, 146, 183n5
Lee, Joung Young, 122–23
Lee, Sang Hyun, 123, 184n15
lenses, 63–64, 103
Levitt, Peggy, 131
Lewis, C. S., 3
liberation, 39, 44, 58, 76–78
liminal, creative, 123–24
lingual equity, 150
the lion, 61–62
literacy: cultural, 19; religious, 19, 174n10
lived experiences, 18, 131
Loomba, Ania, 15, 16
loosening, liberation and theological imagination, 76–78
Lorde, Audre, 170
Los Angeles, California, 42
loss, 135–36; of epistemologies, 146–48; of languages, 121, 150

low context cultures, 65–66, 161

markers, 153, 154
Martin, Trayvon, 85, 185n9
Martínez, Angie Valeria, 115
Martínez Ramírez, Óscar Alberto, 115
mastery, 148; Christian, 33–34; devastation of, 15–20
meaning making, religiocultural, 124
measuring intelligence, 22–24, 175n18
media, 63, 64
mediums, for learning, 80–81
mel-*han*-choly, 120–21
memorials, 87
memories, 115; as knowledge, 157–58; showing up for, 156–59
mental illness, 85, 182n11
metrics, 54
minoritized people, 2, 4, 50, 68, 103; media representing, 64; power dynamics of, 90–94
minority, as code word, 68
mistakes, 27–30
modeling humble modesty, 30–31
model minority stereotypes, 86, 183n7
modesty, humble, x, 11, 23–24, 30–31
modulated disclosure, 125, 186n19
Momaday, N. Scott, 83
Morrison, Toni, 171–72
movies, Hollywood, 64
multilingual learning, 152–53
multiple intelligences, 20–21, 175nn15–16
Muslims: American, 48, 183n17; ethnic minority, 91
myths, racial purity, 46

names, 83, 140, 152, 154
naming, 180n3; exercises on, 154–55; grieving and, 153–55
narratives, 48, 71–72, 135; binding purity, 55–59; disparaging, 126, 136–37; flattened, 51–52, 55; of oppressions, 77; Orientalist, 86–87

nationality, 159
Native peoples, 82–84
navigation, of white and Christian supremacy, 4–6
needs, students, 57
news, world, 178n9
Newsom, Gavin, 35
night/dark (*layl*), 67
noon-chi (eye-measure), 8, 160–61
norms, 59
North American classrooms, 150–51
North Korea, 126
Nu'u'tupu, William, 158

officials, elected, 43, 177n3
opacity, 72, 160
opportunities, 27
Oppression Olympics, 91
oppressions, 3, 9, 12, 39–40, 43, 77
optics, 67
"Oral Traditions" (T. and Nu'u'tupu), 158
orange juice, 161
Orature, 158
ordination, 157
Orientalist narrative, 86–87
origin stories, 111–13
otherness, 104
our Nation (*woori nah rah*), 184n1
our stories, 117–19
outsiders, community, 20, 175n13

pain, 69–71; in classrooms, 70; *han*, 120–21, 125, 187n6; performative, 71–72
paintings, *81*, 81–82
pandemic, COVID-19, xi
Paper Sons, 176n26
paradigms, 49, 76
Park, Gilbert C., 183n7
Patel, Eboo, 51
PC(USA). *See* Presbyterian Church
pedagogy: Indigenized, 157–58; of intercultural and interreligious intelligence, 113, 116, 137–44

people: APIDA, 61, 64, 91, 147;
    BIPOC, 4, 5, 8, 62, 91, 94, 182n15;
    Native, 82–84. *See also* minoritized
    people
peoplehood, 116
"people of color," 93–94, 182n15
perfecting comprehension, 17
perfectionism, 27, 31
performativity, 187n10; in ally-ship
    anxiety, 77; in trauma and pain,
    71–72
perpetual foreigner, 131, 187n3
Personal Practice and Austere Reality
    (Westfield), 95
personhood, 116
pledge of allegiance, 41
plopping, 129
poems, 104, 127, 140, 148, 158, 170
policies, U.S., 42–43
politics: belonging and unbelonging, 92;
    capitalization, 180n3; U.S., 42–43,
    84–85, 123
porous boundaries, 133–37
porous classrooms, 141
Postcolonial Education (Canella), 54
postcolonialism, 40
posture: of intelligence, 8–9, 16; of
    teaching, 95
power, 116; of stories, 113–14; of
    woori, 112
power dynamics: BIPOC
    intersectional, 91; in classrooms,
    94–96; complexities of, 88–89;
    of minoritized people, 90–94;
    uncivilizing, 88–96
practices: hybrid religious, 132, 133–34;
    teaching, 162–63
Pratt, Richard Henry, 82–83
prayer, 134
Presbyterian Church (PC(USA)), 177n3
Presumed Incompetent (Chang), 5
privilege, 85, 116, 139; uncivilizing,
    88–96; walk, 88–89
programs, doctoral, 45

proselytization, 138
Prothero, Stephen, 19, 174n10
psychological development, 118
purity narratives, binding, 55–59

queerness, 109

racial purity, myth of, 46
racism, 50, 67, 171. *See also* antiracism
rage, upsetting, 74–75
reciprocation, 26
reconciliation, 11–12
reconstruction, xi, 7, 96
reformed theology, 156
reframing intelligence, 9–11
reimagining intelligence, 21
relational accountability, 30
religiocultural meaning making, 124
religions, 93; Christianity and,
    32–34; culture entwined with,
    36–37; enculturation of, 165; hybrid
    practices in, 132, 133–34; invitation
    to experience, 34–37; in stories,
    121–23
religious diversity, 34
Religious Ethical Mediation (REM), 52,
    179n20
religious literacy, 19, 174n10
REM. *See* Religious Ethical Mediation
repeating, history, 115
representation, 160
requirements, language, 148–49
research assignments, 22–23
researchers, 37
resentment, 26
restoration, 11–12
reversals, role, 118
Riggs, Marcia Y., 52, 179n20
right, Christian, 84–85, 182n9
risk, 164; in conflict, 52–53
role reversals, 118
roles, 170–71
Rolo, Mark Anthony, 149
romanticizing: stories, 113; *woori*, 108

rose-colored glasses, 136

sacred texts, 155–56
Sano, Roy I., 11–12, 151–52
scan, body, 73–74
scarcity, theology of, 49
scholarships, 29
sciences: social, 19; weaponization of, 18
scripture, 155
A Seat At The Drum, 149
self-determination, 109–10
self-esteem, 122
selfhood, theological, 101
self-reflexivity, 141–42, 147–48
Mr. Seymour (teacher), 63
shared activities, 125
sharing stories, 116
Shindler, John, 138
Shire, Warsan, 127
showing up: for culture, 159–62; for memories, 156–59
Showing Up for Racial Justice (SURJ), 177n8
Sierra Leone, 125–26
significance, of language, 148–52
silence, 65, 90, 159
The Silver Chair (Lewis), 3
Singing the Lord's Song in a New Land (Kim, J.), 184n16
"Sly Civility," 84
Smith, Andrea, 187n13
Smith, Linda Tuhiwai, 40, 54–55, 92, 187n13
soap advertisements, 66, 180n6
social change eco-systems, 170–71
socialization, 42–43
social sciences, 19
solidarity, 90–93, 166
Song, C. S., 130
sonmat (flavor of one's hand), 146
spaces, 8, 61–62, 141–42; anticolonialism, 37, 39–40; for learning, 9, 10, 11; uncivilizing, 82; *woori* across, 105–10

specters, 126–27
stakeholders, 50, 178n15
stereotypes, 62–69, 85, 86, 183n7, 188n5
stories, xi, 10, 55–56, 144; communities and, 126–27; decolonization and, 113–16; dissonance between, 123–26; inquiry and, 129–30; language and, 119–21; origin, 111–13; our, 117–19; power of, 113–14; religion and values in, 121–23; romanticizing of, 113; sharing, 116; in transmission, 116–17; transspiritual and transnational reclamation through, 130–32
strategies: anticolonial, 95; for unbinding, 49–51
students, 50–51, 73–74; binaries and assumptions about, 142–44; interactions, 5; needs, 57; presumed identities of, 139–40
studies: case, 25–27; decolonial, ix
subjugated knowledge, 120
subtexts, 41, 66
support systems, 56
supremacy. *See* Christian supremacy; white supremacy
SURJ. *See* Showing Up for Racial Justice
survival, 118, 119, 172
syllabi, 162–63, 166
symbolism, 82
syndrome, imposter, 4
systems, 39–40; social change eco-systems, 170–71; support, 56

T., Travis, 158
tables, dialogue, 47–49
tacit culture, 19, 20, 117, 174n12
teaching, 23–24, 44–45, 54; borders and boundaries for, 99–100, 102–5; dissonance, 102–5; intercultural and interreligious intelligence, 30–31; posture of, 95; practices, 162–63; questions for, 6–7; *woori*, 100–2

technology, 134–35; accessible, 47; language and, 152–53; transnationalism through, 106
tensions, 116–17
The Term People of Color Erases Black People. Let's Stop Using It (Widatalla), 93–94
terms: Asian American, 181n10; community, 92–93
texts, sacred, 155–56
theft, of knowledge, 54–55
theologians, feminist, 157
theological education, ix, x, 1–4, 61, 171; anticolonialism in, 107, 169–70; competency in, 18; cultural and religious literacy in, 19
theology: of identities, 147; of imagination, 76–78; reformed, 156; of scarcity, 49; selfhood, 101
third-world, 180n7
three Ms, of colonization, 6
time, *woori* across, 105–10
titles, 157
togetherness, 101
tokenization, of educators, 45
Torres, Jessica Vasquez, 63
transformations, 51–53, 58, 170
Transformative Classroom Management (Shindler), 138
translations, 124
transmission: of languages, 119; stories in, 116–17
transnationalism, 47, 186n2; cultivation of, 135–37; of identities, 130, 138–39; stories and, 130–32; through technology, 106
transspiritual identities, 130, 135–39, 186n2
transspiritual reclamation, through stories, 130–32
trauma, 69–71, 75, 83–84; in classrooms, 70; generational, 70–71, 106–7, 137; performative, 71–72

triggers, 100
Trump, Donald, 50, 85, 182n10, 183n1
trust, 73, 167
ttong-song-kido (fervent prayer), 133, 184n16

unbinding, 39–40; binaries, 44–46; complexities, 55–59; conflict toward transformation, 51–53; grading and assessment, 54–55; strategies for, 49–51
uncivilizing: colonial education, 86–87; power, privilege, and vulnerability, 88–96; spaces, 82
undoing competency, 33
United States (U.S.): policies, 42–43; politics, 42–43, 84–85, 123
unity, 147
upsetting, rage and guilt, 74–75
us (*woori*), 10, 103, 149, 183n5, 184n1; epistemology of, 109–10; power of, 112; romanticizing, 108; teaching, 100–2; across time and space, 105–10
U.S. *See* United States

values, 121–23, 167
violence, 53, 84–86, 182n11
vocational differences, 143
vulnerability, 88–96, 167

Waheed, Nayyirah, 100
walk, privilege, 88–89
Warner, R. Stephen, 133
Waters, Mary C., 131
"we," 140–41, 183n5
weaponization, of science, 18
Western Civilizations course, 80
Westfield, Lynne, 95
"where are you from?" question, 99–100
white adjacency, 2
White Christian Privilege (Joshi), 41
white fragility, 68, 96

white-lash, 75
whiteness, 16–17, 42, 132, 179n2; coding of, 64–65; exorcising, 163
white supremacy, 1, 2, 3, 56, 116, 177n8; binding, 40–43; lens of, 63–64; navigating, 4–6
Widatalla, Nadra, 93–94
wilderness, 78, 79
Wilderson, Frank B., III, 53, 173n2
wild imagination, 79
witness, 156
Wittner, Judith G., 133
Wonhee Anne Joh, 184n12
woori (us), 10, 103, 149, 183n5, 184n1; epistemology of, 109–10; power of, 112; romanticizing, 108; teaching, 100–2; across time and space, 105–10
woori nah rah (our Nation), 184n1
words, 149, 152, 175n14. *See also* code words
workshops, antiracism, 63, 176n22
world news, 178n9
worlds, between, 104–5
worship, 146–47, 188n4

Yamazawa, G., 140
Yong, Amos, 141

Zimmerman, George, 185n9

About the Author

The Rev. Dr. Christine J. Hong is assistant professor of educational ministry at Columbia Theological Seminary in Decatur, GA. She has an undergraduate degree in English Literature and Communications from the University of Washington, a Master of Divinity and Master of Theology degrees from Princeton Theological Seminary, and a PhD. from Claremont School of Theology. Her academic interests include anticolonial and decolonial approaches to religious and interreligious education and life. Hong's scholarly interests also include Asian American spiritualities, and the spiritual and theological formation of children and adolescents among BIPOC communities. Hong is a Teaching Elder in the Presbyterian Church (USA) and has spent time as both a religious educator and youth and young adult minister in New York and Southern California. Though she makes her home in Georgia, her heart remains on the west coast and by the ocean. Her first book is called, Youth, Identity, and Gender in the Korean American Church and is published by Palgrave.

ABOUT THE FOREWORD AUTHOR

Dr. Marcia Y. Riggs has an undergraduate degree in religion from Randolph-Macon Woman's College, a Master of Divinity degree from Yale University Divinity School and a PhD in religion/ethics from Vanderbilt University. In April 2006, Dr. Riggs was inaugurated as the first professor to hold the J. Erskine Love Chair in Christian Ethics at Columbia Theological Seminary in Decatur, Georgia. She teaches in the Master of Divinity, Doctor of Ministry, and the Master of Theology Programs at the seminary. Dr. Riggs was awarded 2017–2018 Henry Luce III Fellowship from the Henry Luce

Foundation and the Association of Theological Schools; her research project was entitled: "Envisioning and Practicing Beloved Community in the 21st Century." She received the "Distinction in Theological Education" Award from Yale Divinity School in 2012 and the Alumnae Achievement Award from Randolph-Macon Woman's College in 2006. Dr. Riggs has served on the Editorial Boards for the Encyclopedia on Women and Religion in North America, the Journal of the Society of Christian Ethics, and the Feasting on the Word Lectionary Commentary Series. She has also chaired the Womanist Approaches to Religion and Society Group and has chaired or served on committees of the American Academy of Religion, the Association of Theological Schools, and The Fund for Theological Education (currently, the Forum for Theological Exploration). Dr. Riggs is currently writing a book on an ethical theory and practice called religious ethical mediation. Religious ethical mediation (REM) prepares leaders to address religion, conflict, and violence in a transformative manner. She is the founder of an educational nonprofit: Still Waters: A Center for Ethical Formation and Practices that offers training in REM.

www.ingramcontent.com/pod-product-compliance
Lightning Source LLC
Chambersburg PA
CBHW070829300426
44111CB00014B/2498